THE IDEAL WORLD OF MRS. WIDDER'S
Soirée Musicale

THE IDEAL WORLD OF MRS. WIDDER'S

Soirée Musicale

Social Identity and Musical Life in Nineteenth-Century Ontario

by Kristina Marie Guiguet

Mercury Series
Cultural Studies Paper 77

Canadian Museum of Civilization

National Library of Canada Cataloguing in Publication

Guiguet, Kristina Marie, 1953-

The ideal world of Mrs. Widder's soirée musicale : social identity and musical life in nineteenth-century Ontario

(Mercury series)
(Cultural Studies Paper, ISSN 1707-8970 ; 77)
Includes an abstract in French.
Includes bibliographical references.
ISBN 0-660-19344-2

1. Music – Social aspects – Ontario – Toronto – History – 19th century.
2. Performance practice – Ontario – Toronto – History – 19th century.
3. Toronto (Ont.) – Social life and customs – 19th century.
4. Amusements – Ontario – Toronto – History – 19th century.
I. Canadian Museum Civilization. II. Title.
III. Series: Cultural studies paper (Canadian Museum of Civilization) ; no. 77.

ML205.7O6G942 2004   781.5'35'09713551

C2004-980225-9

PRINTED IN CANADA

Published by the Canadian Museum of Civilization
100 Laurier Street
P.O. Box 3100, Station B
Gatineau, Quebec
J8X 4H2

Technical Editor: Carmelle Bégin
Manager, Publishing: Deborah Brownrigg
Coordinator, Internal Publishing Program and Co-Publications: Sylvie Pelletier
Designer: Digitaljayne

Front Cover Photograph: Achille Devéria, "Soirée Musicale — Musical Party," in *Les heures de la Parisienne: 1840*, ed. Roger-Armand Weigert, coloured by Edmond Vairel (Paris: Éditions Rombaldi, 1957), Plate XXIII. Courtesy National Library of Canada.

Back Cover Photograph: "Soirée Musicale", Interior, Port Dalhousie. Courtesy National Archives of Canada /e002213447

Object of the Mercury Series

The Mercury Series is designed to permit the rapid dissemination of information pertaining to the disciplines in which the Canadian Museum of Civilization is active. Considered an important reference by the scientific community, the Mercury Series comprises 400 specialized publications on Canada's history and prehistory.

In the interest of making information available quickly, normal production procedures have been abbreviated. As a result, grammatical and typographical errors may occur. Your indulgence is requested.

How to Obtain Mercury Series Titles
Telephone: 1-819-776-8387 or, toll-free in North America only, 1-800-555-5621
E-mail: publications@civilization.ca
Web: cyberboutique.civilization.ca
Mail: Mail Order Services
Canadian Museum of Civilization
100 Laurier Street
P.O. Box 3100 Station B
Gatineau, Quebec J8X 4H2
CANADA

But de la collection Mercure

La collection Mercure vise à diffuser rapidement le résultat de travaux dans les disciplines qui relèvent des sphères d'activités du Musée canadien des civilisations. Considérée comme un apport important dans la communauté scientifique, la collection Mercure présente 400 publications spécialisées portant sur l'héritage canadien préhistorique et historique.

Comme la collection s'adresse à un public spécialisé, celle-ci est constituée essentiellement de monographies publiées dans la langue des auteurs.

Comment se procurer les titres parus dans la collection Mercure
Téléphone : 1 819 776-8387 ou sans frais, en Amérique du Nord seulement, 1 800 555-5621
Courriel : publications@civilization.ca
Web : cyberboutique.civilisations.ca
Poste : Service des commandes postales
Musée canadien des civilisations
100, rue Laurier
C.P. 3100, succursale B
Gatineau (Québec) J8X 4H2
CANADA

Canada

For Yvonne Guiguet Johnston, my mother

Abstract

The Ideal World of Mrs. Widder's Soirée Musicale offers a new approach to the concert program as evidence of social, political and business history. This *microhistoire* of Mrs. Frederick Widder's 1844 domestic concert reconstructs the world of one elite group assembled at the home of a prosperous Toronto land developer, but it has implications beyond a single drawing-room extravaganza. Most of the Widder music and the program structure itself were standard fare for all parlour and professional musicians of the time: the Soirée Musicale is just an extreme development of the way musical life affected and reflected contemporary values, thoughts, and beliefs.

A concert form transplanted from imperial London, the Soirée Musicale combined amateurs and professionals performing in a private home or a public venue. The programming of these concerts appears to modern eyes as a laughable stew of mismatched musical genres. This case study suggests instead that mixing parlour ballads, simple piano pieces, and close-harmony glees, all designed for amateurs, with operatic excerpts demanding a professional level of skill required great musical subtlety and a sharp eye to local commercial and personal politics.

Performance conventions of the period linked musical genres with the class and gender of their performers, linkages readily visible in Mrs. Widder's program designed for an intimate social circle, many of whom were central figures in pre-Confederation Canadian political history. The nineteenth-century Ontario Soirée Musicale was a drama of difference, in which stable but sharply distinct categories of class and gender formed an idealized, hierarchical moral universe.

Résumé

L'ouvrage *The Ideal World of Mrs. Widder's Soirée Musicale* présente le programme de concert comme un témoignage d'histoire sociale, politique et commerciale. En cela, il s'agit d'une nouvelle approche. Cette « microhistoire » d'un concert intime offert par Mme Frederick Widder, en 1844, reconstitue le monde d'une élite réunie dans la maison d'un riche promoteur de Toronto. Elle va toutefois au-delà du simple spectacle mondain. Tous les musiciens de salon et les professionnels de l'époque connaissent bien la plus grande partie de la musique de Mme Widder et la structure même du programme. La soirée musicale n'est en fait que l'évolution suprême de la façon dont la vie musicale influence et reflète les valeurs, les idées et les croyances d'alors.

La soirée musicale, une formule empruntée de la Londres impériale, réunit amateurs et professionnels qui se produisent dans une maison privée ou un lieu public. Aux yeux du monde moderne, la programmation de ces concerts semble un mélange absurde de genres musicaux mal assortis. La présente étude de cas avance plutôt l'idée que la combinaison de balades de salon, de simples pièces pour piano et de chants chorals, tous conçus pour des amateurs, mais émaillés d'extraits d'opéra exigeant une habileté professionnelle, demande une grande subtilité musicale et une fine perception de la vie politique locale ainsi que de l'univers commercial et des opinions politiques de chacun.

Les conventions régissant les concerts de l'époque lient les genres musicaux à la classe sociale et au sexe des artistes. Ces liens sont facilement décelables dans le programme de Mme Widder, élaboré pour un cercle social intime où l'on retrouve plusieurs personnalités importantes de l'histoire politique canadienne d'avant la Confédération. La soirée musicale du XIXe siècle, en Ontario, constitue un « théâtre de la différence », où les catégories que représentent les classes sociales et les sexes masculin et féminin, invariables mais nettement distinctes, forment un univers moral hiérarchisé et idéalisé.

Table of Contents

Illustrations

$\mathcal{P}$reface

The "Soirée Musicale" surfaces occasionally in Victorian memoirs and novels, mentioned as if everyone knew what it meant. But what do the domestic Soirées Musicales of 1840s Paris, France (front cover), and 1890s Port Dalhousie, Ontario (back cover), have in common? This study began when an archival envelope unexpectedly revealed a handful of tiny, elegant Soirée Musicale programs from 1880s Toronto. They were utterly mysterious and quite irresistible. My favourite was the Llawbaden Soirée Musicale, printed like the others on a single piece of card three inches by four inches and folded once, but coloured shell pink with a raised, scroll border of exquisite cream. On the outside cover, the name of the location and the date, 1907, were printed above an image of a square grand piano (quite an antique by then), and on the inside, each half of the concert occupied one side of the folded card. On the back, the image of a guitar lying on open sheet music adorned the program.

Like the others in the envelope, the Llawbaden program outlined a formal concert held in what seemed to be a private home, where amateur and professional musicians performed music that, to the eyes of a twentieth-century classical musician like me, was a bizarre mixture of unrelated musical genres. Women and men performed equally difficult material and both sang the vacuous parlour music that is now but a faded memory of naïve sentiment. Formal concerts at home with amateurs and professionals together seemed peculiar: why not get on with it and have the concert in public, or have professionals only, or have the amateurs alone? Though they were few, the programs from that serendipitous archival envelope and the very few others still extant were confusingly different from each other and presented no obvious common ground.

To understand them, I dissected the earliest-known domestic Soirée Musicale in what is now Ontario, Mrs. Widder's private, musical party of 1844, which occupies most of the following pages. After the webs of social meaning in Mrs. Widder's concert program became apparent, the Llawbaden program was finally revealed as a self-conscious revival, held after 1900 and attended by some who had experienced earlier Soirées Musicales. It may have been a similar nostaligia that prompted the 1950s' reprinting of the cover illustration, an image of an 1840s Soirée Musicale in Paris, France (cover illustration).[1] The image, like the nineteenth-century Soirée Musicale itself, charms only if the fluttery femininity of leisured women continues to enchant. The joys of live music making at home, present in the Port Dalhousie image

Programme

OF

MRS. WIDDER'S "SOIREE MUSICALE,"

LYNDHURST, MARCH 12, 1844.

PART I.

CORO—" Plaudite oh Popoli " (Tancredi)		Rossini.
DUET—" Mira oh Norma " (Norma)	Miss Hagerman and Mrs. Nash	Bellini.
CANZONET—" My mother bids me bind my hair "	Mrs. Widder	Haydn.
ARIA—" Come t'adoro " (Beatrice di Tenda)	Miss H. Scott	Bellini.
GLEE—" Lutzow's wild hunt "	Dr. McCaul, Mr. Barron, Mr. Wells and Chorus	Weber.
SCENA ED ARIA—" Vivi tu " (Anna Bolena)	Mr. Humphreys	Donizetti.
BALLAD—" The dream is past "	Miss Hagerman	Glover.
DUET—" Crudel perche finora" (Le Nozze di Figaro)	Mrs. Widder and Captain Haliday	Mozart.
BALLAD—" I ought to tear thee from my heart "	Mrs. Nash	Abrams.
QUARTETTE—" Mi manca la voce "	Mrs. Nash, Mrs. Widder, Mr. Humphreys, and Captain Haliday	Rossini.

PART II.

FANTASIA—Piano Forte	Miss Clara Boulton	Herz.
ARIA—" Trono e corona " (Torquato Tasso)	Mrs. Nash	Donizetti.
BALLAD—" Dermot Astore "	Miss Macaulay	Crouch.
DUET—" Oh, lovely maiden, stay" (Azor & Zemira)	Mrs. Nash and Mr. Humphreys	Spohr.
CAVATINA—" Ah I per sempre io ti perdei " (I Puritani)	Captain Haliday	Bellini.
SONG—" Echo song "	Mrs. Widder	Sir H. R. Bishop.
GLEE—" Come, silent evening "	Dr. McCaul, Mr. Barron, Mr. Wells and Chorus	Call.
ARIA—" Vi ravviso " (Sonnambula)	Miss Hagerman	Bellini.
SONG—" Not a drum was heard "	Mr. Humphreys	Barnett.
TRIO—" Vadasi via di qua "	Mrs. Widder, Mr. Humphreys, and Capt. Haliday	Martini.

Figure 1. Widder Program, 1844, Courtesy Private Colletion

perhaps, are still genuine, but the nineteenth-century ladies and gentlemen who engaged in it were part of a larger world of uncertain allure. I still respond to that shell pink program with a little sigh, but, since making closer acquaintance with Mrs. Widder's Soirée Musicale, it is a sigh of not unmixed delight.

The domestic "Soirée Musicale," as found in nineteenth-century Ontario, was a posh, private party at which a formal concert, complete with printed programs, was performed. Amateurs from the hosts' social circle performed side by side with professional musicians in a mixture of musical genres including opera, parlour ballad, glee, and instrumental salon music. The musical genres of each selection were prominently stated in these programs. Why did hosts, performers and audiences want to know this? And in families that could easily have afforded to pay professionals to provide an entire concert, why were amateurs performing with professional musicians? The Program of Mrs. Widder's Soirée Musicale of 1844 is a window into the way musical life expressed social values.

The Soirée Musicale was a concert format adapted by the rising middle class from the private musical entertainments of the eighteenth century aristocracy. The history of the Soirée Musicale in Britain is not yet written, but perhaps the status-conscious hosts of those English musical parties found the French term captured the perfume of pre-Revolutionary Parisian salons where intellectual women orchestrated political networks during their sophisticated entertainments. The English blended the Soirée Musicale with their existing ballad tradition, and packed it into the cultural baggage of British emigrants to Upper Canada. It was an odd shapeshifter, because it rested on the ironic notion that music, which is so vigorous and unpredictable an art, was suitable as a fluffy, trivial domestic accomplishment for refined women. And yet the Lady Amateurs of these formal, private concerts often performed side by side with professional musicians. True, Soirées Musicales were given on the public stage, but even there the structure of the concert format referred to the blend of amateur and professional musicianship and the atmosphere of exclusive, elite musical leisure. Other concerts, not called by the same name, also combined different musical genres with a relish foreign to the sophisticated aesthetics of later twentieth century programming. There were so many variations of the Soirée Musicale and they were so similar to other concerts that the format was not entirely distinct from the rest of musical life of its time. What made it recognizable was the insistent air of elite, domestic amateurism in which, as this study shows, the assignment of musical genres was appropriate to the class and gender of each performer. The Soirée Musicale performed a kind of opera whose moral was that "natural" differences of gender and class formed a stable universe of interlocking hierarchies. The result was, literally, delightfully harmonious.

Treating a concert program as a portrait of an historical moment allows the historian to explore the non-musical implications of musical life. The art of program building is unfamiliar to most scholarship, but any programmer makes use of music, sequence, and careful casting. The programmer's toolkit is, in effect, a box of cultural building blocks, and the meaning of each of them is particular to the time and place in which the programmer builds each program. As a result, concert programming can change with infinite subtlety in response to microscopic changes of the social world where it occurs. A printed program in 1844 was not just the road map to a concert about to unfold, but was an important commemorative object: it communicated a web of social relationships that could be readily understood wherever it was seen. This was particularly true for a private concert program, designed for an audience largely known to the programmer. The resulting printed program could be used to communicate a variety of different meanings. A teaching tenor could allow a copy to slip out of his music portfolio at the home of a new student - an invitation to her parents to hire him to organise their own Soirée Musicale. An ambitious businessman who had hosted the concert could drop off a copy to a local British Governor, to let him know that devoted citizens who might someday need government support for a business plan were upholding the cream of English culture. An outraged but brilliant opponent of that businessman might be lulled into an erudite chat about the intellectually interesting music performed on the program by one of his own employees who had sung for his rival. A concert program is a portrait of a historic moment that holds a wide range of information.

Since a fundamental argument of this study is that Mrs. Widder's concert was an exhilarating experience, layered with meanings aimed directly at the memories, values, and current public concerns of many of those present, the "Overture" that follows is an imaginative recreation of the evening. It is fully based on the research that forms the body of this study, and weaves together the themes which analysis, perforce, must separate to examine. For the cultural historian, one of the benefits of Victorian social mores is that the respectability of a young, middle-class, Lady Amateur performing in a drawing-room concert in 1844 required the presence of her parents or other respectable members of her parents' social circle. The other good fortune of Mrs. Widder's roster of artists is their political prominence. The "Overture" uses these factors to introduce the performers of Mrs. Widder's concert in the context of their circle of acquaintance and the pressing concerns of the time. Political, commercial, and military networks are all germane to later discussions of the considerations that could have affected the planning of Mrs. Widder's concert.

The Soirée Musicale was a concentrated example of how music making flowed between the banks of public and private life. Amateur musicians in more modest parlours and touring American professionals in public concerts performed the same music. Several of Mrs. Widder's own artists took the music from her March party to the public stage, where those who had not been invited to the Lyndhurst concert could glimpse more glamorous musical lives. Mrs. Widder's private concert was exceptionally fine, but it was no more than an exaggeration of the musical fabric of the time and place. Wherever the Soirée Musicale appeared, its very structure proclaimed the naturalness and beauty of a hierarchy of human difference. It appeared at Lyndhurst, the Widders' home in downtown Toronto, on March 12, 1844.

MRS. WIDDER'S DRAWING ROOM, MARCH 12, 1844

James seems to be getting on pretty well he is getting all the snobs for pupils and has opened a Music Repository for the sale of Music and Piano-Fortes — Mrs. Widder gives a Soirée Musicale next week for which he sings [torn] the great gun.[1]

Figure 2: Lyndhurst Drawing Room (ca. 1890) where the Widder Soirée Musicale was held.
Courtesy Toronto Public Library (TRL) T-11346

They gleamed in the candlelight of Mr. and Mrs. Widder's Corinthian-columned ballroom that mild March evening in 1844 (Figure 2). The occasion was Mrs. Frederick Widder's Soirée Musicale. A passer-by might be forgiven for loitering to watch the guests alighting from the procession of carriages at the gates of Lyndhurst, the gilded upper crust gathering to smooth the way for their commercial alliances at a glittering, private concert. The piano at the far bay window awaited all of its divas, the visible symbol of music as a spiritual, if expensive, respite from the workaday world.

Even men who clashed sharply over politics and religion in this changing society would applaud each other's musical wives and daughters. The hosts, Mr. and Mrs. Widder, were both descended from English royalty, and however distant the clanking of throne and crown in their family trees, their private concert rang with aria after aria about royal politics, the anguish of choosing between "Trono e corona" (throne and crown) and the love of a sincere heart. Frederick Widder was born in 1801 in England, to a family of "Austro-Bavarian royalty," and had named his home "Lyndhurst" after the Widder family home in England. Elizabeth Widder, whose name graced the concert program, was likely the daughter of Sir Henry Moore, and "distantly related to the English Royal Family."[2]

Dr. John McCaul, Vice President of the University of King's College and a prolific classical scholar who had been selected by the Archbishop of Canterbury and exported from King's College Dublin to implement the British education of middle-class boys in Upper Canada, might have been seen striding down Front Street to the concert, with his colleague, the "thoroughly English" Mr. Frederick Barron, the Principal of Upper Canada College, to expand their lungs before they opened the concert by singing an operatic ode to heroism. Barron had studied at Cambridge, and had first been hired as a classics master at Upper Canada College by Colonel Joseph Wells.[3] Both Barron and McCaul owed something of their life work in Canadian education to Justice Christopher Hagerman, who had fought for the inclusion of Upper Canada College with the royal charter of King's, and also to their host, Frederick Widder.[4] Widder, as Commissioner of the Canada Company, had been contibuting to the budget of Upper Canada College. Since 1827, the Canada Company had supported Britain's cost of running the colony in exchange for the right to administer the settlement of some of the remaining farmlands. Canada Company payments to the provincial government included £1,000 annually for "the building of a college," and the full cost of the civil government, "replacing an annual grant from the British parliament."[5] McCaul and Barron would sing together for Mrs. Widder's concert.

There was Miss Hagerman, barely twenty-one and already famous for her gorgeous voice among the social circle of her father, Judge Christopher Hagerman, an old lion of the oligarchic "Family Compact" of Upper Canada. "Handsome Kit" Hagerman might well have walked into Lyndhurst beside the seventy-one-year-old Colonel Joseph Wells, both fathers of amateur musicians listed on Mrs. Widder's program. The Christian name of the Mr. Wells who sang that evening is unknown, but he was likely George Dupont Wells, the musical son of Colonel Joseph Wells. Mr. Wells sang glees with Frederick Barron and Reverend John McCaul, old colleagues of Colonel Joseph Wells. Banished as the incompetent, perhaps criminal, first bursar of the University of King's College and its affiliated prep school, Upper Canada College, Wells had nevertheless supported the Anglican affiliation of both schools. Like Christopher Hagerman, Colonel Wells had fought in the War of 1812 against the American forces seeking to overturn Upper Canada's role as a loyal outpost of British Empire. Wells had sat for years as an appointed member of the tiny, closed Executive and Legislative Councils of Upper Canada. He and the others of the original Family Compact, including Bishop John Strachan and John Beverley Robinson (Sr.), had been appointed to life terms on the governing councils of the pioneer colony of Upper Canada. By 1844, they were being swept out of power by the advent of representative government.[6]

An excited Miss Clara Boulton pattered over the threshold on the arm of her father, Henry John Boulton (Jr.), elected as a Reformer to the Assembly, but a member of a rich and powerful Toronto family. The now-proliferating Boulton clan was moving, like the sons of other Family Compact fathers Robinson, Macaulay, Wells, and Strachan, into the military, legal and medical professions, as well as becoming active in the newly created urban political governments. John Robinson (Jr.), a lawyer like Henry John Boulton, would be Mayor of Toronto before 1850. Robinson (Jr.) might even have slipped into Mrs. Widder's Soirée Musicale, to catch Miss Hagerman's performance. Three years hence, he and Miss Hagerman would marry, two outgoing personalities well suited to each other.

Was the Hon. Dr. Robert W. Scott, a Reformer like John Henry Boulton (Jr.), there to hear Miss H. Scott sing that night? Without knowing Miss Scott's first name it is impossible to tell. The full identities of some other performers are also veiled. Miss Macaulay may well have been the niece of Christopher Hagerman, since his first wife was a Macaulay; and the Mrs. Nash may have been related to the Mr. Nash who sat on the board of directors of the early Toronto Philharmonic Association, but pinpointing with accuracy individuals from large families is not always feasible. There is a record of a Miss Scott, first name unknown, who appeared once in public but this was hardly a professional career, if it was the same person. The records of public performance show that Miss Macaulay and Mrs. Nash did not perform in public in Toronto in the next decade. Like Miss Hagerman, all of Mrs. Widder's women performers were probably middle-class Lady Amateurs.[7]

They must have looked marvellous, every one, dressed for an elegant evening party at one of the largest homes in Toronto. Captain Haliday, the baritone singer of opera for the evening, was probably William Robert Haliday, a Captain of the Regiment of the 93rd Sutherland Highlanders, stationed in Toronto at the time. Although there is no known evidence confirming the singer's Christian names, no other Haliday appears to have lived in Toronto at this time. If he wore full officer's uniform, he dazzled in a scarlet jacket dripping with gold braid, which set off a blue kilt and red plaid socks as the painting of Officers' Uniforms (Figure 3) suggests. The same man who sang for

Figure 3: "Dress of the Officers 1834" by Lieutenant Robert William Haliday Illustration for Roderick Hamilton Burgoyne, ed., Historical Records of the 93rd Sutherland Highlanders, now the 2nd Battalion Princess Louise's Argyle and Sutherland Highlanders *(London: Richard Bentley and Son, 1883), facing p. 62/Courtesy National Library of Canada*

Mrs. Widder's concert may also have painted this picture, since it was credited to a Lieutenant Haliday in the regimental history published in 1883, ample time for a hard-working Captain to rise in the ranks. The Regiment was known for its contributions to local musical life, often, to the chagrin of local professional musicians, charging low fees to entertain at private parties. Captain Haliday must have been known to at least one other person present at Lyndhurst that evening, or he would not have been invited, let alone asked to sing in trios with Mrs. Widder herself. Over the three years in Toronto, Haliday had probably developed social and musical acquaintance through his military connections, which were commonly used as a gateway to developing professional networks.[8]

Civilian and military daily lives were deeply interwoven, so the military references in the music itself resonated among performers and listeners. With the rebellion of 1837 a vivid recent memory, militia service was a common feature for many in Toronto. The tenor of Mrs. Widder's program, Mr. Humphreys, was a Lieutenant in the Third Battalion Incorporated of the Militia from 1838 to 1843, and he may have been a boon companion of Clara Boulton's father, Lieutenant Henry John Boulton (Jr.), from the officers' mess of the same unit in Toronto. The social lives of temporary military residents mingled with those of permanent citizens. A letter to Humphreys' sister, Ellen Foster, implies that the wife of another Captain in the 93rd Sutherland Highlanders, Mrs. Aylmer, had a close friend in Foster's social circle. On 5 March 1844, Charles Harrison wrote that Mrs. Aylmer "was a great friend of your friend Miss Fitzgibbon who will repent her loss much."[9] Perhaps it was this network that introduced the musical Captain Haliday to Mr. Humphreys. One of Mr. Widder's employees in the Canada Company, John McGill of the Fourth Battalion, York, may have met Haliday in informal musical evenings with another musical friend, Captain Thomas Galt, Seventh Battalion, Toronto. Galt's father had been the first Canadian Commissioner of the Canada Land Company until Widder took over in 1839, and Thomas Galt had shared a fine evening of all-male music with professional musician James Dodsley Humphreys. Every person in the room used and understood military references with ease.[10]

James Dodsley Humphreys, the professional tenor who had probably been instrumental in designing the concert program, may have arrived before most of the guests to soothe any pre-performance jitters felt by the Lady Amateurs. Harrison's letter had also mentioned that Humphreys was teaching "all the snobs," some of who might well have been present in this wealthy home. Miss Mary Jane Hagerman studied with him, too, but her nervousness might have been hard to detect. From her father, once described by John Beverley Robinson (Sr.) as "a young man whose bashfulness will never stand in his way," Miss Hagerman had inherited her ringing voice and electric presence.[11] A bouquet of cultured people gathered in the polished drawing room of Lyndhurst to share music.

Tensions simmered beneath this silken surface. In the Toronto of 1844, the battle over representative government was still uncoiling into church, university, town council and commercial enterprise, putting Reform and Tory factions at each other's throats. Frederick Widder himself was a land developer who was trying to attract support from all factions for a bold business plan, angling for control of all the Crown Lands in the newly united Canadas. Among his most determined opponents were Miss Hagerman's future father-in-law, John Beverley Robinson (Sr.) and Robinson's mentor, the Anglican Bishop John Strachan. If John Robinson (Jr.) attended to hear Miss Hagerman, his presence may have provoked his father.

Let us pause for a moment to applaud Mrs. Widder's skill in bringing the daughters of a vituperative old Tory like Christopher Hagerman and the no less passionate Reformer John Henry Boulton (Jr.) onto the same concert stage. In addition to providing a program in which these Lady Amateurs could shine, she had persuaded Bishop Strachan's most senior educational lieutenants, Mr. Barron and Reverend McCaul, to open the concert. Such purposeful entertainment, like business and politics, was a delicate art.

The experience of such a Soirée Musicale is foreign to the twenty-first century. The heterogeneous concert programs of the nineteenth century are assumed by many classical music purists of today to have been aesthetically risible. Much of this study involves not only the detail of the program and the context in which it took place, but the sense of it as an excellent concert, fast-paced, full of variety and built around coherent, secular themes.[12] Cooperative action was the underlying charm of the whole concert. The program of that March evening promised an experience like the one described here.

The assembled company rustled and settled in their seats in the formal reception room of Lyndhurst, the eleven artists clustered in the fringe of seats next to the hallway to allow for a discreet escape to hum before stepping to centre stage. Every eye in the room surely looked up from the programs held in kid-gloved hands, as the three Gentleman Amateurs stepped before them, inhaled together, and sang "Plaudite o populi." Their plain, patriotic chorus, glee-like in its close harmony and narrow vocal range, enacted a grateful populace praising the self-sacrificing heroism of its unelected leader, Tancredi. The musical and dramatic intensity then spiked upwards with two Lady Amateurs singing the virtuoso duet from the opera Norma, their voices in harmony cascading up and down the scale as the two Druidic priestesses, Norma and Adalgisa, vowed friendship despite loving the same man. The intensity dropped suddenly to the elegant simplicity of a Haydn canzonet sung by the hostess, then climbed steadily up through a lyrical operatic aria, "Come t'adoro," unremarkable in range or volume, until the whole room was galvanized with the exhilarating rhythms of the well-known three-man glee, "Lutzow's Wild Hunt." The peak of the first half was reached in the dazzling display of "Vivi tu," loud, fast, and high, sung by a fine professional tenor at the height of his powers. Thematically and musically, this was a marvellous ride to the peak of the first half.

After the operatic brilliance of "Vivi tu" came a dramatic drop into the simplicity of a parlour ballad sung by the Lady Amateur, Miss Hagerman. The sharp contrast in volume, vocal range, and complexity was a masterstroke of programming. It only worked if Miss Hagerman delivered "The dream is past" with great focus and stillness, but the scraps of her reputation which persist from the writing of the time suggest that this was well within her capacity. Whether or not she mesmerized the audience, the simplicity of the ballad offered the audience breathing space before it was embroiled in a piece of complex theatre, an elegant and subtle Mozart scene of aristocratic wickedness being set up for a fall by a clever and charming servant, played by Mrs. Widder. This musically challenging material in a foreign language was sandwiched between easy, English language songs, which plainly stated that good women knew they should control themselves when they were inundated with love for the wrong man. By now, the audience was tiring, and the first half wound down with a simple ballad and a perlescently harmonious quartet, "Mi manca la voce," which was popular at the time and often mentioned in well-known novels like *Rosalie* by Honoré de Balzac. The lyrics mean "My voice fails me," a little quiet humour by silvery-voiced singers approaching an interval in the program. It was a charming finish to a well-wrought first half.

After a welcome trip to the sweets table, perhaps, ready to be entertained but not wounded with undue artistic intensity, the company was greeted in the second half by a young lady from a powerful family showing off her feminine accomplishments with a piano "Fantasia," written by a professor of the English Royal Academy of Music. Social honour was bestowed by placement where it need not be won by virtuosic or musical intensity.

Without knowing which of the many Herz "Fantasias" she played, it is impossible to know how difficult Miss Boulton's selection was. Henri Herz wrote many "Fantasias" both for his own flashy professional concerts and for the student market. In Humphreys' daughter's music folio, held privately, are two examples of simple Herz compositions: "La Belle Allemande" and "La Belle Bohemienne." The same folio holds the Glover ballad sung at Mrs. Widder's concert by Humphreys' student, Miss Hagerman, suggesting that Humphreys assigned music from his own collection to his students. Since he knew some of the simpler Herz works, he could easily have recommended one to Miss Boulton.

Whether she played with bravura or with trembling bravery, Clara Boulton soothed, as every accomplished young lady should. There were no words to consider as sugar was surreptitiously brushed from audience fingertips. This opening number made a promise for the second half of the concert: though its patterns echoed those of the first half, its tone would be lighter and simpler.

After the piano "Fantasia," the intensity of the second number spiked upwards, parallel to the first half but not as loud, with a skilled Lady Amateur enacting a queen torn between love for a commoner and her throne. The operatic work was followed by a simple but affecting ballad common to parlours everywhere, "Dermot Astore," which repeated the theme of the Italian language aria that preceded it: a woman stating her love for a man despite the distance between them. In a lyrical rise in intensity from Miss Macaulay's ballad, but repeating again the theme of anguish at the prospect of lovers parted by their different social stations, the Lady Amateur Mrs. Nash and the professional Mr. Humphreys sang a difficult duet from the opera *Azor and Zemira*, based on the tale of Beauty and the Beast, in which the Beast begs the Beauty to stay. The peak of the anguish of parting in the second half of the concert was reached with the meltingly lovely baritone aria of lost love sung by Captain Haliday, whose voice would have filled the ballroom as it soared to its outer limit, but would not have rattled the chandeliers as the higher-voiced Humphreys had done with "Vivi tu" in the first half.

Mrs. Widder sparkled in a parlour confection just after the midpoint of the second half. She may not have included the same high, florid singing added to the "Echo Song" by professional singers like Adelina Patti, but even if she did, the music itself was not tiring to the ear. It was a pretty rest for the audience who could reduce their attention without mistaking their hostess's charm, and relax even more during the following trio of pleasant male voices in close harmony singing "Come, Silent Evening," a glee about nature's blessed rewards at evening. Miss Hagerman returned with a slow operatic aria of yearning for a better, bygone, decidedly pre-democratic time. Though in Italian, the aria was in the middle of Miss Hagerman's vocal range, hence not very loud. From this luscious if vocally fuzzy romance, the program rose to a penultimate stab of intensity when the excellent Mr. Humphreys recreated the pathos of the dark and gory burial of a war hero whose story was doubtless known to many in the Widder drawing room. In English, not too high or loud, the drum-like beats of the accompaniment helped this Barnett song about the death of General Sir John Moore on a battlefield in Spain to wrap its listeners of every political stripe in noble sorrow for a British leader, before they were rewarded with the final trio of laughing harmony. The repeated refrain of "ha ha ha," in this popular and familiar song, with its jovial reference to quaffing wine, was a clear signal that the concert was ending. If some amateur performances had been lacklustre, the program had finished with Mr. Humphreys as the backbone of the final two items, joined at the very end by his skilled hostess, leaving the audience with the echo of vocal excellence ringing in their ears. The final trio created the ideal atmosphere for alliance building over port, had anyone present been so inclined.

The concert program, smoothly incorporating differences, classically symmetrical and balanced, offered a vision of an orderly and harmonious world. Every artist had sung music appropriate to their natural niche in the social hierarchy recognized by all present. Unhappy and dramatic music had punctuated the program, warning that dangers lurked in this paradise. Irrational desire blotted propriety, causing personal anguish and social chaos, and tales had been told of the barbarism of the invading and often republican foreigner. But the vision framed by the concert program demonstrated that the rewards of overcoming such dangers were enchanting: peace, honour, and harmony for all.

The company parted after the concert was over, the contentious political differences unresolved and yet with them into the mild night departed a shared vision of a harmonious world. Amid rustlings of cloaks and silks, the coachmen holding their stamping horses, the Lady Amateurs and their families clicked carriage doors shut behind them. There may have been satisfaction in the singers' hearts and rosy pride for fathers and husbands tapping top hats into place. Money on singing lessons and an expensive piano was well spent for such universal approbation of the results. As the Gentleman Amateurs strolled back to their academic precincts, a friendly argument about the relative merits of German and English glee composers might have rolled out on those vibrant voices into the night. Mr. Humphreys, after tidying up his copies of the music and possibly tucking a discreet envelope from Frederick Widder into his pocket, may have found a moment to congratulate Mrs. Widder on the evening. Toronto might not be the musical Mecca that London was, but on rare occasions like these it was hard to tell the difference. He threw a silk scarf around his reliable throat, and headed home to his cosy parlour.

As the Lyndhurst door finally swung shut, Frederick and Elizabeth Widder might well have been pleased with their concert. The Canada Company money that helped support Upper Canada College had made Reverend McCaul's and Mr. Barron's melodious singing voices available to adorn the glee harmonies. Without dear Mr. Humphreys, Mrs. Widder could not have managed all the musical details and still managed to sing with any concentration at all. But she sang with such refinement! A faint inhalation hung in the air over the name of Miss Hagerman: really a marvellous voice, and so very, very generous with sharing it so very, very often. Had her formidable father actually blushed with pleasure when complimented on his daughter's singing?

Much had been at stake. Mr. Widder would not grasp all the profitable lands he was aiming at in 1844, but relentless entertaining would continue to facilitate his career as Commissioner of the Canada Company. The core of Mrs. Widder's cast would go on to present Soirées Musicales to the public as examples of the higher order of musical life. Mr. Humphreys, Reverend McCaul, and Mr. Barron would sing often in public, and often with Miss Hagerman. And over the next fifty years, the interlocking layers of music, commerce, and power that had come to life in Mrs. Widder's Soirée Musicale would continue to evolve around stable concepts of gender and class.

Chapter One

THE SCRAMBLED KALEIDOSCOPE
Glimpses of the Ontario Soirée Musicale

For more than fifty years, the many variations of Mrs. Widder's private concert were effortlessly recognized in Ontario as Soirées Musicales, and yet there is no scholarship to explain what they had in common or why they were popular. Musical life, like all culture, did not exist in an autonomous Brigadoon but was an active part of politics, commerce, and personal identity. This case study of Mrs. Widder's Soirée Musicale (Figure 1) offers cultural history an approach to using concert programs as historical, rather than purely musical, evidence. Close analysis of a single concert program unlocks the riddle of what made a concert instantly recognizable as Soirée Musicale from the 1840s until 1910, and in the process shows how public concert life was linked with all domestic parlour music making. The Soirée Musicale was a concert format embodying the idea of a natural hierarchy in which people, distinguished by gender and class, occupied distinct but cooperative niches. It performed a vision of social stability during a period of economic and political upheaval.

A word about sources and method is in order before settling down to Mrs. Widder's concert. All of the information on the program was a starting place for the research, which required a synthesis of scholarship in a range of fields from the pragmatic perspective of performance itself. The work of trying to see the Widder drawing room clearly is like looking through an interpretive kaleidoscope: different academic frameworks emphasize different questions, different sources, and different answers. I drew on my long career as a professional, classical singer who specialized in recitals to pull together a range of academic perspectives and recreate a sense of the whole experience of hearing and performing Mrs. Widder's concert.

The array of sources was daunting. Every performer's name was searched. Each musical selection on the Widder program was found, not always in Canada, and reviewed for the challenges it offered the technical skills of each performer and the emotional and conceptual complexity it offered the audience. The lyrics were translated, read in sequence and summarised thematically. The nineteenth-century habit of binding individual sheet music selections into personal albums allowed the repertoire of Mrs. Widder's 1844 concert to be compared with more than 200 bound albums of sheet music owned in Canada from approximately 1835 to 1900. These volumes, usually containing between ten and thirty selections, show the personal repertoires of their

Programme
OF
MRS. WIDDER'S "SOIRÉE MUSICALE"
LYNDHURST, MARCH 12, 1844

PART I

CORO – "Plaudite oh Popoli" (Tancredi) . . . . *Rossini*

DUET – "Mira, Oh Norma" (Norma) . . . . Miss Hagerman, Mrs. Nash . . . *Bellini*

CANZONET – "My mother bids me bind" . . . . Mrs. Widder . . . . *Haydn*

ARIA – "Come t'adoro" (Beatrice di Tenda) . . . . Miss H. Scott . . . . *Bellini*

GLEE – "Lutzow's wild hunt" . . . . Dr. McCaul, Mr. Barron,
  Mr. Wells and Chorus . . . . *Weber*

SCENA ED ARIA – "Vivi tu" (Anna Bolena) . . . . Mr. Humphreys . . . . *Donizetti*

BALLAD – "The dream is past" . . . . Miss Hagerman . . . . *Glover*

DUET – "Crudel perche finora" (Le Nozze di Figaro) . . . Mrs. Widder, Capt. Haliday . . *Mozart*

BALLAD – "I ought to tear thee from my heart" . . . . Mrs. Nash . . . . *Abrams*

QUARTETTE – "Mi manca la voce" . . . . Mrs. Nash, Mrs. Widder, ... *Rossini*
  Mr. Humphreys, Capt. Haliday

PART II

FANTASIA – Piano Forte . . . . Miss Clara Boulton . . . . *Herz*

ARIA – "Trono e corona" (Torquato Tasso) . . . . Mrs. Nash . . . . *Donizetti*

BALLAD – "Dermot Astore" . . . . Miss Macaulay . . . . *Crouch*

DUET – "Oh, lovely maiden, stay" (Azor & Zemira) . . . . Mrs. Nash, Mr. Humphreys . . . . *Spohr*

CAVATINA – "Ah! Per sempre io ti perdei" (I Puritani) . Captain Haliday . . . . *Bellini*

SONG – "Echo Song" . . . . Mrs. Widder . . . . *Sir H. R. Bishop*

GLEE – "Come, silent evening" . . . . Dr. McCaul, Mr. Barron, ... *Call*
  Mr. Wells and Chorus

ARIA – "Vi Ravviso" (Sonnambula) . . . . Miss Hagerman . . . . *Bellini*

SONG – "Not a drum was heard" . . . . Mr. Humphreys . . . . *Barnett*

TRIO – "Vadasi via di qua" . . . . Mrs. Widder, Mr. Humphreys,
  and Captain Haliday . . . . *Martini*

Widder 1844 Program. Courtesy Private Collection. Reproduced to imitate original.

owners, sometimes mixing generations in a single volume. Three volumes inscribed "Miss Widder" at the National Library of Canada contain music printed before the birth of any of Frederick and Elizabeth Widder's children, and since those earlier works were all printed in England, it is most likely that the music sung by the parents was given to the children.

Not all selections in the volumes were heavily used, but the beloved music was obvious: much-used music was held together with safety pins, strips of newspaper glued over tears, edges rebound. Breath marks, teachers' exasperated comments, and the general level of technical difficulty all give indications of the skill and seriousness of the player. Music within a single bound album tended to show consistent levels of difficulty, so differences in levels of difficulty and taste in repertoire could be seen to vary noticeably between owners. Handwritten indices of the bound volumes occasionally appear, suggesting that some players felt a need for efficient finding aids during performance or frequent personal access. Most albums were inscribed with women's names, but some men's music collections are also present.

The bound music folios available in most collections in the Toronto area did not provide all of the music for Mrs. Widder's concert. Selections like the glees and the Abrams song had to be found in international repositories. This points to the difficulties of using musical sources statistically. A concert program like Mrs. Widder's is evidence of the intention to use specific musical works. Any statistical analysis of existing music collections, however, could not "prove" the full range of repertoire used in the nineteenth century in Canada.

Extant domestic Soirée Musicale programs are few, and in the latter part of the nineteenth century showed confusing variations. Mrs. Widder's, as the earliest known program, was analyzed in the hope that it had emerged prior to the effects of the rise of professionalism in music education and performance after 1880. The interpretive approach developed from the Widder program was tested on a few public programs from Ontario and the solitary English sample held in the British Library, the 1849 private concert in London by the Sandeman family. The Sandeman wealth came from the port wine trade and Widder's from land development, but both were successful merchants. The Widder Soirée Musicale was particularly fine because enormous effort had gone into the construction of the program, and this is perhaps one reason a copy of the program was saved for so long. The analysis of this program has produced an approach that may be a helpful first step in considering the historical but non-musical implications of other nineteenth century concert programs.

Printed Soirée Musicale programs were the often-discarded ephemera of personal life. They are now exceedingly rare. The program of Mrs. Widder's private concert has survived, possibly because it was a pivotal event for more than one participant. The factors that made this concert a Soirée Musicale were common to the Atlantic World, but the Widder programming derived much of its power from the specific local meanings of the music, the performers, and the sequence in which they were presented. Mrs. Widder's Soirée Musicale program printed a picture of social, political, and business networks that were specific to Toronto in 1844. The programs of professional, public concerts cannot provide the historian with the same depth of local information as a private, domestic concert, where the choices and sequence of music on the program were designed to meet the interests of a few individual performers and audience members, most of whom were familiar to the programmer(s).

The history of musical life is as tricky to understand as any other branch of cultural history. As anthropologist Pirkko Moisala suggests, music making is "performative of many ... aspects of culture."[1] Musicologist Christopher Small approaches the same insight slightly differently when he asks, "What does it mean when this performance takes place at this time, in this place, with these people taking part?" Music itself is pure abstraction, but every time it is heard, the words of its songs, the visual aspect of its performance, and the imaginative worlds of those who participate in making and hearing it, imbue the sound of music itself with layers of social meaning.[2]

Trying to understand the every day meaning of "Soirée Musicale" during the nineteenth century is a sizable task, made more manageable by close study of one, rather extreme, example. Even Charles Harrison, writing in 1844 about the Widder evening, described it only as a "Soirée Musicale," evidently requiring no further explanation of the term. Since Mrs. Widder was no eccentric outcast but a lady flourishing in the dead centre of Victorian respectability, her program represents the conventional meaning of the Soirée Musicale in Ontario. The Widder program may provide a model for understanding not only the many variations of the Soirée Musicale, but also the wider horizon of music making in nineteenth-century Ontario.

Gerda Lerner provides the theoretical basis for assembling this kaleidoscope of history when she suggests that "gender, [and] class ... are not separate categories, but different aspects of systems of hierarchy and dominance. They are interdependent ... and inseparable."[3] They are inseparable in function because they share the common premise that there is a biological basis for discriminating a hierarchy of human value. In the Burkean sense that permeated the thinking of the politically powerful in Ontario from 1800 to 1850, innate worthiness to rule was heritable through the bloodlines of aristocracy, or discoverable through resemblance to noble behaviour in a meritocracy. This was the fundamental justification for a hierarchy of access to active political power.[4] Inherited or innate qualities carry the implication that these are somehow biological and natural. Mrs. Widder's Soirée Musicale was a posh party open to the select few.

What little scholarship touches directly on nineteenth-century domestic music making corroborates Lerner's insight that gender and class functioned as interdependent systems of dominance, expressed in musical life as in other forms of culture. It does not always do so intentionally. It is necessary to click the interpretive kaleidoscope abruptly at times from field to field. The patterns shown through the kaleidoscope frame of women's history provide the most flexible theoretical basis for understanding how concepts of gender influenced both men and women in the Soirée Musicale. This history of the Soirée Musicale in Ontario shares one of the important functions of women's history, which is to expand the historical record of women's activities. With another kaleidoscope click to popular culture theory, where the content and commerce of culture are examined in terms of class relationships, the scholarship shares some methodology with feminism but tends to consider gender as a minor factor in the struggle for class power. The history of popular culture has much to offer the Soirée Musicale in Ontario, where the mixture of commerce and class was not an overtone but a bass note. Music was one of the modes of the nineteenth-century economy which bound commerce to private experience. Music was powerful because it could embed the ideas of its lyrics with overtones of the social contexts in which it was performed.

Recognizing the factors at play in Mrs. Widder's drawing room depends on the colourful glass shards poured into the interpretive kaleidoscope from the meticulous research of Canadian historians of music and politics. Without them, Mrs. Widder's program would be a silent document, barely visible in the historical twilight. The distinguished work of Canadian historians on pre-Confederation politics, politicians, and the economy reveals the political landscape of Mrs. Widder's Toronto.[5] More recent analysis of the relationships between Church, State, and education has also been useful.[6] The history of women in nineteenth-century Canadian culture has rarely included music as a topic, but Canadian historians like Katherine McKenna, Elizabeth Jane Errington, and Cecilia Morgan have begun to consolidate the insights of feminist theory with political and cultural history.[7] Mrs. Widder's Soirée Musicale Program pulls all of it into a single drawing room, where musical composition and performance along with the politics, the religious disputes, and the jostle of commerce and idealism, act like so much dust on the eyelashes and coat hems of every person at that musical party in 1844.

Although most of the scholarship about gender, class, and music used here is based on evidence from Britain, Europe, or the United States, it is relevant to the Canadian context in two ways. First, nineteenth-century Canada was in the process of adapting the transplanted cultures of Europe and Britain to its particular geography and circumstance as a British colony with a dominant continental neighbour. British culture still permeated the lives of Ontario's middle class, much of whose economic and political power depended on relationships with the British policy makers based in London, England.

As Canadian historian J.M.S. Careless described public culture, "whatever the ethnic strains in mid-Victorian Toronto [c.1854], its British loyalism remained fully apparent."[8] Edith Firth has shown that the period from 1825 to 1850 was one of rapid and uncomfortable social transformation which put the conservative elites of Ontario in the same position as those in Britain: struggling to maintain a social distance in order to keep a grip on power as the middle classes rose to challenge them. British cultural practice was plopped onto the unpaved streets of muddy York, and with it came the fraught and formal socialising of London, including the idea, the music, and perhaps even some of the players of the London Soirée Musicale.[9]

Second, the economic and class structures at play in middle-class music making in Britain, Europe, and North America were all informed by the similar developments of industrial capitalism throughout the nineteenth century. In terms of the Soirée Musicale, for all but the scholars of music as asocial aesthetic, the relationship between the family and the economy, with its permutations of class and gender, is common ground. The interpretive kaleidoscope includes the study of popular culture as an integral part of the economic forces that contributed to class difference.

A leading proponent of this approach is William Weber, who, in his account of concert life between 1830-1848 in London, Paris and Vienna, *Music and the Middle Class*, explains three important aspects of the Soirée Musicale of London which also apply to Mrs. Widder's event: the mix of musical genres, the class status of the hosts, and the presence of professional, male musicians in the private drawing-room concert. Weber is among the scholars of culture who consider nineteenth-century musical life to be a function of the changing class structure of urban, industrial capitalism. Like many feminist historians, he considers family life to be a necessary part of industrial capitalism. He argues that public concert life in cities emerged from the transition out of aristocratic patronage of musicians with the rise of the middle class, a persistent theme in the history of the nineteenth-century British music profession. His conclusion that professional musicians undertook a range of activities as part of their careers is based in part on noting that private performances were sometimes "planned explicitly as formal concerts" by status-seeking hosts who "put on 'soirées musicales' twice a week 'believing them to create no small sensation in the world of fashion.'" Musicians were often paid to organize and perform at these events, which Weber describes as "the popular music scene." He draws a clear connection between private concerts and those in the public sphere, suggesting that musicians controlled their market and used, among other techniques, "flamboyant performing skills" to squeeze amateurs out of public concert life by 1848.[10] This may have been true for London, but it certainly was not for Ontario, where amateur performers appeared in a variety of public venues beyond 1900.

Weber argues that the mixed genres of the upper crust Soirées Musicales should be regarded as "popular music," which he identifies as music that offered both novelty and ease of performance by amateurs. He suggests that "popular" music in the nineteenth century was a combination of Italian opera after Rossini, and a "revitalized virtuosic style out of various national sources" epitomized by Franz Liszt and Sigismond Thalberg, two internationally famous concert pianists.[11] The commercial symbiosis of professional and amateur performance was a circular integration based on selling simplified versions of virtuosic material for domestic consumption. This explains the financial basis for the tangle of musical genres common to most nineteenth-century concert programs, including the Soirée Musicale of Ontario. Weber is a welcome voice in the fractious debate about the value of "art music" because he accepts real aesthetic differences in musical genres while tracing the differentials of power and money that wove through them. [12]

American historian James Parakilas is in substantial agreement with Weber, but uses the piano rather than the performer as the central symbol of the musical economy in *Piano Roles: Three Hundred Years of Life with the Piano*. The theme of this well-knit group of essays is that "the piano is the instrument, the product around which the modern entertainment industry was created" in the consumer society of the "long nineteenth century." It was not the inventor of the piano, Bartolomeo Cristofori (1655-1732), but Muzio Clementi (1752-1832) who was called "The Father of the Pianoforte." Parakilas credits Clementi with linking "instrument sales, printed music, journal subscriptions, concert tickets, piano lessons, musical keepsakes - and dreams - so that they all promoted one another."[13]

Parakilas, Ehrlich, Scott, and Weber echo Neil McKendrick's conclusions about the implications of personal consumption in *The Birth of a Consumer Society: The Commercialization of Eighteenth-century England*. McKendrick argues that since "the idea of self-improvement through spending implied genuine social mobility," the undeniable differences of class were not innate but "based on little more than purchasing power." Education and refinement were the consumer goods of choice for those who wished to rise socially. The subtle skills and high costs of hosting a Soirée Musicale made it a choice vehicle for manipulating the class status of the newly rich businessmen of the 1840s who, in Weber's view, were the principal purveyors of domestic Soirées Musicales. [14]

The Soirée Musicale on this reading was an example of how the values of capitalist entrepreneurialism structured musical life: Weber's core thesis. Mutual benefit by businessmen in different fields resulted in the musical businessmen manipulating class struggle for its own profit while their clients, the middle-class financiers and manufacturers, appreciative of the display of competitive merit and skill by professional musicians, used musical events as a mode for expanding their social influence. While Weber's assessment of musicians as firmly in control of their economic destiny is at variance with many other historians of the music profession, his description of the typical Soirée Musicale hosts fits Mr. and Mrs. Widder well. Mr. Widder was the director of a commercial land development enterprise in Ontario, and was known for his hospitality. Weber offers valuable context for the Soirée Musicale in Ontario as a sample of mobile English culture, which took root in Ontario because it found appropriate economic and cultural conditions. The music and the practice of the Soirée Musicale emerged in the urban, industrial capitalism of England and Europe and were carried out in Ontario by those who could afford it.

Cyril Ehrlich's groundbreaking history of the English music profession is the flagship for the majority of scholars who, unlike Weber, conclude that most English musicians faced a desperate scramble to make a living from music. Published ten years after Weber's book, Ehrlich's *The Music Profession in Britain since the Eighteenth Century: A Social History* shows that musicians made their living by serving the "utilitarian and culturally impoverished" musical needs of a new, middle-class consumer. Trained as an economist but committed to art music, Ehrlich combined quantitative analysis with prosopography to conclude that amateur music making was "inextricably linked with the commercialization of music and, therefore, the employment of professional musicians." His work shows that only the most successful of British musicians had access to upper-class drawing rooms. Sir George Smart and other successful composers earned part of their living by performing with amateurs at private musical parties. They sometimes waived performance fees to establish a collegial rapport with their employers that could lead to more lucrative teaching engagements and to important commissions from piano makers for successfully promoting the purchase of pianos. [15] This delicate balance between servility and autonomous artistry must have been familiar to nineteenth-century Ontario musicians whose professional basket of activities clearly generated most of its income not in the public practice of the art but by supporting amateur musical interest.

Printed dedications of sheet music to celebrities were part of this integrated musical economy. Derek Scott, whose *The Singing Bourgeois: Songs of the Victorian Drawing Room and Parlour* contributes to the ongoing debate in musicology over the value of popular music, points out that "it was important for publishers to include in advertisements ... details of who they were sung by."[16] Celebrity rather than musicality was the key to the marketing usefulness of a given name, as dedications of music in Toronto to politicians like the Lieutenant-Governor of Ontario in 1884 suggest.[17] Scott recognizes "snob value" as a marketing technique aimed at a middle class that emulated royalty through the purchase of domestic consumables like Wedgwood dinnerware, pianos, and sheet music.

Scott identifies a key premise for this history of the Soirée Musicale in Ontario when he recognizes that the public "soirées musicales" retained an "at home" atmosphere which "aimed to provide impeccably wholesome entertainment" for the increasing numbers of the respectable middle class. One of the clearest examples of this was a commercial production in London, England, of a re-enactment by professional performers. Scott writes that it was advertised as "'Mr. and Mrs. German Reed's Entertainment,' a phrase suggestive of 'at home' functions among polite society."[18] The public Soirée Musicale was a floor model of the private version, and a chance to learn how it was really done, the better to take it home. In Ontario, when public Soirées Musicales were performed, as they often were by well known amateurs who performed similar programs in private settings, it was very much as if a real, not a scripted, drawing room had been transplanted into public view. William Weber's perceptive remark that "cultural experience served as an entry-point into a new class" applies equally to public audiences.[19]

Within this framework, gender as a category of analysis tends to be peripheral rather than constitutive. Although many of these scholars are sensitive to the subordinate role of women, they miss the performers' own perspectives. Amateur women musicians tend to be dismissed as either trivial or tragic, even by feminist historians. Richard Leppert, for instance, in his analysis of the gendered use of music to support class status, *Music and Image: Domesticity, Ideology and Socio-cultural Formation in Eighteenth-century England*, and Eva Öhrstrom, in what appears to be the only existing monograph on the Soirée Musicale, both consider upper-class musical activity by women to be a function of their entrapment as gendered pawns of class and economy.

In her analysis of nineteenth-century Swedish domestic Musicales, Eva Öhrstrom suggests that the higher the social status of the woman's family, the greater her artistic freedom, but that their gender limited even noblewomen to private performance only. Öhrstrom does the important work of reclaiming from invisibility the activities of women musicians, discovering in Elfrida Andrée (1841-1929) an active feminist who built herself a public composing and performing career in the 1890s. Öhrstrom suggests that this "lone pioneer without any followers" broke new ground for women in society. The history of Mrs. Widder's guest singer, Miss Hagerman, outlined in Chapter Five, suggests that, to the contrary, a solitary exception to the rule had no noticeable effect on the access of middle-class women to the music profession. [20]

Still within the gender frame of the kaleidoscope, Richard Leppert's fascinating discussion of music and gender as tropes of middle-class status emphasises the social and conceptual use of the amateur woman musician, but not primarily from the perspective of the amateur herself. Like the expensive keyboards that were their principal instrument, women making music were most important as "icons of privatization, success and respectability." Leppert is a sensitive observer of symptoms of discomfort among the women in the paintings he analyses, and his work is an important step in the process of integrating gender with class and cultural history. His method of deconstructing the layers of semiotic messages in paintings shows that conventions demarking gradations of social and gender status were necessarily upheld in the cultural activities of the upper classes. What Leppert shows for the conventions that underpinned the painted portraits of the musical middle class of England is applied here to the construction of Mrs. Widder's Soirée Musicale program. [21]

The Soirée Musicale, where amateur and professional shared the drawing room as a stage, was perhaps the inevitable outcome of musical accomplishment being ascribed to women in the home. The complex landscape of the Victorian idea of Woman has been revealed by the distinguished scholarship of women's history and feminist musicology. To understand their common conceptual ground, it may be helpful to visualize both Woman and Music as Adam's rib. The rib is natural, physical, and passive. The rib cannot be improved by changing: it protects Adam's heart, and sustains Adam's physical environment and recreation best by continuing to exhibit its naturally stable essence. As Lenore Davidoff suggests, music was one mode in which women, as ladies, were expected to provide "a haven of stability, of exact social classification in the threatening anonymity of the surrounding economic and political upheaval."[22] Adam generates change in the world as he moves purposefully, creating new ideas and things. He relies on the stable services of his rib, which repeats its functions in an unchanging way. The only change possible for a rib is injury or removal, in which case it cannot serve Adam and loses its identity and its nature. It becomes, in fact, a bad rib, incapable of serving its true purpose. Adam's rib is innocent and selfless, since it is not by itself fully human: it cannot have an identity separate from Adam. A good woman was very like a good rib.

So was domestic music. Music in the Victorian home served the creative, productive Adam by protecting his heart and by providing spiritual uplift and moral radiance. The nature of musical performance, and musical performers, was understood to be the body in service to the creative genius of the composer, although, as feminist musicologist as Pirkko Moisala suggests, "music does not exist until bodies make it and/or receive it."[23] Performing music - physical, repetitive, making actual sound - was understood to be different in kind from composing it. Over the nineteenth and into the twentieth centuries, musicology has produced an enormous literature defending the true essence of music as intellectual and masculine. In 1880, Chicago music critic, George Upton, described this in obverse: "woman lacks the mastery of the theoretical intricacies, logical sequences, and the mathematical problems which are the foundation principles of music. She will always be the recipient and interpreter, but there is little hope she will be the creator."[24]

These insights about male and female gender definitions in the Victorian period are not new. The Enlightenment notions of gender persisted through the nineteenth century because they were central to the Industrial Revolution, and have been discussed by many scholars, notably Lenore Davidoff and Catherine Hall who provide an extended analysis of gender, economy and social structure in *Family Fortunes: Men and Women of the English Middle Class, 1780-1850*. Similarly, Deborah Gorham, in *The Victorian Girl and the Feminine Ideal*, emphasizes the economic link between public and private spheres as a key to the Victorian concept of femininity.[25] Masculinity was also associated with persistence through lineage and public service, where lineage is biological, intellectual, and professional. As outsiders to the mainstream of the musical profession, and hence not part of a lineage of transmission by teachers and curriculum, students, publishers, and patrons, women composers were forgotten by music history.[26] Women performers, of course, suffer a similar decapitation of their professional history.

Time differed according to gender as well.[27] Adam strides through time, generating change and progress. Woman, as Adam's rib, is frozen in an eternal "before." This resulted in the feminine ideals of purity, childishness, and innocence, which appeared repeatedly in Victorian song lyrics that associated women with either static or retrospective time.

Deborah Gorham traces how the ideal of perfect femininity persisted through cultural transmission, arguing successfully that women "were seen as fulfilling their function only as they existed in relationship to others."[28] Gorham concurs with Leonore Davidoff, that British women's leisure was essential to the respectable status of the whole family. Davidoff's study suggests that it was a woman's "duty to free herself for the higher sphere," to the degree that the family could afford to have household work done by others. The resulting leisure carried with it a duty to provide cultivated entertainment as a contribution to the family's social advancement.[29] Domestic music making was one expression of Woman's Higher Nature. For all women, as the periodicals published by the music publishers of the time urged, taking the time needed to develop excellent musical skills "is not of a selfish character, but will extend your own to the amusement of others."[30] For women of the upper classes, their musical activity was a demonstration of their leisure, and their musical excellence proof of the superiority of their whole class.

Canadian historian Cecilia Morgan's study of the gendering of civic life in Upper Canada from 1791 to 1850 suggests that in Canada, too, "lady" had a different meaning from "woman" because "gender distinctions were bound up with notions of class and race."[31] Any woman who made money by performing music was thereby not a member of an upper class. The loophole for a Lady Amateur appearing in a public version of the Soirée Musicale of Ontario was that, as an "amateur," she was applying her leisured acquisition of a superior musical skill to civic benefit. If the civic aspects of the domestic drawing room were ambiguous, the presence of upper-class amateurs in a public performance of a Soirée Musicale for charity was not.

As Katherine McKenna's group biography of the Powell family shows, elite women in mid-nineteenth-century Ontario had few options. The lives of two of the Powell daughters, one a wife and mother, the other a self-effacing and helpful spinster, demonstrated that a "good" woman "devoted her life to the care of others." McKenna's chilling example of the third daughter, an eccentric who was outcast because she could not "reconcile herself to her restricted role in life," corroborates most other histories of women of this period. Conformity to the principal tenets of Victorian gender ideology was necessary for survival.

Morgan, McKenna, Gorham, and Davidoff are representative of the scholarship about Victorian gender ideology, agreeing that, despite "contradictions between reality and ideology," a middle-class woman "on her own ... was powerless to act." With the addition of musical accomplishment, however, a special kind of reality intruded. The Soirée Musicale was a variant form of parlour music, which distilled performative excellence into its core purpose.[32]

Feminist musicologist Nancy Reich gives the interpretive kaleidoscope a healthy shake by assuming that performing music, as a paid professional, was important to all women musicians. To account for the difference between amateur and professional, she identifies an "artist-musician class, a category which include actors, artists, artisans, dancers, writers, and practitioners of allied professions." She notes that "almost all professional women musicians were born into families in which members worked together to earn a living and had done so for more than one generation," making explicit for women what has been repeatedly shown to be true for male professional musicians: professional networks were tied to family.[33]

Ann Beedell, author of a vivid case study of the travails of an English family of nineteenth-century musicians, persuasively argues that "apprenticeships in music for women were rare and usually limited to the daughters or sisters of professional musicians."[34] Those women who did receive training had access only to singing, piano and harp study, since the orchestral instruments were thought unsuitable for a woman. Although more research is needed to establish the ratio of female to male professional musicians in Canada in the nineteenth century, Beedell's conclusion is borne out by Canadian music historian Marilynn Smiley, noting that in one North American concert circuit, professional women musicians first appeared in the 1840s.[35]

Nancy Reich shows that even established professional women musicians were professionally hobbled by their gender. Their respectability as good women was conceptually impossible and frankly attacked throughout the nineteenth century in terms which varied little from one German assessment stating that, to the degree that a professional woman musician was artistically superior, she was a bad woman. Even the composer Clara Schumann, perhaps for her own sense of herself as a respectable woman, proclaimed that women did not and could not compose.[36] This is the musical equivalent of historian Natalie Zemon Davis's insight that for the woman whose actions controverted prevailing gender mores, "self-concealment ... was a condition of her liberty."[37] That this applies so readily to women two hundred years later than Davis's seventeenth-century subjects confirms the continuity of certain themes in women's history. The domestic Soirée Musicale of Ontario itself was such a concealment, cloaking in domesticity the artistic authority and skill of its Lady Amateurs.

The kaleidoscope now tumbles the coloured shards of 1844 to the framework of music history, which jitters from the concept of what counts as meaning in music to the history of the music profession in Canada. Any history of the Soirée Musicale that can account for all of the information on Mrs. Widder's 1844 program is a history of what makes music meaningful. Over the nineteenth and into the twentieth centuries, musicology, or the "science" of explaining the meaning of "classical" music, has produced an enormous literature defending the true essence of music as a transcendental aesthetic, described by Christopher Small as "floating through time, untouched by social change."[38] Performance, on this model, is but the handmaiden of the men of genius who channel divine inspiration in the act of composing aesthetically fine music. Canadian musicology has been primarily concerned to trace the rooting of classical music in public, professional performance in the colonial soil. This scholarship provides the essential basis for understanding the Soirée Musicale in Ontario.

Historians of music in Canada have built on Helmut Kallmann's pioneering study, *A History of Music in Canada 1534-1914*, first published in 1960, benefiting from his premise that the meaning of music history in Canada resides, not in its aesthetic, but in "the ever present themes of transplantation, assimilation and search for identity."[39] His work was ground breaking, meticulous, and national in scope. It has launched most of the subsequent musicology of Canada and remains an essential resource for Canadian music history.

Both in this *History* and later in the *Encyclopaedia of Music in Canada*, Kallmann and his colleagues collect a critical and growing body of data.[40] They do not always consider it from the perspective of those whose music making left the data to be found, but their empirical work provides the thoroughly reliable basis for this history of the Soirée Musicale. Looking at the eclectic mix of the professional programs of the time, so similar to those of the domestic Musicale, Kallmann says, "It is easy for us to smile at these programmes with their mixture of styles and circus-like array of entertainers, but we must not forget that even in Europe taste sank to a low ebb in the years after Beethoven's death."[41] The drive to establish an independent Canadian musical identity required a strong-minded challenge to the tenets of existing musicology, claiming the value of investigating the social history of reception and education as part of the proper business of understanding the meaning of music itself. Kallmann and his school understandably define musical excellence in terms of present-day aesthetic criteria, which produces programs at which they would not "smile."

During the 1940s and 1950s, when Kallmann was working on this history, few Canadian musicians were smiling much. The Massey Commission was about to release its report recommending that high culture be promoted to the broad public, in an attempt to distinguish the higher values of Canadian national culture from the sordid materialism of popular American entertainment. The problem for Canadian art musicians was, as broadcasting historian Mary Vipond points out, that Canadians liked American popular culture, and the Canadian "classical" music profession of the time was under threat.[42] Kallmann, discussing nineteenth-century music in Canada, repeatedly defines art music as a "counterbalance ... [to] the influence of cheap and vulgar entertainment."[43] Kallmann's book and Vincent Massey's Commission thus unwittingly share the anti-republican sentiments of Mrs. Widder's Soirée Musicale program, which, as Chapter Two will suggest, may also have been an attempt to distinguish the higher ideals of Canadian culture from the American alternative. Durable indeed are the messages of the Soirée Musicale.

However much it owed to the intellectual concerns of its time, Kallmann's introduction of social history into traditional musicology predated the explosion of musical histories as social texts in the 1980s.[44] Finally based in the music division of the National Library of Canada, Kallmann supported the energetic compilation of data that has resulted in three works without which this history of Mrs. Widder's musical party could not have been written.

The preservation of the record of nineteenth-century musical history in Canada is wonderfully served by David Sale's solid monograph, "Toronto's pre-confederation music societies, 1845-1867."[45] It has but fifty pages of text outlining the short, sharp, squabbling lurches of the first musical societies devoted to "serious" music, but his indices are an Aladdin's cave of the social, religious, business, and political networks of amateur and professional musicians during these early years. Sale has combed an exhaustive array of publications and archival sources to collect the names, repertoire, and performance dates of every public concert in Toronto over the period. Toronto, even in the nineteenth century, dominated the Canadian music profession and music business by importing and manufacturing the greatest volume of musical instruments and sheet music in the country, and by establishing the dominant music training institution in Canada, now the Royal Conservatory of Music, by 1886.[46] Sale's conclusion, that the "indigenous musical life of Toronto in 1846 was largely regimental and dance bands, church choirs and the few professional musicians," is an accurate description of the public work of professional musicians. His careful inclusion of the information from public notices about amateurs and patrons is an important factor in establishing that formal music organisations emerged in Toronto from 1845.[47] His writing is crystalline and his data collection beautifully organized. This thesis is a treasure for the history of music in nineteenth-century Ontario.

Michael Rudman found and reprinted the program for Mrs. Widder's March 12th 1844 Soirée Musicale in his biographical article on James Dodsley Humphreys, a professional tenor resident in Toronto from 1835.[48] Rudman's clear portrait shows that Humphreys' career was typical of working Ontario musicians, and provides the information so necessary for recognizing the parallels between the music professions in Ontario and England.

At every turn of this brilliant kaleidoscope of historiography, the glittering shards of class, gender, politics, and music in Mrs. Widder's musical evening revolve into different patterns. To some degree, any identification of patterning is arbitrary, whether it is in existing framework of particular historiographic fields, or in separating the vast array of information implicit in Mrs. Widder's program into chapters. The following chapters use the historiographic categories as much as possible to sort the evidence. In Chapter Two, the process of constructing the concert program itself is considered in the context of Mr. Frederick Widder's business plans, to suggest how immediate local concerns might contribute to the meaning of musical life. Chapter Three examines class and masculinity by connecting the professional activities of representative male singers with the patterns of musical genre associated with them. The finely shaded social distinctions peculiar to Toronto in 1844 are linked to the English roots of the Soirée Musicale, suggesting that silence of some men spoke as loudly as the singing of others. In Chapter Four, the skilled performing of the amateur women on the program is described in terms of Victorian gender ideology. Peculiar choices of repertoire for two of the women who sang at Mrs. Widder's concert suggest some of the logical contradictions inherent in the Victorian concept of "feminine musical accomplishment." The meaning of music was tightly wrapped in the class and gender of its performers. Lest any mistake the domestic Soirée Musicale as an act of radical feminism, in Chapter Five, the one Lady Amateur who made a break for artistic freedom under the cloak of its domesticity is shown to have failed, magnificently. Finally, in the "Encore," the interpretive model developed from Mrs. Widder's Soirée Musicale program is used to suggest how future research might account for the bewildering range of variations that appeared in Ontario in the later nineteenth and early twentieth centuries.

For the sake of clarity, "Ontario" is used throughout this study to refer to the geographic area known from 1791-1840 as Upper Canada, from 1841-1867 as Canada West in the United Province of Canada, and from 1867 to present as Ontario. "Soirée Musicale" will be capitalized throughout to distinguish the phrase as the title of the concert format, except where other writers or primary sources have used lower case letters or foregone the accent. Capital letters are used for "Lady Amateur" and "Gentleman Amateur" because these were special social roles, not merely factual descriptions. To ease the reader's eye, many footnotes have been removed, but anyone wishing further information may contact the writer for reference details, through the Canadian Museum of Civilisation, Mercury Series Editor.

The clattering components of Mrs. Widder's Soirée Musicale can be sorted into discrete categories of class, gender, music, politics, and economics by the kaleidoscope of historiography. In Mrs. Widder's drawing room, however, they were experienced as the unified complexity of daily life, enlivened by a private concert. Writing about Victorian marriages, Phyllis Rose suggests that "certain imaginative patterns - call them mythologies or ideologies - determine the shape of a writer's life as well as his or her work."[49] The "imaginative pattern" of the Soirée Musicale in Ontario was a drama of difference, an opera of a hierarchical society in which distinctions of class and gender were natural, stable, and harmonious. The importance of this unifying fiction of the Soirée Musicale is its role in sustaining the social acceptance of these differences. The Soirée Musicale was the result of the Victorian fantasies of Music and Woman, colliding in the conceptually incoherent drawing rooms of the rich. No explosion resulted. The tinkling glass shards of the social kaleidoscope clicked and tumbled into familiar, urgent patterns of class, gender, and music. A winking flash of feminine scarlet, a hint of colonial green, gave but richness to the mix.

Chapter Two

PROGRAMMING POLITICS
Musical and Thematic Structure of Mrs. Widder's Program

At the key points in the structure of Mrs. Widder's program appears a single theme: heroic men sacrificing personal interests for the good of the people they lead. These men are without exception unelected leaders who accepted personal sacrifice but were loved and appreciated by the people they governed. This concept of masculine civic virtue was in the air during the transition from colonial oligarchy to representative government, already under way in 1840s Canada.[1] The accompanying debates over the limits of political jurisdiction and what counted as worthiness to rule affected businessmen of great vision like Frederick Widder, who aimed, in 1844, at developing all of the Crown Lands for profit. Mrs. Widder's Soirée Musicale was not just a charming exercise of ingratiating Mr. Widder with the musically-inclined members of a powerful circle of acquaintance. The central themes of the concert supported her husband's commercial purpose. Other music was available in Toronto in 1844, and brief reference will be made to other programs to show that a Soirée Musicale program could be unified by different thematic material. If Mrs. Widder's program was thematically unified, it was by design.

Traditional musicology, if it were to consider performance at all, might suggest that Mrs. Widder's concert program was no more than a hodgepodge of laughable bad taste.[2] This analysis of the concert program structure suggests instead that Mrs. Widder's programmer juggled a mess of unlike factors to create a program of the greatest sophistication. Scholarship about programming techniques is scarce, perhaps because it has not been necessary to the oral tradition of teaching concert skills and perhaps because musicologists have not considered the meaning of individual compositions to be modified by their position in the sequence of a concert program, something no performer would fail to calculate.[3] Technical programming skills are described here from my twenty-five year experience of programming and performing classical recitals, and were learned in the 1980s at the Royal Academy of Music in London, where James Dodsley Humphreys studied in 1832–5.[4] The principles outlined can be verified by listening to the music of Mrs. Widder's program or any other successful concert. The horror of performing a program which exceeds the performer's real abilities or which loses the attention of its audience is a powerful motive for undertaking such complex programming.

Local meanings gave the program much of its power. The music chosen for Mrs. Widder's concert was part of an international repertoire, but local programmers, perhaps most recognizably in programming for intimate concerts among people who knew each other personally, could use subtle local references to communicate with a familiar, local audience. This is not — it cannot be — an exhaustive discussion of all of the repertoire of the program, but examples are discussed to show how the sequence in the Widder program linked separate compositions with each other to create thematic consistency. Subtle engagement with the full range of human feeling is the programmer's art, and a concert program can triumph musically and emotionally without a central, non-musical theme. Audience experience is a complex emotional response rather than a primarily intellectual one, but a conceptual point can be communicated in a concert if it is stated simply and repeated often. Mrs. Widder's concert was programmed as a river of variety and delight from which it would be very difficult for the audience to emerge without understanding its oft-repeated themes of self-sacrificing leadership.

This program could not have been the lucky result of intuition and limited resources: it has a visible architecture which betrays the hand of a programmer experienced at keeping an audience engaged from the beginning to the end of a concert. A brief outline of the programmer's toolbox follows, with a discussion of how the Widder programmer placed a single theme at the structural pillars of the program and carefully filled the spaces between with a range of material that never contradicted that theme. These pragmatic observations about performer and audience experience are then placed in the political context of Toronto in 1844.

One irresistible form of concert program weaves a narrative flow by creating and releasing tension. Audience ability to concentrate decreases steadily from the start to the finish of a concert, but audiences tire more quickly with demanding material. Music is at its most demanding when it is extreme - loud, high, fast, unfamiliar to the audience, musically complex, in a foreign language, or emotionally intense. Interspersing more demanding music with less demanding music allows audiences to rest while remaining attentive. Mrs. Widder's programmer used these factors to create layers of technically perfect patterns designed to engage the audience. The program was symmetrical, with two balanced and parallel halves, each taking approximately forty minutes to present ten works. The summary of technical variations (Figure 4) shows that both halves offered precise alternation of Italian with English language selections and operatic versus song genres. Operatic selections, usually louder and in a foreign language to this English-speaking group, presented challenges of greater intensity to their audiences than did any English language material.

In the second half of the program, these patterns were eased to accommodate the accumulated mental fatigue of the audience. The intensity of the operatic material itself was lower than in the first half. One of the operatic selections, the *Azor and Zemira*

Technical Patterns of Widder Program

Position in Sequence	Genre		Language		Solo/Ensemble	
	PART I	PART II	PART I	PART II	PART I	PART II
1	opera	piano	Italian	Piano	Ensemble	Solo
2	opera	opera	Italian	Italian	Ensemble	Solo
3	song	song	English	English	Solo	Solo
4	opera	opera	Italian	English	Solo	Ensemble
5	song	opera	English	Italian	Ensemble	Solo
6	opera	song	Italian	English	Solo	Solo
7	song	song	English	English	Solo	Ensemble
8	opera	opera	Italian	Italian	Ensemble	Solo
9	song	song	English	English	Solo	Solo
10	opera	song	Italian	Italian	Ensemble	Ensemble

Figure 4. Technical Patterns in Widder Program

duet, was in English. The operatic climax of the second half, "Ah, per sempre," an aria written for a baritone or medium male voice type, was sung by a lower voice than the ringing tenor showpiece "Vivi tu," which was the centrepiece of the first half. (A higher voice type usually sounds louder than a lower voice type, although this depends on training, the physical size of the voices in question, and whether the music being sung requires each voice to sing at the extreme end of its range.) There are other technical factors that may have been considered by the Widder programmer, but, as the chart of "Widder Audience Experience" shows (Figure 5), the sum of such careful planning was a recognizable emotional arc. The shape of the second half of the program mirrored the first, but with muted intensity.

To create the chart, each of the program selections was numbered from one to ten, and given a value based on the same five factors: volume, dramatic intensity, rhythmic vivacity, familiar affection (the "Oh, I know this nice one!" response), and team spirit. The latter is an attempt to capture particular local memories or current enthusiasms. Although each genre created a different kind of emotional excitement, audience enjoyment of all genres was assumed to be real. Each genre was assessed in terms of the net effect of excitement or enthusiasm available with each selection. Parlour music and glees, as well as simple piano music, are all less complex musically and technically than most operatic selections, so for the purpose of assessing complexity, all of these selections were considered to be song-like. While the titles and marching band medleys of the main

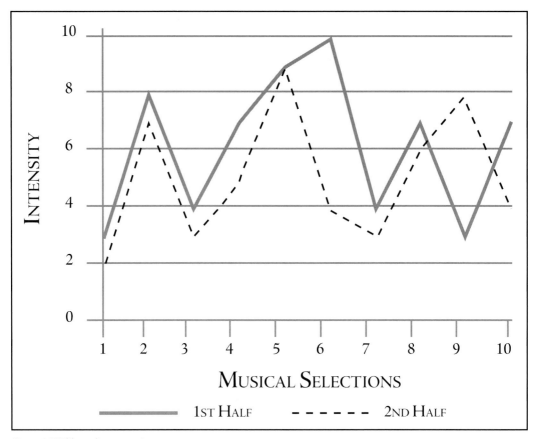

Figure 5: Widder audience experience.

melodies from many of these operas would have been familiar to most of the Widder audience, individual arias and duets were assumed to be much less intimately known, hence "unfamiliar." The parlour songs themselves were either so familiar they could have been hummed by anyone in the room, or they had words and musical shapes so simple and conventional that they resembled other parlour music and were in that sense "familiar." Each work was timed with a stopwatch, except for the Herz "Fantasia," which was assumed to run between three and five minutes. If there was verbal commentary during the concert, an additional ten or fifteen minutes would be needed for each half. Without such commentary, the program ran approximately eighty minutes, with an additional interval between the two halves.

These values are summarised in the Chart of Audience Experience to provide a visual, if subjective, sense of the programmer's expectation of that specific audience's experience of this vanished eighty minutes of music. The original programmer of this concert made a similar calculation, trying to predict and enhance audience experience. The selections in this comparison of the two halves of the concert have been numbered to show that the programmer treated the sequence of both halves in a similar way, as if each point in the sequence of the program had a particular purpose. Similar technical features appear in parallel positions in the two halves. For example, Lady Amateurs sing opera in the second position, men sing opera in the middle, and the glees appear just before or just after the middle of each half. Each ends with a jolly ensemble.

The Widder programmer did all of this technical patterning as well as unifying the whole program with one theme that appeared at each of its architectural pillars. Planning a program is similar to writing well-organised prose. The main points are first plotted in outline and the body of the work then written to move as smoothly as possible from one point to the next. One orderly method of constructing a concert program, which could well have been used for Mrs. Widder's concert, is first to set the music for the structural pillars, or outline, of the program: the opening numbers, the climax of each half, and the closers of each half. Since the highest point of the evening is usually also the most physically taxing for the performer, it is often chosen first. The middle of the second half can then be anchored with a similar, but paler, version of the first climax. On Mrs. Widder's program, the loudest, most complex, dramatic and foreign language selection was "Vivi tu," sung by a man and placed in the middle of the first half. It was echoed by another operatic aria in the middle of the second half, "Ah per sempre," again sung by a man, but in a lower voice type. It was an aria of reflective poignancy rather than stabbing urgency. Once the centre pieces are chosen, the crucial opening selection can be made, to set the tone and state the theme of the whole concert, if it has a theme. The opening is not an emotional peak but a genial warming up by both artists and audience, and the Widder opener, "Plaudite, oh popoli," was a simple, three-man chorus.

The closing numbers in each half can then be chosen to ensure that the audience breaks to chat about the music with the sound of reliably excellent performances of familiar, cheerful music ringing in their ears. As Figure 5 shows, the closing item in the first half bounced up in intensity, a musical indication that the concert was not over, but at the end of the second half, the intensity dropped with great finality, befitting the end of the whole program. In the programming process, once these keystones of structure are fixed, the task is to choose the material to fit between them. Finding each musical work becomes progressively more difficult, as the programmer seeks existing music that meets so many criteria. In a very good program, the emotional world of each musical selection flows from that of the music before it and into the world of the music that follows, without merely repeating it. It is difficult enough to maintain both musical flow and variety, while placing amateurs and professionals a sequence where no amateur was embarrassed by unfavourable contrast with a much better performer. To do so while adhering to absolute thematic unity throughout, as Mrs. Widder's program did, is extraordinary. Some of the performers may not have lived up to expectations, but this program was as foolproof against such vagaries as any program could be, and thematically it never lost focus.

The structural pillars of this program shared the same theme: altruistic unelected leaders working for the good of the people despite their personal unhappiness. The concert opened with a three-man chorus from Rossini's *Tancredi*, an easy but rousing chorus of applause for a military hero, Tancredi, who saved his country from chaos despite his personal unhappiness. The three male voices of the chorus sang Italian lyrics which meant "Applaud, people, the valour of the conqueror with high songs, / The much-celebrated hero of our country." The next line is sung by Tancredi himself, "Sweet are the tones of glory, dear the honourable victory, / But a miserable heart knows no peace."[5]

The theme of a self-sacrificing warrior who saved his country and was, therefore, welcomed as its national leader echoed the convictions of men like Christopher Hagerman who understood the value to their country of their own military service in the War of 1812. It was also of value to Mr. Widder, as we shall see.

The climax of the first half was "Vivi tu," a solo Italian aria that repeated the same theme. For sheer, physical volume of sound in the highest, fully trained voice in the "Vivi tu" in the middle of the first half was the high point of the concert. It was also the most concentrated expression of the central theme. "Vivi tu" was the cry of a truly noble soul for whom death was preferable to dishonour. In the opera, *Anna Bolena*, Henry VIII, corrupted by lust, wrongly sentences his noble wife Anne Boleyn to death, but offers to pardon her two courtiers, Riccardo and Roberto, who were at first condemned to death for collusion with her. After the aria, in the opera, both noblemen reject the pardon, but in "Vivi tu" Riccardo begs his friend to accept the pardon, accepting the pain of living with a false reputation for dishonour to serve the greater cause of telling the truth about the falsely accused Queen. Democratic accountability was not necessary for a truly noble aristocrat who put the good of the people before his own satisfaction.

Of the old Tory oligarchs who may have been in Mrs. Widder's drawing room, Miss Hagerman's father, Christopher Hagerman, had taken precisely this operatic tone in a letter about his own dismissal from office in 1833, claiming that he had been wrongly accused by a fool and intrigued against by a corrupt official:

> I dare say you all think me very ... miserable – I am no such thing – I am a very much injured man – and feel very indignant but by no means unhappy on account of my Lord Ripon – rather my Lord Horwick, very foolish conduct. The former I have good reason to believe is very sorry for what he has done – and the latter is turned out of office as well as me – but for very different reasons – he because he could not be trusted – I because I was too honest.[6]

Hagerman was prone to challenging authority, as he had on this occasion, repeatedly losing lucrative appointments and offending the powerful by wearing his superior idealism as a badge of nobility. Material sacrifice and public opinion were irrelevant to his assessment of his own place in God's human creation, which he closely linked to his political beliefs. Hagerman might well have recognized his own passionate, self-sacrificing idealism as mirrored in "Vivi tu." Both the man and the aria were a product of their times, but that made Christopher Hagerman's experience no less specific to him and no less well known to most Torontonians of the time. Hagerman wore his emotions on his public sleeve.

The opening number of the second half was used to gently return the audience to listening mode, with a wordless piano solo provided by a young Lady Amateur. The main theme returned, however, in the middle of the second half. "Ah per sempre" is the lament of a monarchist nobleman that his beloved has betrayed him for the love of a Puritan republican. In the opera, the woman loses her senses, regaining them only when the monarchy is restored. The title of the opera, I Puritani, plainly marked on the concert program, refers to the English history of monarchical and republican turmoil which would have been well known to the classically educated men in the room and to many of the women.

Concert program structures vary, and some float steadily into undemanding lightness at the end of the second half, but, in Mrs. Widder's program, the theme of heroic leadership was never dropped from view. Just before the end of the program, a man sang the solitary, self-sacrificing heroism of "Not a drum was heard." This was a famous song, the stirring description of the death of British General Sir John Moore, who in 1809 sacrificed himself to protect his retreating troops in the Spanish Peninsular War against the republican French. It was the final repetition of the theme of the noble, non-democratic governance that blazed at the opening of the whole program and the high points of both halves. If the Italian words of "Vivi tu" veiled the thematic content for some of the English-speaking audience who had not seen the operas in London, the plain English of "Lutzow's Wild Hunt" and "Not a drum was heard" delivered the same message.

Both also held references to contemporary preoccupations as well as local history. The military overtones of "Lutzow's Wild Hunt" and "Not a drum was heard" resonated with the recent memories of armed insurrections in 1837. In the 1840s, there was persistent nervousness about American pressure on the Canadian border, as America, defying the spirit of the Rush-Bagot Agreement, which had finally settled the War of 1812, sailed a warship on Lake Ontario. The values shared by Torontonians, whether of Reform or Conservative bent, were, in the words of historian S. F. Wise, an "emotional compound of loyalty to King and Empire, antagonism to the United States, and an acute, if partisan, sense of recent history."[7]

With their references to local history, these two songs might have achieved much for Mr. Widder's business plans if all they did was inspire the cosy feeling that the concert's host was an informed member of the whole community. It was an important defense against accusations by Widder's competitors that he was no more than an opportunistic carpetbagger, the agent of "a few merchants in London, totally ignorant of this country," whose Canada Company "is daily proving ... [that it only wants to make] all it can by hook or by crook, out of the lands which it purchased so cheaply from an ill-advised Administration."[8] Webs of local meaning anchored both "Lutzow's Wild Hunt" and "Not a Drum Was Heard" to the Toronto context of 1844 and to each other. A later

Figure 6: "Lutzow's Wild Hunt" excerpt Carl Maria Von Weber, "Lutzow's Wild Hunt," in *Heart Songs Dear to the American People and by them Contributed in the Search for Treasured Songs Initiated by the National Magazine*, ed., Bea Friedland (Boston: Chapple Publishing Company, Ltd., 1909), p. 331

edition of "Lutzow" was printed in Boston in the 1890s, where perhaps Americans found the reference to Baron von Lützow in the title peripheral to the glee's generic call to conquer tyranny. The meaning of this song was specific to the time and the place of its performance.

At the time of the Widder Soirée Musicale, "Lutzow's Wild Hunt" was a good tune (Figure 6), which would have resonated personally with many who shared what Canadian historian Paul Cornell describes as "a strong 'War of 1812 patriotism' in Upper Canada."[9] The peppy, German glee commemorated Baron von Lützow, who demonstrated his anti-democratic patriotism by continuing to battle on with his personal regiment, or "Freikorps," after Prussia had signed a peace with France in 1813. Von Lützow was as much a Prussian as Major General Baron Francis de Rottenburg, known to the families of some of the Widder guests because in 1813 he was the British Commander of the Forces in Upper Canada.[10] De Rottenburg had brought a "hunter corps," a version of the Prussian "Freikorps," into the British Army in 1797. Perhaps not coincidentally, the German "Lutzow's Wild Hunt" was familiar in Toronto as part of the music played in public concerts by military bands resident in Toronto up to 1845.[11]

Precisely similar associations were repeated in "Not a Drum was Heard," about the death of General Sir John Moore. Moore had revised the standard British infantry-training manual from the original version written by General de Rottenburg.[12] Every member of the Upper Canadian militias of 1837 had been drilled according to Moore's manual, including James Dodsley Humphreys, Mrs. Widder's probable programmer. The song carried particular meaning for Colonel Joseph Wells, who was probably the father of Mrs. Widder's glee singing Mr. Wells and might have enjoyed attending the concert. Colonel Wells had been among the retreating troops in Spain in 1809, whose lives had been saved by General Moore's sacrifice.[13] Moore, von Lützow, de Rottenburg all fought republican threats to non-representative regimes associated with Britain, and all between 1809 and 1813: the same period as the War of 1812.

Mr. Humphreys, working for Mr. Barron and Reverend McCaul, programmed "Lutzow's Wild Hunt" to be sung by the students of Upper Canada College at a public concert in 1851.[14] Its meaning as a parable of the War of 1812 was arguably the same for Barron and McCaul whether they sang it in private or programmed it for their students to share with a public audience. Mrs. Widder's private program thus suggests some of the layers of meaning in public musical life.

Public business and political life also shaped the programming of the Widders' private musical leisure. The central theme of self-sacrificing, civic responsibility was important to the business plans of Frederick Widder, who was trying to establish a public reputation for altruistic, civic manliness. To fully understand the layers of local reference in this program, it is necessary now to sketch the Byzantine maze of politics and history in which Mr. Widder was doing business. Through 1843 and 1844, Frederick Widder, as the director of the Canada Company, was orchestrating his bid to sequester all Canadian Crown Lands, including the Clergy Reserves away from public jurisdiction and into the private, commercial control of the Canada Company. With those lands went significant control over the infrastructure, immigration policy, and the international reputation of Canada. He aimed first at the Clergy Reserves, lands originally designated as the financial support of the Protestant clergy in the colony. Without them, developing the rest of the public lands was doomed to lower profits because the Clergy Reserves parcels were scattered throughout the Province, breaking up natural transportation corridors and development patterns and increasing road building costs and jurisdictional squabbles.[15] Land policy historian Lilian Gates suggests that the need for settlement land was acute by 1843.[16] The lands were a tempting prize while their values were rising.

Widder's strategy was to make the Canada Company perceived as a politically neutral, financially efficient alternative acceptable to "influential parties of every shade of political feeling."[17] Political feeling was particularly combative because the rules of power had been changing since three years before. When the British had changed the governance of Upper Canada (now Ontario) by joining it to Lower Canada (now Québec) in the Act of Union of 1841, they sought to calm the Reform spirit of the 1837 rebellion by replacing the appointed governing councils with representative government. A central issue in the resulting political debate was disagreement over what counted as the right to rule.[18] Reformers like Miss Clara Boulton's father, Henry John Boulton (Jr.) were sharply critical of any action which did not support the authority of the increasingly powerful elected executive, although their commitment was not to the universal suffrage associated with democracy today. When Mrs. Widder had her musical party, the overwhelming political issue was the resignation of most of the elected executive council in protest against the appointed British Governor General Charles Metcalfe's refusal to obey their authority. The unrest that followed forced Metcalfe to call an election in September 1844, but in March, when Mrs. Widder gave her concert, the political debates were intense, rancorous and public.[19] Four days before the Widder concert, a Toronto newspaper had published the Constitution of the new Reform Association of Canada, with the names of the signatories, including Dr. Scott, George Brown, and, as Chair, Miss Clara Boulton's father, Henry John Boulton. Its mandate was "to forward the objects" of responsible Government against the "practical renunciation" of it by Governor Metcalfe.[20]

Those opposed to representative government tended to agree with old Tories like Sir John Beverley Robinson (Sr.), who saw representative government as an unmitigated evil which would lead to inevitable social chaos. If a susceptible public could elect anyone it chose, then unworthy "demagogues" could gain access to power previously available only to the few who had been appointed to power because of their superior talent, experience, and honour.[21] For those who had fought the War of 1812 against such republicanism, like Hagerman, Joseph Wells, and Robinson, the Act of Union of 1841 was a bitter betrayal by the ruling British of their beliefs and their history of service to the people.

In the political debates of 1844 in Canada, the Clergy Reserves were an outstanding reminder of how unelected governance of Upper Canada had been determinedly mingled with the Anglican Church. Other Protestant denominations argued for equal access to the Clergy Reserves, while the Anglican Church fought to keep them at bay. Political Reformers urged that the Clergy Reserves be removed from Church use altogether and dedicated to public education, loosening the tie between Church and State. But the close relationship of Church and State was not merely conceptual for Family Compact Tories like Christopher Hagerman and John Strachan. It was a natural function of divine order on earth. As Canadian historian William Westfall suggests, the great grey mandarin of the Family Compact, Anglican Bishop John Strachan, saw the "carefully ranked hierarchy" of the family as the model for a society in which "the class position, social attitudes, political interests, and religious beliefs they held in common" functioned harmoniously.[22] The fight against republican governance of Canada in the 1840s was, for many, a fight against the overturning of God's natural order.

Land policy was but one of the interwoven issues of government, Church, and education. British imperial policy included promoting British culture, religion and education, appointing to the "local aristocracy" of largely colonial-born administrators only those who wholeheartedly subscribed to British values and governance.[23] Among them was Bishop John Strachan, the Anglican who had educated and influenced the core members of the Family Compact. Strachan worked continuously for the assignment of the benefits of the Crown's Clergy Reserves to the Anglican Church alone, but land was only one aspect of Strachan's vision of an Anglican state. He also ensured that King's College and Upper Canada College both had Anglican theology cemented into their Royal Charters. Strachan engaged all of the Family Compact members to this end, including Christopher Hagerman. As late as 1833, Christopher Hagerman was "laboring hard" [sic] to lock Anglicanism into British colonial policy for Canada, while continuing to support Strachan's personal career. He wrote to Strachan from England:

> *The great point seems to me to be, to get the College into operation, no matter where for the present or under what disadvantages - all things will come right in the end, if you but obtain your proper station and influence in the management. ... I am laboring hard for*

Figure 7: Frederick Widder, ca. 1849
Courtesy Toronto Public Library (TRL), JRR 1002

the accomplishment of your wishes, and proud shall I be if I can assist in bringing them to a satisfactory result.[24]

From 1843 to 1850, political Reformers were trying to disentangle the Church from these state-supported educational institutions, succeeding at last in 1850. In 1844, however, Bishop Strachan was the President of King's College, and thus the immediate authority to whom McCaul and Barron reported. Mr. Humphreys may already have been teaching at Upper Canada College, but in any case it would have been a choice engagement for him to seek.[25] Strachan himself must have been furiously absent from Lyndhurst on March 12th, 1844.

His resistance to Widder's perfidy in reaching for the Clergy Reserves had been fermenting for months, as the battle over the Clergy Reserves mounted. Mr. Widder needed to show the ruling British Governor – and by extension the Colonial Office – that he could make peace in Canada on the subject of the Clergy Reserves by reconciling both political sides and all the religious denominations. The evidence of Mrs. Widder's concert program, in the context of his letters to the Protestant Clergy and William Merritt, suggests that Widder was trying to create a public perception of himself as a trustworthy, altruistic, stable manager who would work for the benefit of all in return for a reasonable rate of return. He was, in effect, suggesting that the commercial sector could do a better job of managing Crown Lands than the government or the Church.

The Clergy Reserves were a necessary first step, but only part of Widder's master plan, as the following excerpt from a letter to his fellow merchant, William Hamilton Merritt, implies:

*I also send you copy of my letter to the Governor General [Metcalfe] ... by which I communicate
to His Excellency what course I have adopted in this question which you will remember formed
a part of the whole Public Lands which we were desirous of placing under the Company's
administration.*[26]

The Merritt to whom Widder wrote in 1844 was William Hamilton Merritt, the
aggressive merchant who had succeeded in forwarding his own, earlier commercial plan
to build the Welland Canal only after winning support from the Family Compact.[27]
Widder might have learned from Merritt's example. Merritt was by now an elected
member of the Legislative Assembly, and hence was among the political gatekeepers with
the right to administer Provincial land, which brought with it influence over significant
aspects of immigration and infrastructure policy. Widder showed, in the same letter, that
he was well aware that, to "administer" as much land as he sought, was in effect to govern.
In the new world of elected government, Widder was constructing what he hoped would
be an acceptable public face for the Canada Company's expanded role. He wrote:
"The whole business will now, I conceive, be brought bodily before the public and
with such fostering and descried patrons as yourself will be sure to succeed according
to our wishes."[28]

Widder's note to Merritt accompanied a copy of his recent proposal to the four
major "Religious Bodies" in the Province of Canada, that the Canada Company should
administer the Clergy Reserves so that a higher net profit could be paid to the Clergy,
free of administrative complication, in return for a "commission" which would include
"all Costs of Agency, and every description of expense." Widder disingenuously
suggested to the Clergy that he could see no reason why the Canada Company, with
its deep pockets, might not even make annual advances to meet the "exigencies of
the Church Society" before such profits had been realised. He presented himself and
his company as disinterested servers of the public good, writing to the clergy, copied
to Merritt, "the object I have in view ... is not one of emolument, but arises from an
anxious desire to render the Canada Company's services available to the Province upon
every opportunity."[29] Widder was offering the Canada Company as an ally to the non-
Anglican Protestant denominations in their ongoing tussle with Bishop Strachan's
insistence that the Clergy Reserves should only support the Anglican Church. But
Widder naturally had to include the Anglicans in his invitation. He addressed his letter
for the Anglican Church to the Secretary of the Anglican Church Society, Dr. Ripley.

Merritt must have laughed and opened his umbrella. Dr. Ripley's response to this
letter was moot. It was Bishop Strachan who had founded the Anglican Church Society
in 1843 in order to bid for the administration of the Clergy Reserves, forcing Widder to
act promptly. Strachan predictably rained brimstone down upon the Canada Company

and upon Widder himself for having dared to touch this "forbidden ground." In four published letters addressed to Widder in early 1845, Strachan accused Widder of "extortion and rapacity in the sale of the lands" (i.e., offering mortgages at six percent) in "a system of vicious concealment which could never have been devised by a person of high principle and manliness of character." Strachan further attacked Widder's masculinity, accusing him of "fulsome coquetry with the Press of the Colony." Widder had been running big front page advertisements about the Canada Company's inducements to immigrants, and Strachan had accurately understood that this was part of a campaign to "render ... conspicuous" the presence and activities of the Canada Company. [30]

Widder's proposal to the Clergy, copies of which he also sent to other interested parties in government, presents the Canada Company as having "incalculably benefited the Colony by attracting public notice to it and inducing settlement" when neither "Crown, Clergy nor King's College have adopted any [such] plan." Widder baldly stated that "the great exertions of the Canada Company who to promote the prosperity of the Colony, spare neither labor nor expense, on both sides of the Atlantic" were "unassisted" and more effective than any other alternative manager.

Merely stating it would not make it true. Widder knew as early as September 1843 that the Canada Company was competing directly with the Anglican Church for the right to govern a large portion of the Province of Canada. Strachan accused Widder of having been present at the opening meeting of the Church Society, where "what you heard on that day suggested your scheme for frustrating the object of the Society and

---

Widder Program Structural Pillars

FIRST HALF

#1. *opening: Tancredi*
Unelected leader is applauded for conquering an invader.

#5. *mid point: "Lutzow"*
Three men cheer baronial leader in fight for freedom

#6. *peak of concert: "Vivi tu"*
Heroic aristocrat urges personal sacrifice for civic benefit.

SECOND HALF

#5 *mid point: "Ah per sempre"*
Aristocrat loses his beloved to anti-monarchist rebel.

#9 *penultimate: "Not a drum"*
Aristocrat, battling republicans, dies saving his men.

Figure 8: Widder Program Structural Pillars

securing it to the Canada Company." Having spent the five years from 1839 to 1843 centralizing the management of the Canada Company in his own person, Widder's personal reputation would be a crucial factor in his bid to control so much land. As Strachan pointed out, "the Canada Company delighted in placing itself ... in opposition to the Church." [31] The trick for Widder was to show that he was a reliable guardian of the public good even if the Church denounced him as corrupt. Widder, by opposing well-known Church objectives, had to rely on the public perception that moral authority in politics did not reside in the Church.

This is a Canadian example of the secularization process of the nineteenth century. In 1844, members of Canadian government, whether they were the British Colonial Office and Governor Metcalfe or the electorate and their newly more accountable houses of government, had to decide whether a sacred or a secular power should govern land and immigration policy concerning the Clergy Reserves but also concerning the university. Widder and the Canada Company understood this issue in these terms, as Widder's own letter suggests. He emphasized to his associate William Merritt the need to persuade public opinion of the appropriateness of these lands being managed by a private commercial interest like the Canada Company.

Elizabeth Widder's program itself was unified by the central theme of honourable, unelected leaders who could be trusted to labour for the good of the people regardless of their personal sacrifices or unhappiness. This theme was placed at the architectural pediments of the program and was supported in subtle ways with every selection that carried the audience from one thematic hammer blow to the next. It offered a vision of an orderly, beautiful, and noble society directed by a classical, secular order rather than a religious one.

In Mrs. Widder's program, no selection undercut the central narrative and simple English songs repeated the thematic or emotional content of Italian arias, in most cases. Examples of English language material clarifying adjacent Italian works include the Mozart duet, in which the Count cannot control his feelings of love, which was followed by the Abrams song that began, "I ought to tear thee from my heart" and ended with "'tis madness great in me, / To ere bestow one thought on thee."

Between the thematic high points of masculine leadership, the women sang only material that supported or clarified this theme. Their music is discussed in detail in Chapters Four and Five, but all of it supported the prevailing gender ideology of women as supportive, loyal, and obedient to their men. The structure of the program reflected the gendered structure of the society. The performance of appropriate gender roles in Mrs. Widder's program reflected well on Mr. Widder's ability to govern his home.

Representative governance was not necessary for harmony in the program, just as Widder's proposal to remove jurisdiction over land, immigration and significant infrastructure policy from government to the private commercial sector perhaps appealed most to those who wanted to reduce the jurisdiction over which an elected government had control. Both Conservatives and many political Reformers did not support universal suffrage or wholly accountable governance, believing that virtuous public men could be trusted to sacrifice personal interests on behalf of the public good. On the delightful Widder Soirée Musicale program, representative government was absent or problematic in the fourteen selections that refer to time. Ten of the twenty musical selections were set in pre-democratic civilisations which offered a vision of a secular, natural law: *Tancredi* - feudal Italy of 1418; *Anna Bolena* — 16th century England; *Le Nozze di Figaro* — 18th century France; *Moïse in Egitto* — Pharaonic Egypt; *Torquato Tasso* — 16th century feudal Italy; *Azor and Zemira* — the mythic, ahistoric fairy tale of Beauty and the Beast; *I Puritani* - set in 17th century England, during the struggle between Puritan government and the Restoration of monarchy; *La Sonnambula* — set in non-democratic Switzerland circa 1800, featuring a good aristocrat who resolves the crisis of the opera by explaining the science behind somnambulism. Four of the nine songs refer more obliquely to historical period. The Haydn and Abrams were first published in England before1800 and the Barnett and Weber refer to heroic battles against republican insurgents.[32]

Widder, by opposing well-known Church objectives, had to show he was a reliable guardian of the public good even if the Anglican Bishop denounced him as corrupt. His proposal to the Churches openly discussed the potential for commercial abuse of public trust. Widder promised that society would be safe from corrupt management if the Canada Company ruled the Clergy Reserves because "were the Company's Officers to attempt such a course regardless of every principle of honor or propriety, inevitable and speedy detection must ensue." Warning tales of loss and immorality on the Widder concert program tended to be the result of overturning a non-democratic hierarchy. Mrs. Widder's programmer placed "Vivi tu," in which a noble man urged personal sacrifice in order to tell the truth about a corrupt monarch, at the highest point in the program. The same message of self-sacrificing civic duty by unelected leaders was reinforced at each of the most memorable moments in the program.

Mr. Widder may have felt a certain kinship with the old Tory oligarchs like Christopher Hagerman who resented what they felt were false accusations of corruption and the political Reformers, who rejected accusations of disloyalty to Britain.[33] Neither old Tories nor new Reformers denied the possibility of corruption among leaders, but both rejected accusations that they themselves were guilty. The theme of mistaken identity or intention in the Widder program is central to seven of the twenty selections. In *Norma*, two women confide in each other without realising they love the same man; in

Sonnambula, Rodolfo is a disguised nobleman whose innate nobility betrays his true identity to the good townsfolk; in *Figaro*, Susannah lies about her intention to cuckold her fiancé by meeting the Count; in *Azor*, the Beast is not truly bestial but deeply human; in *Puritani*, a fiancé is wrongly accused of deceiving his beloved; in the Glover, the singer's hopes of being loved are shown to have been self-deception; in the Crouch, the singer has been wrongly accused by her lover Dermot of not loving him.

Where personal interests distract aristocratic leaders from their duty to act in the public good, moral havoc reigns. In *Norma*, priestesses break their vows and consort with the enemy invader, female – hence, unmanly - rulers acting against their peoples' good; in *Anna Bolena*, the king succumbs to lust and destroys altruistic noblemen and his innocent wife; in *Figaro*, the Count succumbs to adulterous lust, crosses class boundaries, and upsets his whole household, a microcosm of society; in *Torquato Tasso*, a noblewoman loves outside her class and must choose between love and injuring her aristocratic family; in *Puritani*, the woman who deserts her noble lover goes mad until the restoration of monarchy restores her reason. Mrs. Widder's musical selections confirmed the benefits of true nobility in men and women, in their respective spheres, as well as the horrors of corruption.

Many of the guests in the Widder drawing room probably recognized these references from the music they heard that night. The musical genres were familiar, and many of the operas from which excerpts were presented at the Widder concert were common to the great wash of music in Canada, both public and private, as the record of public performances and private music collections in Toronto attests. Military bands were a principal source of entertainment in British North America, only gradually overtaken in the secular sphere by a wider range of professional performers after rail travel was possible, beginning in the 1850s. Band repertoire was broad, including arrangements of operatic material, and familiar to most of the population, since it was played repeatedly in public. Band concerts in Toronto included *Tancredi*, *Norma*, and *Beatrice* medleys as well as "Lutzow's Wild Hunt." The historical references were intrinsic to the opera titles printed on Mrs. Widder's program.

Mr. Widder needed to establish his moral worth in secular terms, and in an era when sacred music was often included in secular concerts, and with repertoire available that held far less political themes, Mrs. Widder's concert program was noticeably secular and political in its texts. In the texts of the Widder concert, tales involving disobedience to secular morality invoked the same moral judgements that Christian religious values would have. For example, in "Lutzow's Wild Hunt," the threat to order is being hunted down; in "Vivi tu," royal corruption is recognized as wrong and noble commitment to truth and honour is passionately stated; in "Crudel perche finora," confusion and humour result from the Count's extra-marital lust and Susanna's inappropriate attempt to manage a man.

In the British-emulating society of Upper Canada at mid-century, what was fashionable in London was desirable in Toronto, as the advertisement by James Humphreys in the *British Colonist*, run the very morning of Mrs. Widder's concert, suggests. "Mr. James D. Humphreys, formerly of the Royal Academy of Music, ... expects to receive from England in the spring and to be regularly supplied with an exclusive selection of the most fashionable and popular piano forte and vocal music."[34] Another Toronto musical entrepreneur trumpeted his wares with an advertisement for the monthly periodical, which promised,

> to offer ... the 'Gems of the Opera' now performing in Europe and America. From the development of Musical taste, which has lately been exhibited throughout this country, those who have engaged in the undertaking have every occasion to flatter themselves that they will meet with liberal patronage, ... as they have engaged Agents in the principal European cities, to forward to them the successful Operas and all Musical compositions of merit as soon as produced, which will give them an opportunity of selecting for this work Music particularly adapted to the taste of ... the amateurs of Music.[35]

These advertisements bore fruit. Music in the personal collections from this period includes arrangements for home performance of operatic selections found on Mrs. Widder's Soirée Musicale program.[36] Toronto music publisher, A. & S. Nordheimer, which depended on profitable sales to thrive, published versions of operatic arias for the local sheet music public, including, in 1846, an English translation of Bellini's "Vi ravviso," which Miss Hagerman had sung at the Widder concert. This pattern in private collections was repeated in public performances of such music at the time: Mrs. Widder's Soirée Musicale reflected the music of private parlours and public stages.

The powerful families who participated in Mrs. Widder's program tended to be loyal to Britain, some of them, like the Widders, McCaul, Barron, and Humphreys, because they were British immigrants. Others visited London, England, often and might have had the opportunity, while socialising there, to attend opera or private Soirées Musicales. Miss Hagerman went with her father in 1846, and again in 1854 with her husband, meeting a working musician, Henry Schallehn, and a dowager countess.[37] Schallehn had performed his own composition entitled "Les soirées musicales" in Toronto in 1848, referring perhaps to his own experiences of domestic concerts. Henry John Boulton, Miss Clara Boulton's father, was in England at the same time as Christopher Hagerman in 1833. Hagerman was delighted by the invitations he received in high society.[38]

For many travelling Canadians, absorbing European culture was part of their purpose. Egerton Ryerson, for instance, went to collect European art for a civic museum in Toronto, in 1855-6, a culturally saturated trip on which his daughter and one of the Miss Widders accompanied him.[39] The locus of political and economic power in Canada still resided primarily in the hands of the British Governors who carried out British imperial policies and who, as individuals, were members of the London society that continued to exert its influence on their own values and culture. Awareness of fashionable London culture was both attractive and important to many prominent Ontarians.

In that London society between 1835 and 1865, seven public Soirées Musicales given by professional musicians of both genders were mentioned in *The Times* in reviews which

---

Mrs. Sandeman's Soirée Musicale, at her residence, 15, Hyde Park Gardens, on Friday Evening, June 8, 1849. Under the direction of Signor Ferrari.

Mr. W. Sterndale Bennett, will preside at the Pianoforte[1]

Duo – Violin and piano, Airs from Oberon – . . . . Blagrove and Benedict
Miss Helen Sandeman and M. le Marquis de Chardonnay
Trio – "Ti prego," – . . . . Curschman
Madame Ferrari, Miss Sandeman and Signor Gallini
Scena – "Ecco il Pegno,"– *Signor Ferrari* . . . . Donizetti
Lieder ohne Worte – Pianoforte – *Miss Helen Sandeman* . . . . Mendelssohn Bartholdy
Aria – "Or la Sull' Onda," – *Miss Sandeman* . . . . Mercadante
Duo – "I Muletieri," – *Made. and Signor Ferrari* . . . . Masini
Fantasia on Airs from "Lucia" Concertina, – . . . . G. Regondi
Signor Giulio Regondi
Glee – "Blow gentle Gales," – *Madame Ferrari,* . . . . Bishop
Miss Sandeman, and Signor Ferrari

PART II

Quartett – "Ecco quel fiero Istante," – *Made. Ferrari,* . . . . Costa
Miss Sandeman, and Signori Gallini and Ferrari
Piano Forte – Solo - *Mr. W. Sterndale Bennett* . . . . Bennett
Scena – "Come per me Sereno," – *Madame Ferrari.* . . . . Bellini
Notturno and Rondo Russe – Concertina – . . . . G. Regondi & de Beriot
Signor G. Regondi
Duo – "Oh di qual Onta," – . . . . Verdi
Miss Sandeman and Signor Ferrari
Morceau de Concert – From "Lucrezia Borgia," Violini –. . . . . Chardonnay
M. le Marquis de Chardonnay
Song – "The Wanderer," – *Miss Sandeman* . . . . Schubert
Quartett – "Over the dark Blue Waters," – . . . . Carl Von Weber
Madame Ferrari, Miss Sandeman, and Signori Gallini and Ferrari

---

Figure 9. Sandeman 1849 Program
Courtesy British Library

noted the formal patronage of ladies as well as gentlemen and described the audiences as "fashionable company."[40] Private Soirées Musicales very much like Mrs. Widder's were also held, although records of them have not yet been systematically compiled. One example was Mrs. Sandeman's 1849 Soirée Musicale (Figure 9) held at her London home, which presented a woman amateur musician of the host family performing alongside the cream of the local music profession, with composer Sterndale Bennett at the piano for her solos, and in quartets with working opera singers. Miss Sandeman was arguably under more pressure to perform at a professional level on this program than was any individual Lady Amateur at Mrs. Widder's house in Canada, since she was the only amateur in a field of well-known professionals. Miss Sandeman demonstrated both singing and piano playing in a program on which the others exhibited but one skill each, except for the composers who played their own works. Signor Ferrari was an opera singer at Her Majesty's Theatre, London, and his wife, probably the "Mme. Ferrari" of this program, was a singer born Johanna Thomson. The singers' performances at her Majesty's Theatre in London were likely fresh in the memories of some who attended the Sandeman evening, since the audience who attended had been invited to performances by these well-known musicians. Bennett was one of the most prominent musicians of the day and Giulio Regondi was a guitarist and composer who had been performing since childhood. The Marquis de Chardonnay, in London, was a French nobleman abroad: his status was ambiguous. He may have been one of the sons of the Marquis de Chardonnay, who, in 1800, applied to enrol his sons, Robert and Jérome, in a school founded by Edmund Burke in 1796 for the sons of French emigré nobility. Perhaps Chardonnay and his fellow exiles after the French Revolution were particularly enthusiastic about recreating salon life in England in the form of private Soirées Musicales.[41]

The repertoire of this concert was considerably more demanding to perform than that of Mrs. Widder's, reflecting the largely professional cast. It mixed genres exactly as Mrs. Widder's program did, however, from Italian opera to glees and parlour piano music. Both programs used works by composers Bishop, Weber, Donizetti, and Bellini. Mr. Sandeman, like Mr. Widder in Toronto in 1844, did not appear as a performer on the program, and although professionals and the Lady Amateur sang the glee, no upper-class Englishman did so. The gradations of status in London, with a much larger and more diverse population, were doubtless slightly different from those in Toronto, but the associations of musical genre with gender and class was congruent with that expressed in Mrs. Widder's Soirée Musicale.

The Sandeman program reveals a unified theme which was quite different from that of the Widder program. At the key structural points on this symmetrical program, the opening and middle numbers of both halves and the penultimate number of the second half, Miss Sandeman performed. Since text, not musical sound, carries non-musical thematic material, to have instrumental works as the opening numbers of both halves of the concert and sharing the mid-point of each half (items four and five of each half, respectively) diminishes the importance of a textual through-line for program unity. The program instead emphasises "pure," abstract musicality. Combined with the presence of Miss Sandeman at the key structural moments, one theme of this programming might have to been to emphasise the seriousness of Miss Sandeman's musicianship.

The preponderance of material emphasising travel by sea at these points and elsewhere, suggests that the unifying textual theme was travel. The opening number is based on the opera *Oberon*, about powerful fairies who travel magically; the Mercadante operatic showpiece is sung by Bianca, a character remembering her past in a distant land; the opening quartet of the second half is entitled in its English version "O the sad moments of parting;" the penultimate work in the whole concert is Schubert's song of the wanderer lamenting separation from home; and the final quartet, "Over the dark Blue Waters," concerns sailing.[42] Further research might answer the intriguing question of why Miss Helen Sandeman delayed marrying until the rather late age of thirty-one: did she, like Miss Hagerman, strive for a professional career? By looking through the interpretive template developed from Mrs. Widder's program, the central theme of the Sandeman concert seems to be that Miss Helen Sandeman was a gifted musician about to travel abroad for further musical study.[43] Mr. and Mrs. Widder broke no new ground in terms of concert structure by presenting a domestic Soirée Musicale with a strong central theme supporting career ambitions in the host family. The music of the period could be adapted to support a range of themes, not all of them political. The Widder theme was a choice.

In London, participating in private concerts as host, guest, or performer was important to the politically and economically ambitious upper crust that emulated royal practice as far as their purses would bear it. One private concert enjoyed by the King of England at St. James's Palace in 1836 "consisted of arias and ensembles by Rossini, Bellini, and Balfe … madrigals, and variations for violin and piano by Czerny."[44] This program was similar to Mrs. Widder's Toronto concert of 1844, where glees, as a development of the madrigal form, replaced madrigals, and Henri Herz replaced the Czerny. Balfe was a popular English ballad opera composer who might well have been represented at Mrs. Widder's house, but the Spohr duet in the arrangement by Sir George Smart was equally central to the same genre and equally popular in London in 1844.[45] Particularly among those who had or aspired to have, political and economic power in Upper Canada's colonial society, some familiarity with the political plots and historic periods of the well-known operas on Mrs. Widder's program was likely, even without spoken commentary by a master of ceremonies.

With or without a formal master of ceremonies, the presence at the Widder Soirée Musicale of three teachers, McCaul, Barron, and Humphreys, suggests that conversation of some kind would follow their musical performances. Spoken commentary during the performance would have served Humphreys, the freelancer who depended for his teaching and concert-advising livelihood on his reputation as "the Professor," very well.[46] Or perhaps Dr. McCaul, a classical scholar more noted for the "occult, magnetic force of his personal influence" than for shyness, introduced the arias.[47] Even if there were no erudite guide, the classical educations of all the elite men present would have supplied much of the intellectual resonance of the operatic music itself.[48] No overt discussion of the concert's themes was necessary. By using their own home for the concert, Mr. and Mrs. Widder implicitly presented the values and themes in the program as their own. It cannot be known whether the assembled company all consciously identified the themes of the program or whether there was simply a deep glow of satisfaction in the orderly beauties of the hierarchical universe, which the program itself had embodied. The relentless relevance of the music of this program to local political issues, so difficult to achieve however, strongly suggests that a programmer who was aware of their immediate implications made the musical choices.

The most likely candidate for the hard work of selecting specific repertoire for the difficult interstices between the structural pillars of the program was James Dodsley

Mr. Humphreys' 1851 Program

CONCERT BY THE PUPILS OF UPPER CANADA COLLEGE, ST. LAWRENCE HALL, 19 DEC.

PART I

1. *Quadrilles* – Victoria . . . . CZERNY
2. *Chorus* – "Lutzow's Wild Hunt" . . . . WEBER
3. *Piano Solo* – Fantasies from 'Lucrezia Borgia" . . . . BEYER
4. *Glee* – "When wearied wretches" . . . . BISHOP
5. *Waltz* – "Queen of the Flowers" . . . . SIEBOTH
6. *Violin Solo* – Swiss Air and Variations . . . . PRAEGER
7. *Chorus* – "The Pilot" . . . . NELSON
8. *Song* – Mr. Humphreys . . . . LEE
9. *"Rauber Galop"* [Thieves' Gallop] . . . . KREUTZER

PART II

1. *Quadrilles* – "Fête au Couvent" [Convent Celebration] . . . . BERGMULLER
2. *Glee* – "The Old Bell" . . . . ALLEGHANIANS
3. *Flute Solo* – "È vezzosa si la rosa". . . . . VACCIA
4. *Chorus* – "The brave old Oak" . . . . NELSON
5. *The College Polka* . . . . MAULE
6. *"Some love to roam"*. . . . . RUSSELL
7. *The Railroad Galop* . . . . GUNGLE
8. *Chorus* – "See our Oars" . . . . STEVENSON
9. *Finale* – "GOD SAVE THE QUEEN" . . . . JOHN BULL

Figure 10: Humphreys 1851 Program

Humphreys. Humphreys had the formal training, and his business was performing. He has been credited as the programmer of the 1851 concert by the Upper Canada College students which used similar materials, he owned some of the music on the Widder program, and, as the teacher of one or more of the singers, he knew the capacities of his singing students intimately.[49] He may not have supplied all of the music, since the Harriett Abrams song was not among his known music collection and had in any case been published and forgotten in London before he was born. Soirées Musicales were known, in part, for presenting new music, a feature noted in the 1840s in England that was found as late as the 1890s in Toronto. It would have been to the advantage of a professional musician to introduce, and sell, recently published material.[50] It was common practice in England for a professional musician to arrange the program in consultation with the hostess. Mrs. Sandeman's 1849 Soirée Musicale program announced that Signor Ferrari, a well-known musician, had "arranged" the program. Mrs. Widder did not have to invent the Soirée Musicale in Ontario, when she could simply have remembered it from London and worked to recreate it with Mr. Humphreys.

Choosing the particular political themes, however, was not necessarily the work of Mr. Humphreys. He had nothing to gain politically from such themes, and his other known program, created in 1851, reveals quite a different thematic emphasis. That program shows similar technical patterns, with symmetry achieved by having nine selections in each half, by repeating the mix of solo voice, solo instrument, and ensemble singing in each half, by beginning each half with a "quadrille," and by including in each half an ensemble sung about the joys of a roving band of independently-minded iconoclasts ("Lutzow's Wild Hunt" and "Some love to roam"). The 1851 program highlighted abstract, instrumental dance music at the centre point of each half (a waltz in the first half, and a polka by a Toronto composer, Maule, in the second), in the opening numbers of each half (the quadrilles), with the dance form called the "galop" as the end of the first half and the seventh selection in the second half. The third selection in each half was a solo, instrumental work. The two halves of the program were noticeably symmetrically patterned.

Thematically, the concert emphasised a jolly good time and social virtue. The emphasis on enjoyable group activities like dancing, hunting, and roaming was suitable for boys at school. The textual theme was steadfastness, expressed by loyalty to England and God ("Victoria" as the opening selection's title, "The Pilot," "The brave old Oak" as a metaphor for England, and "God Save the Queen") and by long-term faithfulness (Humphrey's song in the first half, and the "Old Bell" glee in the second half). Unlike the secularity of the Widder program, overtly sacred references are present ("The Pilot," "The Old Bell").

Humphreys' thematic intentions as programmer were underscored by having the words for the English language vocal material printed in the program. This 1851 program used the political theme of loyalty to Britain as part of masculine team experience, but compared to the Widder program had less controversial political content. The specific local overtones of "Lutzow's Wild Hunt" may have influenced the use of this glee on the 1851 school program as an underlying reminder of the historic military roots of the connection between colonial Canada and England. As in Mrs. Widder's 1844 program, the weight of history was present in the emphasis on English national identity as ancient and organic. The "brave old Oak" was a symbol of England, which had "ruled in the greenwood long." Mr. Humphreys' 1851 program showed thematic coherence and symmetrical use of musical genres similar to Mrs. Widder's 1844 program, but the themes themselves were different. The Widder program of 1844 was more intense, and emphasised unelected leadership. The themes that unified Mrs. Widder's program were a matter of choice.

Oh, to discover a note from Frederick to Elizabeth Widder outlining what he would have liked to see in this program, and why! Whatever Mr. Humphreys' contributions to the planning, Mrs. Widder, as the named hostess on the printed program, was formally responsible for the final choices. Her precise input is unknowable, but this program was extraordinarily apt for her husband's business plans at the time. While Frederick Widder would have benefited if all persons, even of the most democratic stripe, supported his goals, he could only successfully appeal to those who were in favour of the governance implications of private sector control of Crown lands. No Soirée Musicale program, indeed no argument in any form, would have been likely to change the allegiances of the most democratic of the political Reformers of the time. Yet the structure of this concert program was poised on the notion that harmony resulted if private and public morality were fully integrated on the basis of a hierarchy of human difference. This, in turn, was consistent both with conservative notions of proper governance and with the implications of Mr. Widder's apparent notions of appropriate commercial jurisdiction. Mrs. Widder's Soirée Musicale program might be seen as a little opera in which civic manly virtue could be carried out in the world of commerce. Whether or not Frederick Widder had suggested to his wife that she might design a Soirée Musicale program thematically aimed at fostering his bold attempt to shift Crown lands from state governance into the control of private commerce, the program she oversaw on March 12, 1844 could only have delighted him. The relevance of the program to local business and politics, whether intentional or unconscious, was real.

Chapter Three
MR. WIDDER SAT SILENT WHILE OTHER MEN SANG
Musical Genre, Masculinity, and Class

Five of Mrs. Widder's eleven singers were men. Why were they there? Why was Mr. Widder not among them? It was socially acceptable for his wife to sing at the Soirée Musicale that bore her name as the hostess of the event. The answer is that the decision to perform music in a formal concert setting, domestic or public, had as much to do with the variations of masculinity and social status as it did with musical ability. Just as women and men of the same class did not experience their leisure in the same way, so men of different classes did not experience the domestic Soirée Musicale in the same way. Men who held, or could reasonably aspire to hold, real political or economic power in the upper middle class or the aristocracy, did not devote time to developing a professional level of musical skill, nor did they perform music for others. Conversely, the men listed on Mrs. Widder's concert program belonged to different gradations of that "artist-musician class" defined by musicologist Nancy Reich to include "the practitioners of allied professions."[1]

The nuances of social rank among the men of Mrs. Widder's Musicale are revealed by the musical genres in which they sang and are confirmed by scholarship about elite socialising and the political implications of musical life in Britain and Europe. The patterning of Mrs. Widder's program suggests that McCaul and Barron, as professional educators, were practising one of those "allied professions," and thus shared the ambiguous social status of the professional musician. McCaul, Barron, and Wells were the only singers of glees, and they sang nothing else. If this Wells was George Dupont Wells, he was a barrister, but may have experienced reduced social status as the son of a disgraced college bursar. Mrs. Widder's star tenor, James Dodsley Humphreys, was a working professional musician who sang different musical genres and solo selections, as well as performing with the amateur women, who, not coincidentally, sang identical kinds of repertoire.

Captain Haliday shared Humphreys' musical territory, singing a solo aria requiring significant vocal and musical skill. His position in Toronto society in 1844 is difficult to pinpoint because conclusive proof of his identity is lacking. If he was the Haliday on temporary posting to Toronto with the 93rd Sutherland Highlanders, his professional background outside the military is unknown. Music was noted as a "trade" in the personnel rolls of the Regiment at this time, along with other working-class trades like baking and painting, and Haliday may have been the solitary professional musician in his regiment.[2] Part of his function, official or unofficial, may have been to use his special skills to engage with the local population. As historian Elinor Kyte Senior suggests, officers' "contributions to musical and dramatic performances ... showed that the garrison's role as an agency of cultural refinement came close to equalling the importance of its role as protector and aid to civil power."[3] If Mrs. Widder's singing Captain Haliday was not the William Robert Haliday of the 93rd Sutherland Highlanders, he was also not influential enough in the local society to have been noticed in the thorough scholarship that addresses pre-Confederation Canadian commerce and politics.

Middle class musical life in Ontario in 1844 was a compendium of the music, the trained musicians, and the patterns of musical leisure exported from London, England, the metropolitan centre of the British Empire. Fortunately for the professional tenor in the room and hostesses like Mrs. Widder, the idea of the Soirée Musicale had also been transferred from London, where it was an integral part of the basket of activities that provided professional musicians with their livelihood. Even the most eminent British musicians were charmingly available to assist their amateur hosts by teaching, performing with or for them, composing music dedicated to them, and brokering their purchases of pianos. Josef Haydn, for instance, sometimes accompanied composer and performer Harriet Abrams at the aristocratic soirées she organised. Musicians were often paid to perform at British Soirées Musicales, although they occasionally declined a fee in order to negotiate long-term teaching engagements.[4]

Despite these opportunities, however, most musicians in England struggled with unreliable incomes on the fringes of the respectability and comfort of the middle class. Although they were largely unable to compete with the influx of European musicians in the changing economy of English music, many fled Britain for the colonies rather than abandon their musical vocations in the face of the declining English music profession.[5] Ann Beedell's biography of the family of one such musician, William Castell, describes a flight to Australia, not to Canada, but her study may explain the sudden appearance, in the 1830s in Toronto, of emigrant British musicians like Mr. Humphreys.

The career of Mrs. Widder's star tenor, James Dodsley Humphreys, in the words of Michael Rudman, "provides an excellent perspective from which to view the general musical life of Toronto in the nineteenth century."[6] Rudman's biographical essay on Humphreys makes it clear that, like the lowly Castell and the lofty Haydn in England, Humphreys' busy career was full of variety. Wherever they worked, professional musicians did not just perform on professional concert stages for their living.

Figure 11. James Dodsley Humphreys, Courtesy Private Collection

James Dodsley Humphreys (1810–1877) lived by teaching, composing, perhaps selling music and instruments occasionally, producing concerts, and performing. He had left England for the less contested margin of the colony of Upper Canada, arriving at the age of twenty-five and quickly developing a network among the educated middle class.[7] As Beedell points out, a well-developed middle class was crucial to the financial survival of the professional musician, and, in Toronto, Humphreys cultivated a reputation among the middle class for reliability and musical expertise. Like his other qualified colleagues, he seldom failed to mention to this British-emulating public that he had trained at the Royal Academy of Music in London, a professional training school founded in 1822 by aristocrats, not musicians, ostensibly to foster a national musical identity for England. Humphrey's colleagues there included Henry J. Haycraft, whose friendly affection was mixed with canny marketing in his dedication of a song he wrote for Humphreys: "dedicated to his fellow Academician and friend, J. Dodsley Humphreys."[8] Unpretentious and wholly charming, Mr. Humphreys supported informal music making both because he liked it and because it served him well. The networking he found so enjoyable resulted in important appointments as church musician, teacher, and performer.

He advised the musical organisations founded and run by the musical amateurs who could fund the concerts, and wrote and performed incidental music for the dinners of local organisations like the Mechanics' Institute. He produced, sometimes with other local professionals, tours and subscription concerts for profit, to which the middle class led the way in purchasing tickets. He appeared "in public more often and over a longer period than any other Toronto artist of the mid-nineteenth century," by singing with everybody, from drawing-room amateurs to visiting professional troupes.[9]

Humphreys did well for a musician, but he was constantly seeking new income streams. While there may have been fewer musical competitors in his new community, there were also correspondingly fewer clients. Like virtually all musicians, he taught, but the teaching income was not always reliable. In 1857, although the family was comfortable enough to have their own greenhouse "with lots of roses in bloom," Mrs. Humphreys had "a great many things to pay for" and in a letter worriedly asked, "What think you of your nice pupils never having sent me one penny since you left."[10]

Just as in Australia, where well-known musicians tried, not always successfully, to boost their incomes with retail sales of instruments and music, in Canada, James Humphreys made a fleeting attempt at a retail music store. Despite his newspaper announcement in 1844, there is no record of it ever being opened. The formidable Nordheimer brothers, one a violinist and the other an excellent businessman, had also opened a music shop in Toronto that year, hedging their bets by selling sewing machines as well as pianos, and by 1857 had monopolized the piano business of Canada, "an immense trade." Humphreys may have made arrangements with A. & S. Nordheimer Company for commission on whatever music and instrument sales he encouraged among his students rather than persist with a store front of his own.[11]

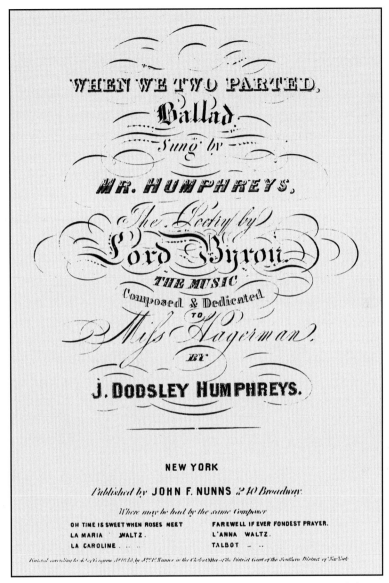

Figure 12: Song Dedication,Cover of J. Dodsley Humphreys, "When We Two Parted" (New York: John F. Nunns, 1843), Courtesy Rare Books and Special Collections, University of Windsor Library, University of Windsor

Humphreys certainly combined his teaching with composing music for the amateur musician, dedicating compositions to his students, who included not only Miss Hagerman (Figure 12), but also Miss M. Powell, niece of the sourly proper Mrs. Jarvis. These dedications were important marketing tools for composer and publisher, who depended on potential dedicatees to respond as, for instance, Miss Hagerman did. She wrote to him: "I am flattered by the consideration which has led you to offer the dedication of your most effective and beautiful Ballad to an old friend and pupil. I may certainly call myself the latter as it is to you I owe my first instruction in the vocal art – ... I accept with pleasure your proposed flattering dedication." [12] Since Miss Hagerman was answering a request for permission for the dedication, it had clearly been the composer rather than his dedicatee that had raised the possibility. Humphreys himself was famous enough to promote the music of others. A. & S. Nordheimer Company's first publication in 1844 announced that the song had been "Sung with much applause by Mr. Humphreys." Domestic performances also inspired music purchases, however, which may be why it was useful for publishers to print dedications to amateur singers who sang only in private. Inscribed by hand on a copy of an 1843 edition of "Kathleen Mavourneen" is, "This is just the one you wanted, that the young Lady sang at Mrs. ...." [13] Dedications to local celebrities continued into the 1880s in Toronto, with composers like Henry Martin following Humphreys' lead to associate a composition with Mrs. Robinson's reputation as an excellent singer. [14]

The warm, reciprocal collegiality between Humphreys and his client and friend, Miss Hagerman, suggested by her note, seems to have endured throughout their careers, which marched in tandem, his professional and hers amateur, until the end. Quiet desperation for a better livelihood in music may have moved Mr. Humphreys to emigrate to Canada, but his life and work there left the sweet odour of kindness and genuine delight in music hovering in his wake. His obituary described him as "so skilled a musician, so genial a gentleman and so true a friend and ... perhaps the best performer in our midst." Humphreys seems to have been a performer rather than a businessman, as the records of his professional activities show. Like many performers, he may have found the performing of music to be his principal satisfaction, and used creative strategies, including emigration, rather than abandon his training, identity, and vocation as a musician. [15]

Humphreys, so typical of nineteenth-century Canadian musicians, seems to have come from a family of the working artist-musician class. It was as true in Ontario as it was in Europe that professional musicians were usually born into such families, and developed not only musical skills from childhood but the professional connections without which access to paid musical work was rare and difficult. In Canada, there were several families of musicians who worked together in just this way. Humphreys and his sister Ermine both studied music at the Royal Academy of Music in London, a professional training school at this time. Annotated student lists show J. D. Humphreys and Ermine Humphreys as students, noting for them, as for all other students of both sexes, their professional status. While women's careers were often noted as being terminated by marriage, this 1848 publication clearly emphasized that the school provided training for professionals, not entertainment for amateurs. Humphreys' daughter Eliza was a Toronto singer who performed in public by singing a duet with her father, as did the daughter of local musician Mr. R.G. Paige. The common practice in Toronto, as in England, was for professional musicians to introduce their children to the profession. [16]

The ready acceptance by their fathers of the women's paid performing was a function of their shared family business rather than an indication of wide social acceptance of music as a profession respectable enough for middle-class women. The careers of famous professional women musicians did not make the musical profession a suitable alternative for all women. Male musicians themselves were outside the pale of professional respectability. As Richard Leppert points out in his discussion of one English portrait of a father teaching his daughter how to play the harpsichord, what was appropriate for a family of artist-musicians "would have severely violated portrait - hence social - convention" if it had been a portrait of a "'true' gentleman." Without addressing gender in such detail, Cyril Ehrlich's analysis of the British music profession simply concludes that the low incomes and spotty social reputations of working musicians meant that they were intellectually, personally, and financially suspect in England throughout the nineteenth century. [17]

Toronto's favourite tenor may have taught and performed in the grand drawing rooms of Widder or Robinson, but his wife perfectly understood that her husband's presence there was not a sign of peer status. Although Caroline Ridout Humphreys' birth family was well connected in Toronto society, her social status was determined by her husband's status. As Leonore Davidoff suggests, when a woman married, her status changed in accordance with that of her husband. In 1842, newly married, Caroline Humphreys wrote, "I found *my house* very comfortable and I assure you I should not be ashamed to see any visitors however *grand*." Thirteen years later, invited to a private concert at Government House while her husband was out of town, Mrs. Humphreys wrote to her husband, "But of course I did not go. I heard it was quite a concert they had printed programmes." The domestic Soirée Musicale was socially comfortable for her husband, as a work environment, but without him, she "of course" did not attend. [18]

Humphreys' constant association with amateur musicians, as teacher, as producer of their concerts, and as their fellow performer in Soirées Musicales, meant that, like any English musician, he had to have "the careful mentality of a burgher but the manners of a courtier." Whereas, in England, private concerts were "often full-scale affairs, with orchestras, singers, and even whole ballet companies being engaged," the Soirée Musicale of Toronto could draw on no such wealth of professional artistry. [19] Kallmann points out that only twenty-five musicians and nineteen music sellers were listed for Toronto. [20] Humphreys was lucky to have so few competitors, but doubtless worked hard to ensure his welcome among the families who could afford to hire the best musicians in town to teach their daughters and perform. Even after Toronto's concert life expanded in the 1850s, with the influx of travelling professionals and another wave of immigrant musicians, Humphreys' professional performances regularly included sharing the stage with amateurs. In 1844, his only known engagement was Mrs. Widder's private Soirée Musicale, where he performed with the men who were his potential employers from Upper Canada College, and the Lady Amateurs.

The work of Mr. Humphreys closely resembled the leisure of Mrs. Widder's Lady Amateurs. Both professional musician and Lady Amateur sang music that displayed the advanced vocal technique of operatic showpieces and dripped with the dramatic emotionalism of intellectually vacuous parlour ballads. Both musical genres were as emphatically feminine as the Victorian notion of musical performance itself.

In Victorian culture, the semiotic femininity of music as sound was unambiguous As Cyril Ehrlich makes clear, by 1850, "music was virtually forbidden to boys of 'good family,' particularly if they betrayed signs of talent or serious interest." At the same time, "pupils at all levels of society were predominantly female."[21] A compelling explanation for this is offered by Richard Leppert, who analyses the use of music as a trope of social meanings in eighteenth and nineteenth century family portraits commissioned by the English upper middle class. The representation of music making in these paintings shows that domesticity was intended to entrench a way of life by presenting the relationships it embodied as the natural pattern for the future. Leppert suggests that music was an effective symbol of prevailing ideas of gender difference because the paintings associated music primarily with the leisured women of these families. The exception Leppert notes was the association of masculinity with military instruments like the flute, the drum, and the trumpet, all instruments of the battlefield. The nature of domestic musical performance and musical performers was understood to be doubly feminine: mechanical repetitions by the body and service to the creative genius of the composer.

The corollary, as Leppert suggests from his large sample of English portraits, was that music was consistently deemed to be "improper for a man." Masculine leisure ought to produce tangible, rational outcomes, but the sound of music vanished as soon as it was made, a temporary fizz of emotional excess. Musical skill took too much time for important people to develop, in a period when "time was money was power." Leppert concludes that any man who demonstrated a high level of musical performance skill thereby proved that he had spent more time outside the mainstream of economic activity than anyone but a leisured woman or professional musician could literally afford. Hence, "any male presenting himself as a devoted, and not merely recreative, musician was suspect."[22] This had painful consequences for the musical profession, but it also presented a challenge to those powerful men who found singing irresistible.

Enter the English glee. The delights of music making do not depend upon the sex of the musician, so elite men who were musically inclined developed the glee. Glees, being more refined than the bawdy, witty "catches" that had emerged in the fifteenth century, were written by and for the members of all-male glee and catch clubs where noblemen, gentlemen, and professional musicians sang in close harmony, drinking hard until they could sing no more. It demonstrated the masculine features of low technical performance demands, intellectual complexity, and tangible outcomes, without compromising the commanding position of men who could not perform for their social inferiors without losing caste. As musicologist Gloria Delamere suggests, most glee clubs imitated the structure of the original Noblemen and Gentlemen's Catch Club of London, founded in 1761, at which the "regular members" were the noblemen and gentlemen who paid dues and had voting rights. The "privileged members" were the professional musicians who wrote and performed competitive glees, and provided skilled singing to improve the sound at the club meetings, but had no voting voice in directing the club.[23] Just as in Mrs. Widder's drawing room, the experience of making music in private glee clubs varied with the social status of the participant.

The written mandate of the Noblemen and Gentlemen's Catch club was "for the encouragement of the composition and performance of canons, catches, and glees," complete with a written plan for implementation.[24] The product of this musical leisure was tangible, printed music, with professional musicians competing for prize money, and the subsequent publication to a wider market of the glees they wrote for the glee clubs. The right to assess its quality was restricted to the regular club members who made it clear that the judgements of the trained musicians in the club were irrelevant to their deliberations. It was only natural that the upper-class men of these clubs should claim to be authorities on the glee, which was considered to be the musical form that gave eighteenth and nineteenth-century England its national musical identity. Nineteenth-century English musicologist William Alexander Barrett (1836-1891) claimed that the English glee was so intellectually rich that, "The study of it will insensibly lead to the accumulation of other knowledge, and if rightly used will be found available for the highest purpose ... Every kind of mental power, once evoked and applied to a worthy purpose, becomes available for other purposes." The musical leisure of upper-class Englishmen claimed significant results: stylistic innovation, tangible new publications, cash, and musical nationalism. Fun was not enough. [25]

Glees were more amusing to sing than to listen to, as a review of their close harmonies and simple melodies will confirm, precisely because they were primarily designed to please their singers. Tucked away in private meeting rooms, the elite men of the glee clubs sang to please themselves, not others. (The working musicians, of course, had to always please the "regular members.") With its emphasis on the intellectual skill of sight-reading rather than the time-consuming skill of polished vocal technique and emphatically masculine lyrics, the English glee offered manly musical recreation appropriate for elite English men. When glees did appear on concert programs, as they often did in the nineteenth century in Canada, students, teachers, and professional musicians performed them, and they served as reminders of the private musical amusements peculiar to British men. Powerful men did not perform glees at concerts; glee performers were homage to them. They were also unmistakable confirmation of class and gender differences.

The all-male glee club was the masculine equivalent of feminine domestic musical accomplishment. Both were leisured pursuits for middle and upper-class amateurs who engaged professional musicians to teach and sing with them. A critical difference was that elite women could achieve far higher levels of skill because they had the time to spend practising. This is reflected in the predominance of solo ballads, rather than ensemble glees, for women. The elite men of the glee club, singing songs for three or more voices, occasionally accepted instruction from the "privileged members" but bad singing or being musically unprepared was such a constant feature that club regulations provided for suitable punishments. Since the price of musical sin was usually to drink "a bumper of wine," and try again, with predictable results, the regular club members were obviously less interested in their own musical excellence than in the opportunity for enjoyable self-indulgence.[26]

Mrs. Widder's program was framed and punctuated by three intellectual Gentleman Amateurs singing unusual glees. The beauty of Barron's and McCaul's voices was noted in memoirs of the time, and both men sang in public often, so their singing was probably reliably good, an important consideration for Mrs. Widder's event. Glees gave Mrs. Widder's program intellectual sheen. It is unlikely that these singers would have used the musically rather dull *Tancredi* chorus for pleasure at convivial musical meetings, but for such skilled readers of music, this male-voice chorus would have been very easy to learn. The *Tancredi* chorus may have been chosen for this program because it was thematically consistent with the works selected for the climactic moments. It was also a suitable vehicle that allowed the intellectually distinguished McCaul and Barron to open the program. The two men were probably important enough to Mrs. Widder's guest list that they could have performed any material they liked, but because the glees they sang were so very apt, thematically, selecting them may have posed an enjoyable intellectual puzzle.

The presence of McCaul and Barron in Mrs. Widder's drawing room was highly charged, hence extremely important, because of the bitter dispute between Bishop Strachan and Mr. Widder. It might have been difficult to refuse a Widder request to sing, since Widder's firm, the Canada Company, had contributed financial support to their schools, but tact may have been necessary in managing their boss, the Bishop. The use of an irresistible musical entertainment to facilitate political bridge building was common at the time. As one music critic wrote in 1842, "Music has become ... a juste milieu, as an art of reconciliation between all the classes of society. When one listens, no discussions ... are possible. Music stimulates goodwill."[27] In the same way, emphasising the apolitical nature of abstract, intellectual refinement may have provided McCaul and Barron with a politically neutral bridge between warring factions. Like the professional musician in the room, these educators had to serve many masters.

Thematically, it was unnecessary to use the German composer Leonhard von Call's glee to achieve the atmosphere of "Come, silent evening." The same sentiments were readily available in music held by Mr. Humphreys, like Joseph Knight's song which opens with "Give me the night! The calm, beautiful night."[28] Most glees in Canadian collections, like the vast preponderance of glees in Britain, were by English composers. Englishman Edward Rimbault patriotically, but wrongly, claims that no search could "produce a foreign glee ... no such thing exists."[29] The German glees of Mrs. Widder's program were recondite variations of the more customary English glee.

The programmer used the glees to unify the program with a symmetrical repetition of the sound and spectacle of three men singing in close cooperation. As musicologist Lawrence Kramer has suggested, masculinity in music has been associated with overall structural unity, as opposed to the "feminine" absorption in the more fragmentary experience of the momentary.[30] The programmer of the Widder Soirée Musicale used men, all singing thematically unified material appropriate to their social stations, to support the principal architectural pediments of the program structure. The glee singers' status as amateur musicians was well known to all present. Their performance of the glees was a complex representation of their professional function as directors of the intellectual and cultural training for the next generation of Ontario's leaders. They maintained the intellectual masculinity of elite men by singing music that did not require the same degree of physical or vocal skill as the lower class professional musician in glee club, Musicale, and concert hall. But they shared with James Humphreys the status of the hired artist-musician by virtue of (probably excellent!) performing on a formal concert program.

Mr. Widder sat silent, his name not even on the printed program of the musical entertainment produced by his wife in his home. Mrs. Widder was the perfect hostess, juggling a myriad of small but critical details. The very date of her Soirée Musicale was sensitive, changed at the very last minute to the 12th of March. On Tuesday, the 5th of March, 1844, a friend of Humphreys wrote that the Widder Soirée Musicale "was to have taken place tonight but has been postponed owing to the melancholy loss of

Mrs. Aylmer who died on Monday Morning as you have doubtless heard … no one can help feeling some degree of sorrow at the death of so young a person, a wife and mother too." Mrs. Aylmer's husband was a colleague of Captain William Robert Haliday in the 93rd Sutherland Highlanders stationed in Toronto. [31] Mrs. Widder allowed a respectful week to mark the death, but did not cancel her Soirée Musicale. Never a woman to do things by halves, she had programs printed with the new date, March 12th, 1844.[32] Since there were printed programs with the correct date of the postponed Musicale, March 12, programs for the original date, March 5, had probably already been printed when it was suddenly cancelled. The smallest details of this program werAs e given careful attention.

The performers' names also suggest careful calculation. As Katherine McKenna has shown for Toronto in this period, the social lives of the powerful "were not mere diversions but battlegrounds upon which fights over social position were won and lost."[33] Mrs. Widder's ingenious social strategy brought Miss Hagerman and Miss Boulton, the daughters of one old Family Compact member and one prominent Reformer, onto the same stage. The appeal of a special musical party overcame, for a moment, hot political antipathies remembered by whole families for generations. Miss Hagerman's own daughter wrote, in 1917, that the name of Reform journalist George Brown, a sharp critic of old Tories like Christopher Hagerman, "had always been represented to me as something vile and too horrible to live, and the idea that, as my playmate said, he was a kindly gentleman, was one which could not be allowed to exist for a moment. Accordingly, we had a violent quarrel, which ended in a forcible separation by the governess."[34] Some members of the families of the Lady Amateurs on the program were almost certainly in attendance at Mrs. Widder's concert.

All of these men and women were acutely aware of subtle distinctions of social position, and with them, gender-appropriate activities. For these people, Mrs. Widder, but not Mr. Widder, was the only possible nominal host on the Musicale program. Sheer propriety made it impossible for men to invite women to their homes unless a mature female were present as hostess. Some men initiated entertainments, which probably included Soirées Musicales, but even later in the century, Toronto bachelor George Beardmore had his sister-in-law preside as hostess.[35] Whether the Lyndhurst Soirée Musicale was performed at Mr. Widder's request is not known, but like any man with a musical wife, Frederick Widder need look no further than his own breakfast table for his guarantor of propriety.

His wife was not just a chaperone. Mrs. Widder, as organizer, hostess, and performer of a Soirée Musicale that involved her husband's commercial and political associates, was setting an example of superior feminine behaviour by entertaining beautifully. The Soirée Musicale was more elaborate than ordinary domestic music making, partly because it was special bait in the competitive socialising of the powerful. Sought-after guests had their choice of parties, and music could tip the balance.

Silences, as well as sounds, rang out from her program. Mrs. Widder's name in the title of the program captured the silent absence of her husband from the far end of the drawing room, which had become a concert stage. Men who were politically or economically powerful did not perform on Mrs. Widder's program. Their names, like Mr. Widder's, were associated with music in Ontario as patrons of concerts or directors of musical organisations. The printed program captured in amber the fact that each performer had performed, and Mr. Widder was not among them. Carefully printed for every selection was its musical genre, glee, ballad, or opera, and on the same line, the name of each performer. The sole exception was the curious *Tancredi* chorus, glee-like in its simplicity, but in fact, an operatic selection: the program was silent about these performers. No lies were told, but the three glee gentlemen left no record of having sung it. To perform glees was quite enough. Every person who might read the program in 1844, whether a glee singer in that Toronto drawing room, a working tenor propping the program up on the mantel of his teaching studio, or an ambitious business man genially sharing the program of a missed concert with a British colonial governor, would have been intimately familiar with each of these musical genres. The combination of musical genre with the gender and class of the performers reflected precisely not only their own status but their relationships with their audience and fellow-performers. The five male performers of Mrs. Widder's Soirée Musicale, like the six Lady Amateurs, were singing for their supper.

Chapter Four

MRS. WIDDER SANG AWFULLY WELL
the Dignified Struggle of the Lady Amateur

The domestic Soirée Musicale of nineteenth-century Ontario was completely unnecessary for dutiful feminine accomplishment. The families who could afford to train their daughters in music, buy high-priced pianos, and pay for the catering and service for a Soirée Musicale held in a large formal drawing room could as easily have engaged only professional musicians to perform the entire concert. Why did formal concert programs in these homes include the amateur women musicians of the family circle? The domestic Soirée Musicale in Ontario depended upon the superior musicality of its Lady Amateurs. Without them, it would have been very different.

The Soirée Musicale was one of few options for profound self-development available to its Lady Amateur performers. The male musicians who performed with them were working, directly or indirectly, for pay, and the Gentleman Amateurs who performed had other professional sources of satisfaction, income, and public identity. It was the Lady Amateurs who were uniquely displayed - and uniquely satisfied - in these formal domestic concerts. The Soirée Musicale was no more than an extreme version of the ordinary domestic musical duties common to all parlour music making. Most women left no trace of their parlour music making, but the evidence of the few who performed in the Soirée Musicale suggests that the range of amateur women's musical accomplishments was greater than the monolithic mediocrity so often assumed.

Mrs. Widder's 1844 Soirée Musicale is an example of how music making entrenched restrictive notions of femininity even as it activated the slight elasticity of Victorian gender ideology. There were contradictions in Mrs. Widder's evening, as there were in the great body of musical life as the century progressed, but no mere logical muddle could overwhelm the apparent naturalness of the Soirée Musicale. It was a drama of difference in which "ladies" and "gentlemen" were always musical "amateurs" whose performances compared favourably with those given by the professional musicians of a different social class. It is ironic that a woman oversaw the placement of masculine leadership at the conceptual high points of the program, and ensured that the women's music was programmed as essential, supportive filler. Mrs. Widder's program reflected what were likely her own ideas about gendered difference.

Figure 13: Parlour Music: "Unidentified couple in living room, Three Rivers, Q.C.," about 1895, copied ca. 1975 Notman Photographic Archives, MP-0000.1571.24, Courtesy McCord Museum of Canadian History, Montreal

Mrs. Widder's musical selections, representative as they are of the women's music on her 1844 Soirée Musicale program, are discussed here in the context of domestic musical life of the period. The two arresting choices of operatic arias written for male characters but sung at Mrs. Widder's house by women are used to show that although the Soirée Musicale developed in part to give newly skilled Lady Amateurs a more rewarding platform on which to exercise their skills, it broke no new path for them in the music profession. The Lady Amateur was doing her feminine part to maintain the status quo.

Convention assigned musical accomplishment to women, "for that domestic comfort, they were by Providence designed to promote."[1] For some, it was a joyless duty, incapable of rewarding the player with pleasure. Helen McNicoll (1879-1915), deaf by age two, was trained to provide musical entertainment at home.[2] The powerlessness of women to refuse their musical duty in the home was poignantly stated by American pianist Amy Fay, who wrote of a family visit in 1866: "Since I have been here I have been converted into a sort of hand organ, for they make me play morning, noon, and night until I am completely worn out."[3] As the photograph of informal parlour music making

Figure 14: "Music Lesson", Illustration by Lamoureux [sic] in *The Aldine Magazine: The Art Journal of America*, vol VII, no. 20 (1874-5), p. 391/Courtesy National Library of Canada

suggests (Figure 13), parlour musicians were not always accorded the full attention of their listeners. Whether or not it pleased the player, musical accomplishment was *de rigeur* for respectable nineteenth-century women.

"The Music Lesson," (Figure 14) found in the family collection of an Ontario home, summarises the similarity of the Victorian concepts of Music and Woman. The rapt pose of the small dog at the left, so similar to the woman pianist with hands like front paws and train in place of tail, suggests that the woman's music making was governed by her non-rational, physical nature rather than her conscious, intellectual awareness. The standing man is intellectually aware, identifying the spiritual authenticity of the moment and controlling the other man in the room, who is a music teacher. The woman playing, however, is as utterly absorbed in the physical experience of the music as the dog. The accompanying article asks, "What is it in the 'music lesson' that has stirred ... his quick gesture of silence and attention? ... What has drawn the calm eyes from the duplicate sheet of music and filled them with a far-away, absorbed light that does infinite credit to the taste and skill of his fair daughter?"[4] The father has been transported to spiritual awareness by the music making of his daughter.

As the 1844 *Musical Times* of London put it, "That, without which there can be no truly beautiful performance of any kind is — Faith."[5] Both Music and Woman, as vehicles for divine inspiration, were intended to provide men with spiritual improvement; hence the familiar notion of the Victorian Angel of the Hearth who provided music at home as soothing respite from the masculine world. On Mrs. Widder's program, in the duet from the Spohr opera *Azor and Zemira*, which is the tale of Beauty and the Beast, Man, as "Beast," longs to be elevated by Woman's mere presence. Azor (Beast) sings "Oh, lovely Maiden stay … 'tis all I ask, for love I may not seek from thee!" Zemira (Beauty) accepts her part in the relationship in the self-effacing words, "for my father's sake."[6] The essential, biological difference between Man (Beast) and Woman (Beauty) is explicit in the title of the myth. The duet is a parable of the Victorian conventions of gender as an expression of natural order.

Domestic music, and by extension the Soirée Musicale, had a spiritual function. As parlour music specialist Derek Scott notes, "the entertainment of the drawing room came to uphold 'the ideal of the week of seven Sabbaths.'"[7] During the 1840s, popular parlour music supplanted traditional hymn singing at home partly by adapting the forms of sacred music to secular texts.[8] Part of the social stability provided by parlour music was its maintenance of religious values in secular form, and, closely related to those religious values, was the definition of Woman as subordinate to Man. The music sung by the women on Mrs. Widder's program was representative of the prevailing norms of femininity, and typical of most nineteenth-century drawing room and parlour music in Ontario.

Mrs. Widder's whole program was composed of selections largely consistent with the daily hum of music popular throughout the English-speaking world. Although there were local resonances to all music, and although some music was not distributed internationally, the major producers of sheet music fed an international market. Music historians James Parakilas and Gretchen Wheelock date international marketing of English parlour music to 1815, when Muzio Clementi began publishing simultaneously in England, France and Germany. International copyright law only began with the Berne Convention in 1886, so local publishers could - and did - reissue most works published elsewhere with impunity.[9] There were variations in American publishing law, which made it worthwhile for Samuel Nordheimer, of A. & S. Nordheimer in Toronto, Canada's most prolific music publisher from 1844 to 1900, to join the American Board of Music Trade in 1859.[10] Nordheimer's expansion into the larger American market place was typical of the porous borders through which the imprints of sheet music flowed. Musically, Mrs. Widder's Soirée Musicale was no more than a subset of the every day musical culture.

If informal performances were meant to be an especially feminine aspect of home life, the domestic Soirée Musicale was a forum for demonstrating particularly fine femininity. The collision between the superior "nature" of a lady and the intrinsic inferiority of being female had logically incoherent outcomes. The upper-class lady had to demonstrate class superiority, and, in music making, that meant singing better music better while remaining modest.[11] The result in Mrs. Widder's drawing room was that ladies sang both difficult operatic works and simple parlour ballads. The greater technical difficulties of opera required more leisure time and more expensive training to master than did the simpler ballads of the workaday parlour. In formal concert formats, "amateur" was actually code for "leisured," and implied that the performer was merely amusing herself with music. In the case of a lady, "amateur" could also mean a performer who combined nearly professional proficiency with the pristine spiritual authenticity of "true womanhood."

Compare, for example, the technical difficulty of the two vocal lines in "Oh, lovely maiden stay" (Figure 15). Lady Amateur Mrs. Nash sang the top line and the second line was sung by the professional tenor Mr. Humphreys. Both require extended vocal range, great vocal flexibility, and excellent ensemble singing skills. This excerpt captures the kind of technical demands made by the *Norma* duet and the tenor aria "Vivi tu." By contrast, ballads like "Not a Drum was Heard," sung by Mr. Humphreys, and "Dermot Astore" (Figure 16), sung by Lady Amateur Miss Macaulay are technically modest. The vocal technique necessary for the three Gentleman Amateurs to give a fine performance of their glees, "Lutzow's Wild Hunt" (Figure 6) and "Come, silent evening" (Figure 17) is similar to that required by most parlour ballads sung by women. The interpretive demands of the glee are different from those required by solo parlour music, however, because singing in close harmony blurs the distinction between individual voices. For two or more voices to sing close harmony well, the ensemble skills of the glee were similar to those required by the operatic duets like "Oh, lovely maiden, stay" and "Mira, oh Norma." Both women and men who sang difficult operatic material and simple parlour songs required more musical and vocal skills than the singers of glees.

By delivering the same ideas in the musically complex and often technically difficult genre of opera, the importance of a hierarchy of human difference was presented as

Figure 15: Opera Duet: *Azor & Zemira* excerpt. Louis Spohr, "Oh, lovely maiden stay, duet from *Grand Opera of Azor & Zemira*," arr. Sir George Smart (London: D'Almaine & Co., n.d. [104 New Bond Street, c. 1811]), p. 126, Courtesy British Library

Figure 16: Parlour Ballad: "Dermot Astore" excerpt. F. W. Nichols Crouch, "Dermot Astore" (New York: Hewitt & Jaques, 239 Broadway, n.d.), p. 2/Courtesy National Library of Canada

Figure 17: Glee: "Come, Silent Evening" excerpt. Originally a trio

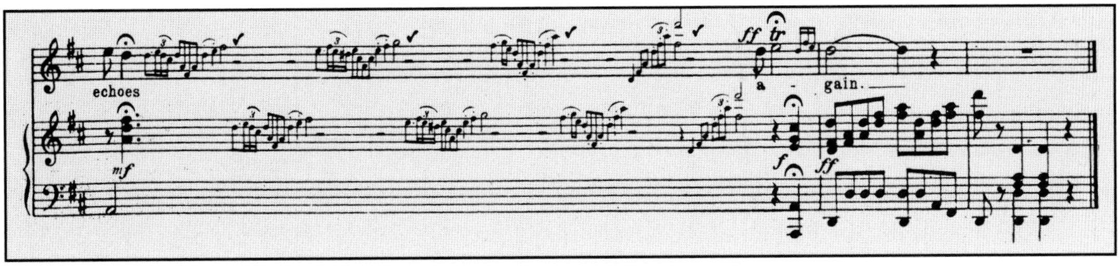

Figure 18: Glee: "Echo Song" excerpt.

worthy of elevated musical effort. Both opera and ballad delivered the same messages about gender and class. The performers with enough skill to master "Vivi tu" or "Mira O Norma" also presented simple songs, using technique far in excess of what was needed to satisfy their audience's affection for simple ballads, which were loved as familiar, restful expressions of charming sentiments. The musical and intellectual vacuity of such songs as "The Dream is Past," found on Mrs. Widder's program, confirmed that this musical genre and its performers were non-intellectual. In the domestic Soirée Musicale, a real lady set an example of femininity.

Derek Scott, in his history of the nineteenth-century parlour ballad, notes that there were two types of woman in the texts of drawing room ballads, the "'perfect lady' or 'honest country maiden.'"[12] Cultivation made the difference between the two. One Canadian piano advertisement in 1872 urged farmers to buy pianos for their daughters rather than live like animals.[13] Even a lady retained the essential female nature: physical rather than intellectual, and dependent on her relationship with others for her identity. At Mrs. Widder's Soirée Musicale, her own final solo was Bishop's "Echo Song." The song is as innocent of intellectual content as an "honest country maiden," and enacts the physicality of music. The words are merely a stage direction to make plain that the music re-creates the physical experience of hearing an echo. In performance, the audience experience of this song is the singer's voice as an embodied "Spirit" that "floats sweetly around," musically "echoing" the airy strain. The singer's voice emerges from nowhere else but from her body, and is experienced by the listener as evidence of the authentic inner self of the performer. The accompanying instrument imitates the vocal phrases from the beginning to the pyrotechnical end (Figure 18) when the singer wordlessly trills bird-like vocalism after the final "echoes." Voice and instrument utter identical musical phrases, allowing listeners to experience a woman's voice as an instrument. This song embodies Woman as pure physicality, like the uncultivated fauna in the natural world. The technical cultivation necessary for enjoyable performance of this song made it a perfect choice for a refined, musical Lady Amateur.

Music was seen as a mode of spiritual and moral elevation, as this description from an 1844 periodical suggests: "its powers to soften, to purify the heart ... are divinely authenticated and bestowed."[14] The music business, of which this trade magazine was a part, marketed domestic consumption by women of music, teaching, and instruments in the 1840s.[15] It made use of the connections between the concepts of music, spirituality, and domestic feminine responsibility, but it did not create them. Music was recommended as a mode of transcendental spirituality in this secularising Victorian world. The spiritual responsibility assigned to women in the home was expressed in secular parlour music in part as an emotionalism, maternal warmth, a decorative charm collected in the innocent purity of the "true" nature of womanhood. Spiritual life was shifting from the public to the private realm, using recognizable musical and textual Christian tropes in apparently secular terms.

In the non-Christian "fairy land" of the "Echo Song," Mrs. Widder's voice embodied a secular form of the soul, the indisputably "inner" essence of her self. The secular universe so important to Frederick Widder's commercial enterprise thus retained the stable social values of Christian spirituality in the form of female subordination to male authority, a microcosm of the human relationship with God. The questions "Is't Fairy land? Are Spirits round?" create, in the asking, an imagined sanctuary which could be enjoyed effortlessly as feminine, domestic, innocent, and tidily boxed out of the daily reality of non-domestic, non-feminine activity. The performance of Bishop's "Echo Song" allowed the audience to relax in the benevolent stability of woman's essential nature. Mrs. Widder the singer was performing in song the same social role she performed as a hostess at home.

Throughout the evening of March 12, 1844, the lyrics sung by the women presented a number of the conventional variations of that essential nature, from the painful stasis of self-injuring love and the passive yearning for the impossible, to eternal girlishness and unending loyalty. Mrs. Widder herself provided the spectacle of a middle-aged mother of four playing the part of young girls in works by Haydn, Mozart, and Spohr. As Deborah Gorham shows, the mid-Victorian ideal of a good mother was that she remained "childlike even in maturity."[16] The high, light, girlish voice needed for the "Echo Song" would also be well suited to a convincing performance of Haydn's "My mother bids me bind my hair," in which a young girl defies her mother to stay true to her absent lover. In the song, a mother is recommending, quite sensibly, that the singer, a young girl, provide for her future and find a husband. The Haydn character is emotional, not rational, and innocent of selfish scheming, as well as selflessly devoted to her man. She cannot "help herself while Lindoro is away." Self-injuring loyalty, a form of the innocent self-sacrifice of the ideal woman, was a common theme in Victorian parlour songs. In this program, the Glover and Abrams songs are based on the same theme. The characters in both songs are static, not prompted to remedial action by their circumstance, but fulfilled by grieving, passive, self-injuring love.

The character of Susanna in the Mozart duet, another young girl sung by Mrs. Widder, emphasizes feminine intellectual fogginess and irresistible sexuality. Susanna is a wily servant, a dangerous temptation to her lascivious boss, the Count who, in this duet, is extracting a promise of an illicit sexual encounter from her. The scene performed at Mrs. Widder's Soirée Musicale is part of a plan to teach the wicked Count a lesson about true love. But, dear creature that she is, Susanna is easily confused by the Count, and nearly gives away the plan by mistake. Silly, sexy, Susanna! She will do the right thing because she feels a true moral impulse and is following the leadership of her fiancé, but her intellectual confusion makes it dangerous for her to take action against any man. The gendered subtext is that a woman is unreliable when she ventures into thought or tries to control a man.

While the lyrics of their selections were intensely conventional about the nature of being female, the Lady Amateurs were the heart of the Soirée Musicale as a form. The quality of the performances in a formal musical evening like a Soirée Musicale had to be reliable and superior to less formal musical gatherings or this kind of concert would not have been repeated, as it was in Ontario for over fifty years.[17] The quality of the professional musicians' performances were reliable because they were steeped in experience and training. The quality of singing demonstrated by the Amateur Gentlemen in their glees was probably reasonable within the narrower technical and musical demands of that genre. But the Lady Amateurs sang difficult music alone, and carried a large proportion of the program. At Mrs. Widder's Soirée Musicale, fourteen of the twenty selections featured women performers, and of twelve solo selections, women performed nine. If two thirds of the concert were dull or embarrassingly bad, the purpose of the evening would have been better served by the men trotting off to a spirituous glee-club meeting or the whole company gathering, as legend has it they often did, "around the piano for a lusty sing through the voyageur melodies with Mrs. Widder at the piano."[18] The Soirée Musicale, as a form of amateur concert, was a unique vehicle for the display of the highly-skilled Lady Amateur.

As such, the domestic Soirée Musicale brought the internal contradictions of nineteenth-century gender ideology to something of a boil. Here lies the fertile weakness of the concept of idealised "Woman" engaging in music as a trivial, private activity: the tidy containment of aroused musicianship is impossible. There were doubtless tormentingly persistent performers untouched by talent, but women who too warmly loved musical performing made many uneasy. The Lady Amateurs of Ontario were not immune from social censure. One of Mrs. Widder's Lady Amateurs, Miss Hagerman, was criticized for her musical zeal in private circles before her marriage. (Although there is extensive evidence of Miss Hagerman singing in public after her marriage, there is no trace of her doing so before.) In 1843, Samuel Jarvis wrote, "I am glad [our daughter Ellen] has been giving her attention to music again. Ellen's intimacy in that respect with Miss Hagerman will be very beneficial, for I really think her the best private performer in Toronto." Mary Jarvis, Samuel's wife, acidulously replied, "Eliza Fitzgerald … is a very nice young woman, and a much better companion for Ellen than Miss Hagerman, although she cannot play or sing."[19]

These were not idle exchanges but part of the serious business of marrying well. The competition for the position of wife to the sons of prominent families could be

Figure 19: "Miss Windeat, Artiste." Adelaide Macdonald (attrib.), bound music album #22, flyleaf inscribed 1863/ Courtesy National Library of Canada

brutal. In the diary she left open for all to read in her home, Mrs. Harris of London, Ontario, viciously mocked Mrs. Widder's attempts to have the Widder daughters dance with the visiting Prince of Wales in 1860, after her son, Edward Harris, had thrown over Blanche Widder's affections to marry Sophia Ryerson. Mrs. Harris later cooled towards Sophia and demonstrated her disapproval in part by declining to attend her daughter-in-law's large Soirée Musicale. The cultural diversity of a large urban centre perhaps gave Mrs. Widder more license to take centre stage in formal domestic concerts than was available to the unhappy Sophia Ryerson Harris in a smaller urban setting.[20]

The convention of musical accomplishment as feminine activated the faint elasticity of the Victorian notion of femininity, but simultaneously set up a thrum of contradictory tension. As Deborah Gorham has shown, a Victorian daughter was bad if she were "vulgar, self-seeking." Sharp-nosed enforcers like Mrs. Jarvis recognized musical accomplishment as problematic partly because no respectable nineteenth-century woman should have displayed such dazzling musicality that she outshone father or husband.[21] Worse, perhaps: a woman who really enjoyed performing, like Miss Hagerman, was pleasing herself, rather than directing her energies to pleasing others. As the portrait one young lady drew on the flyleaf of her own music folio, "Miss Windeat, Artiste" suggests, Miss Hagerman was not the only amateur musician who enjoyed the attention she received for performing (Figure 19).

Mrs. Jarvis' resistance to Miss Hagerman's musical brilliance was consistent with a hostile strand of public discourse about feminine musical accomplishment. Perhaps the most ironic expression is found in the lyrics of this 1842 parlour song:

> *How I wish that my husband would let me alone,*
> *And not want me always to play!*
> *Oh! I've never a minute to call my own;*
> *I'm playing and singing all day!*
>
> *...*
>
> *I seldom can get to the nursery now,*
> *For practising fills every hour;*
> *I've never seen Susan or Willy, I vow,*
> *Since Wednesday evening at four:*
> *For if ever I enter the school room to hear*
> *How much they have pleased Madame Lisle,*
> *My husband comes in with, "now Mary, my dear,*
> *Come and practise Herz's newest quadrille."*[22]

This "nice" woman did not want to be distracted from her children, but placed her husband's wishes ahead of her maternal devotion. The female singer of "The Musical Husband" trumpeted her femininity by denigrating her own singing even as she sang: truly "feminine" self-injury.

Mrs. Jarvis was right about the dangers of music. No prescriptive attempt to limit the actual dynamics of music making can change the fact that making music is active, a powerful transformative mode of self-exploration and communication. The Soirée Musicale existed in Ontario, however, as an extension of prevailing mores of gender and class. For the domestic Soirée Musicale to persist as an appealing entertainment, the quality of the amateur women's performances had to belie the notion of music as trivial and women's musical accomplishment as mediocre, mechanical, and trite.

If it went wrong, a Soirée Musicale could be a social disaster, as embarrassment led to distraction and a rising volume of chatter while the musicians ploughed on. This happened often enough for satirical comment to be made, as it is in "Amateur Concert," (Figure 20) from an American fine arts publication subscribed to by some nineteenth-

Figure 20: "Amateur Concert" – a Soirée Musicale in disarray. F. Simm/National Library of Canada/ e002283002

century Ontario families.[23] Mrs. Widder could not afford such a flop. The programming of a truly excellent Soirée Musicale could tempt the hostess to trump gender propriety with high concept. Mrs. Widder probably did not create the whole program herself, but she agreed to it, and on that March evening in 1844, two women sang operatic arias written expressly for men: Miss H. Scott singing Filippo's aria of lust, "Come t'adoro," and Miss Hagerman singing Rodolpho's wistful, "Vi ravviso."

In both cases, placing an operatic aria sung by a woman where these arias occur on Mrs. Widder's program allowed the programmer to continue the disciplined alternations of three different factors, genre, language, and gender. "Come t'adoro" and "Vi ravviso" are Italian arias, each sandwiched between an English song and an English language glee. "Vi ravviso," sung by a woman, broke up what would otherwise be a solid streak of men-only singing at the end of the program (Figure 1 "Widder Program", 1844). The rigorous programming undertaken for this concert created demands for music that was thematically apt, gender appropriate, readily mastered by each performer, and supplying patterned variation of genre, language, and gender. Finding music to meet so many criteria may have outstripped the repertoires of the evening's performers, requiring that at least one singer learn new material.

Of the two male arias sung by women, "Vi ravviso" may have been chosen first, as part of the dazzlingly continuous musical fabric of the warmly elegiac second half of the concert. The aria seems to have been paired with "Ah per sempre" to bookend a thematic unit, since the two arias sound similar. Both are in A flat major as originally written, they share a rolling, triplet rhythm, and both open with precisely the same melodic figure, starting on the fifth of the chord and rising to the tonic. For the first few bars, the words of either aria could be sung to the notes of the other. Thematically, the texts of the two arias, both yearning for the better life of a bygone time, frame first the female, then the male version of an enchanting, natural world. The first aria, "Ah, per sempre," laments a lost beloved; the second, "Vi ravviso," mourns a beloved person as a symbol of a lovely past, now gone forever. Between them, first a woman sang the "Echo Song," which expressed her affinity with nature, and then a trinity of men sang close harmony about the welcome peace bestowed by benevolent nature, in "Come, Silent Evening." Fabulously apt in this sequence, the latter ends with a reference to the birdlike trills of the Echo Song, "While nightingales complaining, / Their melting notes prolong." These two selections gave voice to the gender differences of ballad and glee, the woman puzzled but enchanting, the men enjoying the beauty but understanding it. The mathematical perfection of the patterns of this unit of music was maintained as long as a woman sang "Vi ravviso": the alternation of male and female performers was particularly telling in this tightly-woven section. The programmer drove on from there, punctuating this yearning for a paradise on earth with the melodramatic "Not a drum was heard," a reminder, in

English, of the masculine heroism that was necessary to protect this beautiful world. If, indeed, the programmer had set the Barnett song, which had to be sung by a man, in the penultimate position on this program in order to maintain thematic unity, assigning a woman to sing "Vi ravviso" was a masterful stroke of programming.

That there was a woman singing a male aria in each half of this program suggests yet another layer of conscious symmetry in the programming. Miss Hagerman, an eager and gifted singer, would have been able to tackle the technical demands of "Vi ravviso" competently; after all, she sang the *Norma* duet in the first half. Selecting Miss H. Scott to sing another male aria, "Come t'adoro," meant that the daughter of an important Tory, Miss Hagerman, was not singled out to sing arguably anomalous material.

There are no known records describing Miss Scott's singing ability. Her only selection, "Come t'adoro," however, is vocally easy, with a narrow range similar to that of the Glover ballad, and could be unobtrusively shortened by omitting the repeat if she lacked vocal stamina. Placing any Italian language operatic aria in this position on the program allowed the programmer to continue the disciplined alternation of genre and language, but arias written for women in the Italian operatic repertoire on this program are either not easy or not interesting. "Come t'adoro" offered the cachet of opera without technical tears to a politically crucial performer.

Even if there were qualms about assigning a male aria to a woman, the text and melody of this particular aria would have been experienced as a warm embrace of gender ideology in 1844. "Come t'adoro" was written for the male character Filippo to express the adulterous lust which distracts him from his public duties as ruler. The aria has been described by music historian Charles Osborne as "both ardent and graceful, surprisingly so for such a deeply unattractive character" and the composer, Vincenzo Bellini, himself wrote, "by colouring the music ... I tried to correct and get rid of the disgust that the character of Filippo arouses."[24] Even as an exciting plot element, a male ruler saturated with blinding love arouses "disgust," but its lyrics, which begin "How I adore you, and how much / My heart alone could say to you: / Joy is mine in my weeping, / Peace in my distress," read effortlessly like a parlour song about a good woman's love. Compare this with the self-injuring love of the Glover ballad, in which the singer explains that "the joys which gone come not again" were composed of cherishing an unrequited love "for many years" in "silence and in tears." Both share the "feminine" behaviour of finding delight in painful love. The "Vi ravviso" lyrics are also "feminine," recalling "the happy, carefree days" of childhood which are now "beyond recall!" The male character singing "Vi ravviso" is an older man who yearns for an irretrievable past without attempting to change the circumstances that caused his pain, arguably not a man at his virile prime.

It was the performer who determined much of the meaning of the music, even to the point of changing the intended gender of the character being sung. The perception of gender in music is socially constructed. As musicologist John Shepherd suggests, gender as such is not intrinsic to the abstract structures of musical sound, although musical sounds can be readily associated with gender and other social categories of non-musical meaning.[25] The audience perception of music as feminine or masculine depends on a complex relationship between composer, performer and audience, and is influenced as much by the lyrics and the visual dimension of the performance as by the music itself.[26] The same musical sounds of "Come t'adoro" could be understood as charming femininity or masculinity so corrupt it was "disgusting," depending on who sang it and when: what made Filippo a bad man made Miss H. Scott acceptably feminine.

Feminist musicologist Carolyn Abbate suggests that live musical performance causes singers to be "refigured subtly in the listener-spectator's mind as creating what they sing." The transgressive act of co-opting male arias for female singers happened offstage at Mrs. Widder's Soirée Musicale, first in the selection and then in the performers' preparation of the music, but onstage in performance, a different kind of transgressive shift occurred. Abbate's principal insight about a woman singing is that "as a voice she slips into the 'male/active/subject' position." This was what underlay Mrs. Jarvis's objections to Miss Hagerman's music making, and it became particularly acute in the formal concert format of the domestic Soirée Musicale. As Abbate puts it, "Musical performance enacts a bizarre drama, in which the performers ... shout out that they are creating the work literally before our ears (and eyes.)" Since most composers were male, and indeed composition itself was gendered masculine at this time, whether a Lady Amateur sang a man's aria or any other work composed by a man, her act of singing was "a little drama of usurpation that powerfully disperse[d] the 'composer's voice.'"[27]

The issue of the performer's authorship of the music in the act of performance was stated differently by a Toronto critic, who wrote of one of Mrs. Widder's Lady Amateurs, albeit on another occasion, "Equally delightful was the *effusion*, the rapture with which she poured forth the noble composition 'The Death of Diarmid.'... Mrs. Robinson [née Miss Hagerman] possesses the faculty of throwing herself heart and soul into the music. This thorough identification with the spirit of the composer, was observable in all her utterances."[28] This listener perceived the singer as pouring forth, in the same singing utterance, a parlour ballad, the spirit of the composer, and her own "heart and soul." The listener did not distinguish between the singer and the song. He thought Mrs. Robinson had somehow merged with the spirit of the composer.

That was not what she was doing. She was acting with her singing, inventing the moment. She sang songs about widows, but she died before her husband — whose name was not Diarmid. In the same way, on March 12, 1844, she had sung an old man's mourning for his child, when she herself had none. The work of a performer is to make an audience believe that what she is singing is real, by first imagining that construct in detail, herself, in rehearsal. The more specific the performer's imaginative work of preparation, the more natural and inevitable her performance will seem to her audience. This is not the fanciful channelling of genius of "The Music Lesson" (Figure 14), above, and it is no accident. The performer has to develop and apply concrete technical skills in order to internalise the song. Although simple music can be presented accurately enough with minimal craft or ability, an emotionally committed performance by a technically developed singer can turn the simplest ballad into a spine-chilling thrill. The Lady Amateur, Miss Hagerman, received "thunderous applause" for her ballads, time and again. Even when the singer's gift is more modest than Miss Hagerman's, the rehearsal process is the same. To the degree that they give good performances, singers internalise the material, infuse it with their imagination, and recreate it as their own, natural expression in performance.

Abbate is analysing audience experience, but for the singer there is a corresponding experience of authorship. Any musician can enjoy the intellectual, emotional, and physical challenges of identifying and mastering the performing demands of a piece of music during the rehearsal process, but recreating that imaginative world in the moment of performance for an attentive and appreciative audience offers a different order of intensity. This did not depend on whether the music being performed was complex or as simple as any parlour ballad. As another of Miss Hagerman's reviews suggests: "To the old and somewhat hackneyed song ... she gave full evidence of the exalted spirit that stirs her inner life ... thunders of applause for the fair cantatice [sic] who had done it such justice."[29] Domestic feminine musical accomplishment was intended for domestic performing, but not all such performances gave the performer the full attention of their audience or the artistic scope of a formal concert format. The Soirée Musicale distilled the performative aspect of feminine musical accomplishment into its most concentrated form.

For any amateur woman musician, the Soirée Musicale offered unique opportunities for engaging, personal experience. Mrs. Widder could enjoy her participation in the fascinating process of building a concert program, could savour the stimulation of rehearsing and performing with skilled professional musicians, and could bask in the applause of the people who mattered to her. For most of the women who performed in the Soirée Musicale, the wealth of their families meant they could live in comfort. But even for these comfortable Lady Amateurs, the need for self-realisation was always present. Carolyn Abbate's valuable insight – that the audience experiences the singer as the creator of the music – applies, too, to the performer's own experience of authorship.

This was surely one of the shocking improprieties that so offended the proper Mrs. Jarvis. Performing music well was an active, creative experience at variance with the passivity of Victorian notions for feminine musical accomplishment.

The Soirée Musicale was stretching the limits of feminine musical accomplishment, but not altering its foundations. The Soirée Musicale could exist because it was understood by most to conform to prevailing mores of gender and class. The imaginative world of the music through which Mrs. Widder's Lady Amateurs experienced authorial control trumpeted the Victorian ideas of gender and class. The amateur women musicians enacted Ideal Womanhood with every song, inhaling it, infusing it with their energies and skills, and pouring it forth to be believed as natural. For a woman to create the imaginative world of the Victorian Ideal Woman was at least to own the self she could not escape.

Every guest who applauded the Lady Amateurs of Mrs. Widder's private concert demonstrated that transgressive implications of their performances were absorbed without changing the prevailing norms of gender. As long as the Lady Amateur engaged in activities that were commonly understood to be appropriate to her gender, she made not an iota of real change in the status of women. As they sang and played that March evening, Mrs. Widder, Mrs. Nash, Miss Macaulay, Miss H. Scott, Miss Clara Boulton, and Miss Mary Jane Hagerman embodied the conventional meaning of "femininity." Most of the well-dressed Ontario women who caught the wind of the Soirée Musicale in their billowing sails remained firmly anchored in the drawing room. Miss Hagerman picked up a paddle.

Chapter Five

SINGING TIGHT HER CHAINS
Miss Hagerman, Mrs. Widder's Exceptional Lady Amateur

"as I lay green and dying ... I sang in my chains like the sea."

"Fern Hill," Dylan Thomas

If the Soirée Musicale was the most extreme development of women's domestic musical accomplishment in Ontario, then Miss Mary Jane Hagerman was the most remarkable of its Lady Amateurs. Miss Hagerman wanted to change but one link in the golden chains of her middle-class femininity: she wanted to become a professional singer. She failed but struck an extraordinary compromise, incorporating her public activity with her identity as a Victorian wife. As her granddaughter, Stewart Bagnani, recounted a hundred years later, "My grandmother had professional yearnings. ... At almost all the endless charitable concerts in Toronto she was in demand. Her fame lasted in many peoples' memories even to my childhood. She apparently had that strange quality in a singer born, rather than made, which moved her audience often to tears." [1] Miss Hagerman, after her marriage to John Beverley Robinson (Jr.) transformed her into Mrs. Robinson, had a performing career that was in many respects indistinguishable from that of her teacher, the professional musician Mr. Humphreys. As the indices of David Sale's exhaustive listings of Toronto concerts for the period show, they both sang in public for thirty years or more, shared much of the same repertoire, knew the same people - and each other - and were resident in Toronto during the mid-nineteenth century. Except for one brief moment her career was entirely amateur, but it was, in Ontario, unique. Did Miss Hagerman/Mrs. Robinson merely take the internal contradictions of domestic musical performance, so concentrated in the domestic Soirée Musicale, to their logical conclusion? Did her efforts mean that a professional career in music was widely acceptable as an option for upper-class, respectable women?

Despite her extraordinary achievements, Mrs. Robinson never became more than a slightly soiled floor model of the Ideal Woman who was so central to the structure of the Soirée Musicale. She negotiated a special public space for which the domestic Soirée Musicale was the protective cloak, but she was unable to change the basic terms of engagement. As musicologist Nancy Reich suggests of professional women musicians, "Those professionals who married into the bourgeoisie or aristocracy were expected to abandon their careers and cross over into the ranks of the non-professionals, thus gaining social status and respectability but relinquishing earning power."[2] No lady could cross in the other direction: a lady was only a lady so long as she did not formally earn an income independent of her father or her husband.

The singing career of Miss Hagerman, the glittering amateur star of Mrs. Widder's 1844 Soirée Musicale, can be best understood in three phases. Until her marriage in 1847, she sang only in private. This domestic music making continued throughout her life.[3] The second phase began within moments of being married, when she began to sing in public, apparently with a view to becoming a professional singer. The third phase began in 1854, when Mrs. Robinson emerged from a silence of twenty-three months, and performed steadily in public as a Lady Amateur until 1871.

Three telling features of Mrs. Robinson's musical life suggest that she consciously adapted her wish for a professional career to the prevailing constraints of gender and class. First, she fought hard for her husband's permission to allow their daughter, Augusta, to become a professional singer in the 1890s, leaving a trail of letters which detail the fight and her personal feelings about her own performing. She identified herself as a good singer, and wanted to make it possible for her daughter to have a fully professional singing career. Second, Mrs. Robinson tested the outside edge of social tolerance when she left town to perform with a professional troupe under an assumed name in 1852. The March 6th, 1852, edition of the *Buffalo Morning Express* contained an advertisement for "Wm. Vincent Wallace Soiree Musicale on Wednesday Evening, March 10th, assisted by the distinguished Amateur English Ballad Singer, Madame Beverly."[4] Social tolerance seems to have snapped at this, because, for nearly two years thereafter, what had been her steady pace of public performances stopped cold. She had been performing one public concert each year until 1852, when she sang two. She reappeared in late 1854, singing more often and emphasizing the charitable, civic benefits of her performances as a highly visible Lady Amateur. Mrs. Robinson accepted a permanent taint as, at best "eccentric" and at worst "flirting with the Scarlet Woman," as the price for what must have been an irresistible drive to sing.[5] To fully understand the risk and the triumph of this career, Mrs. Robinson must be situated in her social context.

Mrs. Robinson (1823-1892), née Mary Jane Hagerman, grew up in a faintly liminal middle-class family. Her father was Christopher Hagerman, a prominent judge and politician. Mary Jane's mother was Elizabeth Macaulay Hagerman, who died when her daughter was nine years old. Mary Jane's father remarried in 1835, and, widowed again, married his third wife in 1846. Less than a year after his final marriage, Christopher Hagerman died. Six weeks later, on June 30, 1847, his daughter, Mary Jane, married John Beverley Robinson (Jr.).[6]

Miss Hagerman's unmarried life was therefore full of uncertainty. Within two months of her mother's death, her father was away working as a circuit-riding judge, and wrote a touching letter to "My dear little vole," showing concern that his children not feel abandoned by him as well. Outside his family life, Hagerman was often abrasively assertive of his right to be governed only by his own understanding of correct behaviour. As he taught his daughter in 1832, "I trust they [his children] will never do anything that they know to be wrong. They will in such case be loved by everybody."[7] The unconventional singing career of that "little vole" appears to have been governed by her own understanding that she was not doing anything she knew "to be wrong." As her granddaughter described it, "She was ... inclined to be unconventional, but she would never have allowed [her daughter] to behave except in a seemly manner, both for her own sake and because of her father's position."[8] Like her father, Mrs. Robinson answered to her own judgement. As a woman, hence legally and financially more vulnerable than a man of the same class, she was perhaps more careful than he to maintain a critical mass of supportive allies. She succeeded, where her father had failed, to be "loved by everybody" at the end of her career, but, like him, she was willing to defy mainstream opinion even at some cost to herself.

Her father had always been on the fringe of power, irresistible to those in governance because of his gifts of intellect, oratory, and conservative principle, but prickly with unconventional independence and a loud public personality. Literary scholar Carolyn Heilbrun, writing about patterns of women's lives before 1950, suggests that "the efforts of fathers to be accepted in the male world they do not question or challenge are vitally connected with their efforts to imprison their female children."[9] Christopher Hagerman repeatedly risked his livelihood to challenge the male world of colonial power, and this independence may have helped to foster his daughter's independent spirit.[10] From the time she was nine, Miss Hagerman's only consistent parent was her father, whom she observed as he repeatedly questioned the "male world" of British colonial power on which his livelihood depended. She grew up making the best of ambiguous social status, taught by her father's example to lead with her talents and act on her own understanding of her ideals.

Miss Hagerman was single at a time when respectable women restricted their musical activities to the home or religious services. By 1843, however, Miss Hagerman's musicality had been leaking beyond the home and her name was famous enough to be useful as a dedication on one of her teacher's compositions (Figure 12). The printed cover of "When We Two Parted" included the notice, "Sung by Mr. Humphreys ... Composed and dedicated to Miss Hagerman." Samuel Nordheimer, Canada's most prolific music publisher, 1844-1900, once told Mrs. Robinson "she (as Miss Hagerman) had given him his first large order for music. The undertaking had been a venture, so much music having to be copied in those days, but she and her beautiful singing were so well known that it really established the business in this part of Canada."[11] In precisely this period, the internal contradictions in the ideas of "feminine" and "music" had produced the domestic Soirée Musicale as a stage for those women whose training for musical accomplishment unleashed both talent and desire for formal performance. Although in her public performances Miss Hagerman/Mrs. Robinson dared more than any other Lady Amateur of her own circle, she may not have been the only simmering renegade.

She stepped out of the drawing room with care. Mrs. Robinson's first known public concert in Toronto, in 1848, seems to have been a cautious public debut. Structured like a domestic Soirée Musicale, it was a conventional image of appropriate relationships (Figure 21).[12] In its domestic setting, where Mrs. Robinson was a familiar member of the cast, the Soirée Musicale was an acceptable vehicle for high levels of performance by amateur women musicians. Mrs. Robinson, however, floated the whole drawing room into public view.

"Amateur Concert in aid of the funds of St. George's Church"[1]

DECEMBER 13, 1848 (ST. GEORGE'S CHURCH) MRS. (JOHN) BEVERLEY ROBINSON, SINGER

PART I

1. Trio "Could I hush a lover's sigh" . . . . Mrs. Robinson, Messrs. Humphreys and Barron
2. Romance *Les Mousquetaires de la Reine* (Halévy) . . . . Mr. Humphreys
3. "From the alps the horn resounding" (Proch) . . . . . . Mrs. Robinson with Mr. Clarke, piano, and Mr. Schallehn, obbligato (violin)
4. "Tema con variazione" . . . . Mr. Schallehn (violin)
5. "Bid me discourse" (Bishop) . . . . Miss Staines
6. Clarinet solo "Les soirées musicales" . . . . Composed/performed by Mr. Schallehn
7. "Ah per sempre" *I Puritani* (Bellini) . . . . Mrs. Robinson
8. Comic song . . . . Mr. Ettrick
9. Comic Song "The man that couldn't get warm" . . . . Mr. Ettrick
10. "Singing lesson duet" (Barnett) . . . . Mrs. Robinson and Mr. Humphreys

PART II

1. Duet "I've wandered through dreams" (Wade) . . . . Miss Staines, Mr. Humphreys
2. "Angels ever bright and fair" *Theodora* (Handel) . . . . Mrs. Robinson
3. Divertimento "Mary Blane" . . . . Mr. Schallehn
4. "Rocked in the cradle of the deep" (Knight) . . . . Mr. Humphreys
5. Violin and Piano Fantasia . . . . Messrs. Schallehn and Clarke
6. Ballad "The death of Dermot" (Crouch) . . . . Mrs. Robinson
7. "Bold Robin Hood" (Balfe, Nelson?) . . . . Mr. Humphreys

Figure 21: Mrs. Robinson's 1848 Program

Her 1848 concert differed in other ways from a domestic Musicale. It was a showcase for Mrs. Robinson, who sang six items, which was an unusual emphasis on a single artist in a program. Touring celebrities like Jenny Lind sang no more than six selections.[13] Mrs. Robinson was further distinguished as the only singer to be accompanied by both piano and an additional instrument in one selection. She sang alone and with all three professional musicians (Humphreys, Schallehn, and Clarke), as well as with Mr. Barron, the principal of Upper Canada College.

Both Mrs. Robinson and Miss Staines, who also sang, were on public display as samples of their teachers' instruction, but Mrs. Robinson was demonstrating a wider range of skills. Miss Staines studied with Clarke and sang in public in Toronto between 1847 and 1849, most notably in an all-professional series of subscription concerts, which suggests that she may have been trying to establish a professional career. Miss Staines sang two selections, a ballad and an English duet. Mrs. Robinson, by contrast, sang ballads both virtuosic (Proch) and simple (Crouch, Barnett), a sacred Handel aria from the standard professional repertoire of the time, and she sang, in Italian, the male character operatic aria, "Ah per sempre," which she knew from Captain Haliday's performance at Mrs. Widder's concert. This sampler of styles, languages, and musical genres was not repeated in any of her other known programs. It was more consistent with the repertoire of trained professional singers than with the single, usually simple, musical selections offered by other amateurs in public.

When Mrs. Robinson first stepped onto the public stage, she was accompanied physically by Mr. Barron, an acknowledged local intellectual of great influence, and her teacher, Mr. Humphreys, a musical expert who was trusted to teach and perform in the homes of many of those in the audience. Mrs. Robinson literally played the part of the student with her teacher before the crowd, singing Barnett's "Singing Lesson Duet" with Mr. Humphreys. To crown her feminine duty in matters spiritual, Mrs. Robinson also sang sacred music. Her role on the public stage was conventionally subordinate, spiritual, and feminine.

Respectability and civic duty were served by performing for the benefit of the church where the concert was held. St. George's Church was already known as the venue for the first concerts of the Toronto Philharmonic Society, an organisation peppered with names like Widder and Boulton, familiar from Mrs. Widder's 1844 Soirée Musicale. Philharmonic tickets were available only through members in the Society, and were not sold to the general public. In 1848, when Mrs. Robinson's father-in-law first presided over its Board of Directors, their published mandate was that "no person will object to take part in the concerts ... when it is known that ... even the Royal family, join in the performances of the similarly private society in London."[14] This atmosphere of private, exclusive entertainment was like the Soirée Musicale. The care taken to ensure an atmosphere of sanctified, elite domesticity of the most educational sort protected Mrs. Robinson's respectability. By stepping into the public space to perform, Mrs. Robinson was stretching the corset of respectable Victorian femininity.

Mrs. Robinson's "professional yearnings" came to a decisive point between 1848 and 1854. She had been expanding her horizons beyond appearing in churches, by singing in Toronto theatres in mixed concerts which resembled the domestic Soirée Musicale in fact, if not always in name. In 1852, she assumed a false name and left town to sing with the famous William Vincent Wallace and his professional troupe in Buffalo as "the well-known English ballad singer, Madame Beverley."[15] By naming herself for her chosen activity, but choosing her husband's middle name, Mrs. Robinson combined her independence with her identity as the wife of Mr. John Beverley Robinson.

Mrs. Robinson's gratification from public performance must have been significant to make up for the social price she paid. Her reputation of "flirting with the Scarlet Woman" was handed down in her own family lore to her granddaughter's generation, and since there are existing records of members of her social network disapproving of her performing, it is difficult to imagine that Mrs. Robinson herself was unaware of the criticism. Her first known public performance was on her honeymoon, away from Toronto, and it generated enough talk in Toronto social circles that one bachelor butterfly could not resist confiding to his diary: "We all thought it very heartless of her."[16] In 1848, her husband's aunt, Mrs. Stephen Heward, "pronounced an acid comment upon her voice and social graces."[17] Mrs. Jarvis seems unlikely to have restricted her criticism of Miss Hagerman/Mrs. Robinson's singing to oblique notes to her husband. She had many opportunities to convey her feelings to Miss Hagerman/Mrs. Robinson, since the two families knew each other well.[18] It was Mrs. Jarvis's husband who wrote home about Mrs. Robinson's Buffalo performance in 1852. Whether or not she had been paid to perform, Mrs. Robinson had lost the protection of singing surrounded by musicians known to be respectable when she sang with strangers in a foreign city, and under a false name. The circumstances were too suspicious to be respectable. If Miss Hagerman, performing only in private while she was single, had not realised how people like the Jarvises whispered about her singing, Mrs. Robinson, singing on the public stage, could not have failed to feel the sting.

"Opinion," formed, bruited, conveyed to the transgressor, and dangerous to a social or political career was perhaps the reason why Mrs. Robinson abruptly stopped performing in public for twenty-three months after her 1852 excursion to the professional stage in Buffalo. As Nancy Reich suggests, "The appearance of a woman on the concert stage could undermine the hard-won social status of her bourgeois family; consequently, even the most gifted were expected to confine their musical activities to the home."[19] Buffalo seems to have been the breaking point that taught Mrs. Robinson the limits of her professionalism. It may also have been the catalyst for a new public persona, which would enable her to continue to perform in public.

After living through the reaction to her attempt at professional performance from 1852-1854, Mrs. Robinson emerged with a public persona as an ultra-feminine Lady Amateur. Her first concert after nearly two years of public silence was for the "Society for Supplying the Poor of the City with Wood" and at it she sang a modest two items on a program shared with the Band of the Royal Canadian Rifles. The following year, all three of her public concerts were shared with the leaders of British culture. Like Reverend McCaul and Mr. Barron, she sang overtly British, military material, like Arne's "Rule Britannia," for charitable objects like "the Widows and Orphans of the Fallen Heroes of Sebastopol."[20] Her role on stage was uniformly that of the ideal woman: loyal, self-sacrificing, and emotional. Her public repertoire between 1854 and 1870 was a unified blend of military, British nationalism, and domestic, retrospective, and self-injuring femininity.

Mrs. Robinson may have modelled her public persona on Jenny Lind, for whom she was reputed to have auditioned in 1851. Robinson was sometimes called "the Canadian Jenny Lind," and, by accident or design, her public career resembled Lind's in three important ways. Like Lind, Mrs. Robinson's public loved her; she emphasised maternal, rather than erotic, femininity; and she tithed the financial proceeds of her concerts for charity.[21]

Jenny Lind was one of the early celebrities in the nineteenth-century concert world. As a woman, she faced the same conflicts over respectability that Nancy Reich suggests were common to women who were paid to perform in public.[22] Lind developed a public persona as the embodiment of feminine virtue. She renounced the operatic stage in favour of concert and oratorio work because of her religious convictions, and sang programs that focussed on spiritual and domestic femininity rather than eroticism. She was so beloved as a performer that the great opportunist, P. T. Barnum, made $500,000 by producing Lind's North American tour in 1850. Lind herself made nearly $200,000 on that tour, but unlike Barnum, she made a well-publicized point of contributing £500 to an orphanage during her 1851 stay in Toronto.[23] The earning of money by women for their public appearance in any capacity was extremely sensitive, and Lind addressed the sensitivity directly, with cash for a suitably maternal concern.

So did Mrs. Robinson, whose only public Soirée Musicale in her own name, in 1856, was advertised to be "in aid of the City Industrial Farm."[24] The concert raised

Figure 22: Mrs. Robinson, Courtesy Trent University, Archives, Stewart and Gilbert Bagnani Fonds, 97-003/81

£200.15.6, but a "suitable charity" to receive the money was not announced until 1875, when the money, doubled in size after being invested for the intervening twenty years, went to the Hospital for Incurables.[25] The precise dollar amounts were publicized in both 1856 and 1875, the press clippings firmly pasted into her scrapbook. Perhaps Mrs. Robinson valued the monetary value of her performances as a benchmark of professionalism, measured in the literal currency of the commercial market place and compared directly with Lind's donation. Her efforts to perform in public were complicated, and, while she recognized that "one *can't* have *all* they want so there is no use in bothering about it!" she may have wanted to confirm, if only to herself, what signposts of professionalism she had in fact achieved.[26]

Like Lind, Mrs. Robinson cultivated a stage presence often remarked upon as "her dignified bearing" or a "graceful bearing" [which] ... secure[d] for her the sympathy and admiration of an audience."[27] A Cobourg reviewer wrote, "Mrs. Robinson, apart from her brilliant talents, quite enchanted her hearers with her grace and elegance of manner."[28] This stillness may have been her normal mode, but it was strong visual evidence of the control she had over her body. No juicy jiggling distracted the audience from Mrs. Robinson's constant demonstration that her performances were respectable.

Mrs. Robinson seems to have been committed to the conservative values of her circle. She enjoyed the advantages of her wealth and her busy family life, and there is no evidence that she wanted to change any of its values, but one. What she wanted, but could not add, was genuine membership in the musical profession. Instead, her record shows samples of different kinds of performing venues, even going to Cobourg as a kind of mini-tour in 1867, as if she were challenging herself to match any criterion of professionalism. When it came to her choice of fellow musicians, after her first tentative steps into the public realm, "she refused to discriminate between the religions to the disapproval of many."[29] She crossed political lines, too, and performed with the excellent flautist James McCarroll, whose political journalism was heavily weighted on the side of Reform, anathema to the conservative politics of Mrs. Robinson's social circle.[30] Her performance record is that of a musician who made as many decisions as she could solely on the musical or professional merits of the opportunity.

The dissonance between Mrs. Robinson's work and the terminology used to describe it is striking. In 1866, she sang, unamplified of course, in a military drill shed for an audience of 5000. A reviewer described her "exquisitely sweet and well trained voice" as "distinctly audible at the furthest end of the Drill Shed." The feisty competitiveness of being the "only musician to attempt" the feat brought this middle-aged woman amateur to sing to a vast crowd, extremely loudly.[31] How "sweet" she sounded as she cranked up the volume can only be imagined. Carolyn Heilbrun suggests "well into the 20th century, it continued to be impossible for women to admit into their autobiographical narratives the claim of achievement, the admission of ambition, the recognition that accomplishment was neither luck nor the result of the efforts or generosity of others."[32] This was equally true for biographical accounts written by the fans of ambitious, powerful women whose actions contradicted the prevailing norms of what made a woman "good."

Another important brick in the edifice of respectability was her repertoire, which, like Lind's, was primarily standard popular songs, perfectly acceptable in any drawing room.[33] The exceptional use she made of male operatic arias was restricted to those with lyrics indistinguishable from conventionally "feminine" parlour songs. It is worth noting that the most famous parlour song of all, "Home Sweet Home," is actually written from the perspective of a man wandering far from home, but tone and content were "feminine" to the legions of nineteenth-century people who loved it. The song was a staple for most of the professional women singers who performed in Toronto between 1845 and 1856. "Home Sweet Home" presented a compelling image of an ideal world, which maintained a safe, stable, feminine home as lodestar for masculine adventure. The retrospective longing of "Home Sweet Home" is the thematic core of Mrs. Robinson's nominally masculine arias, "Come t'adoro" and "Vi ravviso." What Lind and Mrs. Robinson both avoided was the erotic, operatic material written for women characters who took risks for personal gratification. Respectability was crucial to their respective success on stage, and the conservative values of that respectability seem to have been sincerely held by both singers.

While Mrs. Robinson's desire to sing professionally was at its height, she had no class or financial advantage to gain by becoming a professional performer; the reverse was true. She sailed with ease in the elite salons that intimidated her teacher's wife. The large home, the servants, the travel abroad, all suggest that, between 1847 and 1871, her family was relatively wealthy. For a woman of the comfortable middle class to try to step into the financially dubious world of the artist-musician class would have been to seek a lower standard of living and the life of a social pariah. Only women whose family income had suddenly dropped turned to performance for a livelihood. Lily Langtree is a famous example of a woman for whom "the next step, to becoming a professional actress, would never have been taken ... except for sudden bankruptcy and desperate need for money."[34] Mrs. Robinson, in the comfortable bosom of her prominent family, did not need the money. Her drive to be a professional musician was about something else.

Performing is a sufficient reward for many musicians, but only professional, public performance with musical peers can develop full, professional artistry. As Nancy Reich suggests about women amateurs who were fine musicians but performed only in private, "because they did not undergo the scrutiny of reviewers and compete for the attention and money of audiences, they did not grow artistically and sharpen their skills as the professionals did."[35] In 1836, Fanny Mendelssohn Hensel, constrained to domestic amateur status despite her serious musicianship, wrote: "If nobody ever ... takes the slightest interest in one's productions, one loses in time not only all pleasure in them, but all power of judging their value."[36] Working with those of the same or a better skill level, and performing for audiences under a wide range of demanding circumstances fostered artistic maturity.

Whether or not Mrs. Robinson's singing skills and gifts were really of professional standard is difficult to assess. Perhaps one of the reasons she tilted at the Buffalo stage in 1852 was to test her mettle in a town where her family name was unknown and her singing alone would determine first whether she got the engagement, and second how the public responded. There are no reviews of that performance, but her Canadian reviews were rapturous and echoed in personal memoirs from the time.[37] Her singing was remembered vividly. One old friend wrote to John Beverley Robinson (Jr.): "Of course I remember every song your dear wife used to sing in the merry merry days when we were young. I know most of them by heart now and often repeat them, though I am not gifted with a voice of song!"[38]

Mrs. Robinson's reviews suggest that even though age diminished her vocal powers from a rapturous height in 1861, she never lost her charismatic stage presence. In 1862, even the reviewer who refrains from "detailed criticism" because the vocalists, "being all amateurs, or persons having a mere local celebrity, it would perhaps be invidious to notice the special merits or defects of each," cannot "avoid expressing our especial admiration" for Mrs. Robinson's performance.[39] Another reviewer writhed to cope with the social awkwardness of singling out only one of an assortment of amateurs: "Mrs. John Beverley Robinson was, without doubt or disparagement whatever of the merits of any of the other singers, the great attraction."[40] Some of the reviewers may have been influenced by her family's prominence and power, but the intensity of the reviews went beyond what was necessary for decorum. Her daughter Augusta was never reviewed so warmly, even during her father's tenure as Lieutenant-Governor of Ontario. When mother and daughter appeared together, Mrs. Robinson in a cameo and Augusta as the lead in *Patience*, reviews described Augusta as having "a very sweet and well trained voice, completely under her control," but said "Mrs. Robinson's 'Home Sweet Home' received a perfect ovation and had to be repeated."[41] Mrs. Robinson's teacher, James Humphreys, was praised for "a remarkable distinctness of enunciation" and for being a genuinely charming performer who "will always please an audience whether critical or not - musical or general." When Mrs. Robinson was in her prime, she "electrified" her audiences, "poured forth an effusion of rapture," "threw herself heart and soul" into her music. As an unidentified newspaper clipping from "1862," stated, "Mrs. Robinson's performances were the chief attraction ... Mrs. Robinson sung it with a force and power which fairly electrified the audience. It was a grand performance."[42]

This seems to have been how Mrs. Robinson experienced her singing. It is rare to catch a glimpse of a performer's perception of their performance of performing. But Mrs. Robinson described her experience to calm her daughter's stage nerves: "May you be able to keep your nerve dear and then after the first few bars you will have nothing to fear. You will forget yourself and only remember your art and its interpretation."[43]

Mrs. Robinson seems to have been able to fuse imagination and skill with the energy of an audience into utter absorption at the moment of performing. She could forget her "self" by rapt focus on her "art and its interpretation."

Such imaginative transformation onstage did not stop Mrs. Robinson from a shrewd offstage understanding of precisely what she achieved in performance and how to manage audience and career considerations. When her daughter Augusta had a successful concert, Mrs. Robinson wrote, "let me tell you how delighted I was with your letters telling me of your great success at the Liverpool Entertainments. I really shed a few tears of joy! It took me back to former triumphs of my own and a remembrance of that feeling of delight which success always brings."[44] Mrs. Robinson clearly recognized her successes, which were repeated often enough to form a pattern, as the "always" suggests. Repeated triumphs tend not to be accidental, but the product of hard work and careful planning.

Her large but limited repertoire was consciously selected. This may have reflected a shallow musical education or a narrow vocal range, but she also clearly understood that her audiences wanted to hear respectable music, which could thrill the heart without taxing the mind. She advised Augusta, "I also am glad to hear that your ballad singing brought you such applause don't belittle that style Gussie - for after all - the greatest artists have to condescend to it very often before the most cultivated audiences."[45] Mrs. Robinson's reviews repeatedly emphasize her ability to transform the simplest of hackneyed sugarplums into magic.

The conservative femininity of the inspirational parlour ballad may have been the ideal world which engaged her attention to its fullest extent. Imagining that vision to the point where she could "forget" her "self" meant imagining something other than what she was. Apart from conjuring circumstances at variance with her own – for instance, she was never a widow, though repeatedly successful in singing the song of an officer's widow – there is a hint here of the underlying theatricality of the prevailing norms of femininity. This theatricality was overtly recognized in 1886, when Canadian composer, Susan Frances Harrison, wrote a short story in which her character, Cecilia, "found she had to learn to play a part, the part of a woman, which all women who have just left off being girls find so hard to play at first."[46] Literary scholar Nina Auerbach developed this theme in her biography of Ellen Terry (1847-1928), an English actress whose work was contemporary with the latter half of Mrs. Robinson's career. Auerbach suggests that the roles available to Terry were limited to conventional stereotypes of femininity, but that, as she grew through her career, Terry could not control her opposition to them. She was primarily useful to the theatre business as an icon of conventional femininity, but her abilities outstripped the roles she was assigned. Auerbach suggests that it was Terry's body that expressed her rejection of that feminine ideal, a rejection visible in Terry's disruptive involuntary laughter and terror on stage.[47] Mrs. Robinson was a lady, not a professional actress, whose musical capacity outstripped the confines of the drawing room as a performance venue. Although she, too, performed conventionally feminine material, her response was to become wholly absorbed by acting it out, imagining the feminine conventions to be real as she performed.

Where Ellen Terry was "held down and fought back unconsciously," Mrs. Robinson was liberated by the physical act of performing publicly. She fought consciously for two opposing ideals. Ideal femininity as an ineradicable component of an orderly society was the message she literally embodied; her right to decide what she stood for and how she stood for it was the antithetical ideal she never considered abandoning. Unlike Ellen Terry, Mrs. Robinson was not auditioning for existing stage roles, but creating her own role, play, and venue. Her career as a public Lady Amateur perfectly performed the masque of the Victorian Ideal Woman. The women of the ideally "sweet home" were not to display themselves for personal satisfaction by singing on a public stage, but Mrs. Robinson managed to be so *perfectly* domestic on stage that by her presence she made that stage domestic. The fact that these two ideals were logically inconsistent should not distract from the fact that they jostled together throughout Mrs. Robinson's musical life.

If the man she married had not agreed to her public performing, she could not have done it at all. The Robinsons must have been accustomed to negotiating frankly as, groping without a model, they created their own method of balancing propriety with Mrs. Robinson's public singing. John Beverley Robinson (Jr.) (1821-1896) was a lawyer and a politician, first elected to Toronto municipal government in 1851, and, by 1857, Mayor of Toronto. His electoral success depended on the public reputation of his whole family, but he accompanied his wife to Buffalo for her only known professional performance.[48] Thirty-five years later, in 1888, it was John Beverley Robinson (Jr.) who accepted a public tribute on his wife's behalf for her public services as a singer and official hostess.[49] This was not stiff-necked resignation, but what seems to have been warm enthusiasm for her singing. After her death in 1892, he was able to write an accurate list of his wife's repertoire, and on February 14, 1860, it must have been he who wrote a long poem to Mrs. Robinson, entitled "From One Who Heard Thee Lately," which said in part:

> ... But stream, nor bird, nor flow'r conveys
> Such thrilling peace of mind,
> As thy soul-utter'd soothing lays
> Which leave the world behind -
> If Heav'n indeed rejoice in Song
> Of everlasting praise,
> May I be there to hear thee sing
> Such everlasting lays.[50]

Mr. Robinson may sometimes have found his wife's performing beneficial to his career as an elected official, but it is clear that he loved and encouraged her singing.[51] Without her husband's permission, Mrs. Robinson could never have performed in public.

She nevertheless had to negotiate with her husband when her goals were too sharply different from prevailing norms. Her husband was conscious of the social constraints on his wife's performance. Mrs. Robinson wrote in 1891 that he had agreed to his daughter's professional singing because "opinion in this way has undergone such a change since the old days!!"[52] There is no known documentation of any discussions between husband and wife about Mrs. Robinson's own career in the 1850s, but the record of her performances shows that after the hiatus of 1852-54 she always sang as an unpaid amateur. Between 1889 and 1892, however, Mrs. Robinson pressed her husband to give their daughter permission to sing for money. To her surprise, he gave it. As she wrote to her daughter:

> [Y]our father had [agreed?] to leave everything to me as regards your great desire to study and etc. ... you have at last been permitted to fulfill your laudable ambition! I have upheld you all the way through - certain that your desire to study was worthy of all encouragement ... It has really been rather a hard fight but never mind - 'all's well that ends well' _Now_ we shall have the immense happiness of looking forward to the development of your beautiful voice - and the corresponding [joy?] of a great success in _that_ music world to which all may laudably aspire without any derogatory or impertinent remark.[53]

There is a sense in this letter of long-familiar arguments about what kind of "music world" might be free of "derogatory or impertinent remark." Four months later, she still sounded surprised that, after such a "hard fight," her husband had agreed.

> It is quite astonishing how your father seems to have got over his objections to your exerting your talents. It was only the other day he said "I had no idea ... [illegible] ... be all right now - for opinion in this way has undergone such a change since the old days!! You may be sure I rejoiced to hear him make these remarks - not to me but to some man (I think it was Jock Macdonald) who was calling here one Sunday."[54]

If Mrs. Robinson was right, then "Jock" could have been Sir John A. Macdonald, upon whom John Beverley Robinson (Jr.) was dependent for reappointment as Lieutenant-Governor of Ontario, a post which brought with it the handsome residence in which the Robinsons had lived from 1880 until 1887.

In 1889-90, as they debated their daughter's singing, they were in the process of selling their own home because, as Mrs. Robinson stoically wrote, the proceeds "would make things easy and comfortable for everyone of the family." Her grand-daughter later suggested of this period that, "after seven years as the first Canadian-born Lieutenant-Governor of Ontario ... [John Beverley Robinson (Jr.)] was in debt because he had spent so much of his own money on what he considered necessary to the dignity of the Office."[55] Their generous hospitality had included full-scale theatricals reminiscent of the pace-setting entertainments of Lady Dufferin in the 1870s, as wife of the Governor General.[56] The Robinsons had probably attended some of these events: Lady Dufferin had invited Mrs. Robinson to sing at one, although it is unknown whether the invitation was accepted.[57]

Although Mr. Robinson (Jr.) agreed to his daughter pursuing a singing career, his doubts persisted. After Mrs. Robinson died, in 1892, her husband received a letter from General Sam Jarvis, clearly replying to a question about the propriety of Augusta's singing. Jarvis wrote, "I think Gussie is quite right to cultivate an accomplishment so universally charming. Public singing too must be a great incentive to striving for excellence - and she is in good company!"[58] Mrs. Robinson was perfectly willing to argue forcefully with her husband when she thought she was right and he was wrong. It is a testament to the strength and collegiality of their partnership that he acceded to her judgement even when he was not fully convinced.

After Lady Dufferin, wife of the Governor General, invited her to sing at a private Soirée Musicale in the 1870s, Mrs. Robinson stopped performing publicly. Faced with an amateur Soirée Musicale after all the musical mountains and performance venues she had scaled, she may have realised that her path had, after all, been locked into a circle. The heroic effort needed to continue, particularly the physical effort of maintaining her vocal skills, may have seemed pointless after well over twenty years.

In some crucial respects, Mrs. Robinson's performances amounted to a professional career. She and her teacher, Mr. Humphreys, shared the same repertoire, often gave the same small number of performances in a year, and often shared the same stage. Their circles of acquaintance overlapped, and they performed in private homes together for people they both knew well. Humphreys came from a musical family that supported his musical aims; Mrs. Robinson did not, but her husband was remarkably supportive and their daughter carried her mother's musical torch, however briefly. If their reviews are a reliable indicator, both were well liked by their audiences, but Mrs. Robinson was the more compelling performer. But the differences were precise. Humphreys received a formal credential through training at an institution; Mrs. Robinson studied privately. Humphreys' skills included piano playing, composition, and conducting as well as singing; Mrs. Robinson only sang. Humphreys was a paid professional and Mrs. Robinson was a Lady Amateur.

Gender accounted for much of this difference. Even if she had studied for a formal credential, Mrs. Robinson would have been excluded from classes in composition, conducting, and, had she been so inclined, playing orchestral instruments.[59] Even those women who worked in music by the late nineteenth century had restricted access to the full range of income opportunities available to men. Humphreys depended on being able to participate, without supervision, in all-male networks. He advised the directors of the Toronto Philharmonic Society, he conducted military bands, he played the roistering toasts he composed at the end of the liquorous banquets of all-male clubs, unchaperoned. Imagine a solitary woman musician in such company in 1848 or even in 1948!

Class was the other key divide. A woman might have run her own retail music shop, if that woman were not a member of the social and family circles of Mary Jane Beverley Robinson, née Hagerman. Mrs. Robinson and her circle were the market for Mr. Humphreys as for all other musicians, whether hiring him to perform with her at a Soirée Musicale, walking into his music shop to complain that her music was late in arriving, or taking lessons from him for which her father paid. Mrs. Robinson's daughter Augusta made a small career as a salon singer but only in England, something she could not have begun to do for fees in the Toronto salons of her parents and friends.[60]

Mrs. Robinson's persistent public performing could have been awkward for Mr. Humphreys, but perhaps the warm, reciprocal collegiality so evident in her note to him explains much of the success of her career. Like Mr. Humphreys, Mrs. Robinson was as nice as she was utterly determined to sing. She was freer than most to make up her own mind, and successful in enlisting allies. Mrs. Robinson had the gift and the curse of a charismatic need for the imaginative transcendence of performing. She recognized in the Soirée Musicale a mobile idea, a vehicle that could transfer the cloistered domesticity of the drawing room to the public stage.

The Soirée Musicale was a necessary first step in the career she carved out. It gave her important initial experience and, as all music making does, it "performed" an alternative reality, in which a Lady Amateur sang as well as her professional colleague. Perhaps it was singing next to Mr. Humphreys at a private concert that Mrs. Robinson first recognized the similarity between the skills of the professional singer and those of some Lady Amateurs. Mrs. Robinson used the domesticity of the Soirée Musicale as a cloak for her ambitions of a fully professional, public career.

This could only have worked if the nineteenth-century Ontario the Soirée Musicale was really enjoyable. Excellence was promised by the presence of reliable professionals, a glimpse of authentic upper-class life by the amateurs. As long as she performed as an amateur, the excellence of her singing made Mrs. Robinson a particularly convincing sample of the ideally feminine Lady Amateur for public consumption. Her unique public presence served her class well. If she was, as some thought, the best domestic singer in Toronto, then she was a suitable display model of the superiority of her class. The tarnish that accrued to her reputation was no more than might accumulate on any public sample of an object intended for domestic use. Mary Jane Hagerman/Robinson managed to have a singing career because she was willing to say she did not. She was loved by her audiences and accepted by her professional colleagues because of course she was not an object that could be locked in the drawing room. She worked with the circumstances at her disposal. Some find such Lady Amateurs too clean to be heroic, too comfortable to be tragic, too peripheral to matter, but Mary Jane Robinson managed to defy a stultifying convention and earn "that feeling of delight which success always brings."

Mrs. Robinson was only the most visible of the Lady Amateurs of the Soirée Musicale in Ontario. In every parlour where women performed Victorian music, they tightened their own chains by entrenching the sense of the naturalness of the Victorian concepts of femininity and of music. That does not mean that all amateur women musicians of the parlour were performing dull music badly. The Lady Amateur of the Soirée Musicale could not break her chains. But perhaps by singing in them, she made her life her own.

Encore

TURNING THE KALEIDOSCOPE
Evolving Patterns of Meaning 1844–1910

The kaleidoscope of meanings in Mrs. Widder's Soirée Musicale can be turned to show how the same clutter of components found in that single concert program formed interlocking patterns of gender, class, and professionalism that shifted as the nineteenth century wore on. The program itself was a representation of interlocking social networks expressed by the casting, the sequence, and the musical genre of each selection. Printing the musical genres performed by each member of the Widder program turned the sound of that music into a stylized presentation of the social status implicit in amateur or professional musicianship. "Amateur" was a code word for superior class status. "Glee" referred to the private musical leisure of those Gentleman Amateurs who would never perform on formal programs for others, and when a woman of the upper middle class performed highly emotional music, operatic or of the parlour persuasion, it confirmed her status as a "Lady Amateur." The history of women in the Canadian music profession has yet to find its historian, but professional male musicians sang the same music as the Lady Amateurs. Understanding the Widder Soirée Musicale as a function of idealized differences between men and women of subtly different social niches makes it possible to suggest how future research might approach the later manifestations of the Soirée Musicale in Ontario.

As Lawrence Levine, scholar of culture and class in America, suggests, in "the second half of the nineteenth century American culture was undergoing a process of fragmentation ... manifest in the rise of professionalization, which ... saw people who had once inhabited common ground ... increasingly separated ... into discrete neighbourhoods."[1] The components of gender, musical genre, and class revealed by the patterns in Mrs. Widder's Soirée Musicale separated as the century wore on into such discrete conceptual neighbourhoods. The few remaining programs of Ontario Musicales from 1880 to 1910 suggest that the underlying concepts of gender and class remained stable. Without the clarity of Mrs. Widder's 1844 program, the colourful chaos of the later variations of the Soirée Musicale would obscure what changed and what remained the same as the Soirée Musicale in Ontario evolved into the twentieth century.

The Soirée Musicale as a form at mid-century provided a special opportunity for some women to experience the stresses and pleasures of presenting their imaginative musical performances of the idea of "true womanhood." The domestic Soirée Musicale in Ontario shifted and adapted after 1844, but it did not challenge the amateur status of the upper-class woman musician. Records of private musicales that resembled Mrs. Widder's concert appear occasionally in diaries or reminiscences of the time. Mrs. Widder's 1844 concert may have been unusually fine, but it functioned within a set of well-established cultural continuums. Despite the social criticism of music as a feminine accomplishment, Mrs. Widder's private concert was not an isolated gesture. Nor could it be generally disapproved of: Mrs. Widder's husband was too powerful, her fellow artists too numerous, her networks too varied and entrenched. The claim of social propriety, even if it were contested, was central to the Widders' social goals.

For the seeker of protofeminist activism, the Lady Amateurs of Ontario are a sorry disappointment. The Soirée Musicale may have crystallized the collision of the Victorian fantasies of Woman and Music with the more muscular realities of both, but it was used by most of its Lady Amateurs as an opportunity for active participation in a conservative ideal of society. As Canadian historian Cecilia Morgan suggests, it is a mistake to consider the maternalism of middle-class women "as somehow 'apolitical' ... [or] as disconnected from political thought and theory."[2] Music was but one mode through which upper-class women promoted their ideas. For instance, in 1859, Mrs. Robinson capitalized on the public recognition she had gained as a singing Lady Amateur to speak publicly on behalf of the organic unity of a diverse society. She opened a football match, intoning with delphic clarity the higher purpose of having two teams in a football game: "The one would scarcely be perfect without the other, for though beautiful apart they are more beautiful together and the Branch of an Oak upholds the ball ... [to] remind you that strength with union forms the bond which holds nations together."[3] Like other women of her circle, including Mrs. Frederick Widder and the wives of senior government officials like Governor General Bond Head's wife, Lady Head, Mrs. Robinson appeared as patron of public musical events in addition to her private hostess work.[4] The conclusions Leonore Davidoff reached about the active, civic purpose of elite women's domestic entertainments in Britain find a close parallel in the musical lives of these upper-class Ontario women, and continued to do so beyond the turn of the century. The domestic Soirée Musicale met most of the performance needs of Lady Amateurs, but even transferring it to the public arena did not make the Soirée Musicale a launching platform for social acceptance of such women as paid, professional musicians. Whether in public or private, a Lady Amateur was living testimony of the benefits of conservative political and social values.

The one known glimmer of opposition to the gendered constraints of the Victorian feminine ideal among the ladies of the Soirée Musicale was Mrs. Robinson's singing career. Her presence in public Soirées Musicales was perhaps a logical extension of the role of performing hostess in a domestic Soirée Musicale, but Mrs. Robinson was the only such hostess recorded in Toronto as having developed her public identity to such a high pitch for over thirty years. Perhaps unique in the history of the nineteenth-century Soirée Musicale, the long career of Mrs. Robinson suggests that amateur status was the only conceivable mode for public musical activity by an upper-class woman. Her public concerts were not always called "Soirées Musicales," but, in their mix of gender, genre, and professional with amateur performers, they carried the same overtone of domesticity. Mrs. Robinson herself was always recognized as a Lady Amateur, a public persona she seems to have cultivated. With every note, every Soirée Musicale proclaimed an ideal world of human hierarchy. In that ideal world, good women were happy to be the sweetly-singing angels of the domestic hearth. The fact that the Soirée Musicale did not free its Lady Amateurs for professional careers is a testament to the cultural power of the music they sang, and to their abilities to sing it.

Perhaps Mrs. Robinson was responsible for putting the authentic version of elite private musical leisure onto public stages in Ontario. She was the genuine Lady Amateur who sang with real Gentleman Amateurs and professional musicians of her acquaintance, in just the same kind of programming they enjoyed in private. Later public concerts, whether or not they were called "Soirées Musicales," sometimes resembled Mrs. Widder's private concert, with the same mix of musical genres and sometimes the same performers in exactly the same repertoire. The proceeds of public concerts with amateurs were usually donated to charity, just as the presentation of exemplary music by exemplary people was a contribution to the civic benefit of demonstrating morally uplifting music to inspire the populace. In England in the same period, as British performance artists Nick Till and Kandis Cook suggest, civic-minded middle-class Victorians used public entertainments "to promote the Victorian ideals of progress, self-improvement, patriotism, empire and monarchy."[5] In Ontario, Mrs. Robinson was a fine ambassador for the joys of a properly managed social hierarchy. The important sense of genuine elite experience was not separate from the atmosphere of domestic education implicit in all parlour music. The public Soirée Musicale gave those who could not afford the private version a peek inside the life of privilege.

The Soirée Musicale was identified as musical leisure, which was worthwhile in part because of its association with education. For the women of Mrs. Widder's domestic concert, it had been an opportunity to display the musical education their fathers had paid for, bolstered by the presence of their teacher. Throughout the nineteenth century, musical accomplishment remained important for genteel young ladies, but it became available to an expanding population as part of the curriculum of private girls' schools, as the Soirée Musicale programs of Mrs. Neville's girls' school, Rolleston House, in 1881 and 1894 attest. More could be done to investigate the networks expressed by these

concert programs, but the unusual name of one performer at this private girls' school concert, Miss Beardmore, suggests that such retrospective musical accomplishment was still considered to be an important indicator of upper middle-class status and conservative gender values. Members of the conservative Beardmore family included Walter Beardmore, an 1890s "leather goods manufacturer and Conservative Party bagman" and George Beardmore, known for entertaining at his large home.[6]
The common modern assumption that the Soirée Musicale was the exclusive province of women speaks to the gender segregation evident in the all-female girls' school Soirée Musicale. This musical education was not aimed at providing middle-class girls with saleable skills but with demonstrable, musical femininity.[7]

By 1900, domestic Soirées Musicales with amateurs seem to have become acts of self-conscious historical memory. This may be true of the private Llawbaden Soirées Musicales of 1907, the programs of which found their way into the collection of Sarah Murray, former president of the Women's Historical Association. Another amateur musician, Mary Austin, probably attended the Llawbaden evenings – one of the programs is still among her family files - and the self-conscious historicism of so much of Mrs. Widder's 1844 repertoire was echoed in the costumed nostalgia of Mary Austin's 1900 Christmas Musicale.[8] Mrs. Widder's program emphasised the eternal verity of girlish Victorian femininity in her own musical selections and in the presence of so many young, unmarried women of her social circle. The handwritten program entitled "Spadina Christmas 1900" shows children of both sexes performing a mixed entertainment of songs, piano music, recitations, and dance, in the family drawing room of the Austins' Toronto home, Spadina. It would be interesting to trace the patterns of professional and amateur music making in this family, since Mary Kerr Austin (1860-1942) had left her career as a professional pianist to marry in 1882. Her family roots were in the artist-musician class, since her father was a schoolmaster, and, like Augusta Beverley Robinson, Mary Kerr abandoned her own professional career when she married.[9] More research would be needed to show when, or whether, wealthy, middle-class women began to work as professional musicians without losing their social place.

This persistence, indeed the intensification, of the Victorian images of ideal femininity, as Deborah Gorham so pointedly notes, withstood the "onslaught of bicycle, competitive examinations, and financial independence" not because the ideal reflected a reality but because education and cultural experience embedded it in the psyches of individuals and hence as a force in society.[10] Mid-nineteenth-century domestic music was a means of reproducing social values guided by women in the home, not only through the memorable melodies chiming the tenets of femininity, but through the feminine functions of transmitting social and spiritual values. The domestic Soirée Musicale, usually organized by women, displayed the musical education of the household and required cooperative organizing. It also assisted the careers of professional musicians. As the century progressed and professionals took over many functions previously carried out at home, these aspects of the domestic Soirée Musicale evolved into music programs at girls' schools and women's musical clubs.

At mid-century, Mrs. Robinson had had to choose between professional status and her place in her society and family. She was able to hold open the professional stage door for her daughter Augusta for a time, but for Augusta only, and not for long. By the late 1890s, still unable to perform professionally after marrying unless the family fell on hard financial times, middle-class women musicians continued to make music in private circles, which now included club membership. Both Mary Kerr Austin and Augusta Robinson/Houston continued to perform after marriage, but as amateurs. Both were early members of the Women's Musical Club of Toronto and of the private Fortnightly Musical Club. An 1898 program announced that the Fortnightly Musical Club would meet "at the residence of Mrs. Brouse, 91 St. George Street [Toronto]," for a concert of ballads, German art songs, and piano and harp music on which Robinson/Houston and Austin performed together.[11] The Fortnightly was active at the same time as the faster-growing Women's Musical Club of Toronto (WMCT), which was producing public concerts by 1904. Both clubs continued the tradition of the domestic Soirée Musicale by isolating upper middle-class women who wanted to perform in private, amateur venues, away from the paid music profession. Private Soirées Musicales, like Mrs. Widder's in 1844, had provided important performance opportunities for skilled amateur women, but they had not launched those women into professional performing careers. Mrs. Robinson always had to cloak her professional ambitions with the aura of domesticity.

Women's musical clubs, emerging after 1888 in Canada, inverted this pattern, and used their amateur participation in the public sphere as a sign of their persistent domesticity. As Canadian musicologist Robin Elliott suggests, the typical member of the WMCT at the turn of the century was a woman "of a certain class" who had professional training and had often pursued an active public career until marrying, when "it was common for these women to abandon their public careers." The WMCT, founded in 1898, had dropped the requirement that active club members perform, in favour of producing professional, public concerts, by 1914. Just as the truly powerful men of the mid-nineteenth century did not perform for others, but contented themselves musically with formally organized glee clubs laden with constitutions, rules of procedure, and public outcomes, so the WMCT produced annual reports about a formal plan of work, in accordance with "Rules for Active Members."[12] The WMCT increasingly emphasized administrative, patronal, and intellectual opportunities for its members. The entrance of more women into the musical profession in the early twentieth century seems not to have changed the options for these upper-class women, whose cultured leisure continued to require amateur status.

This had not changed from 1844, when amateur status was code for upper-class leisure. The "greatest achievement" described in the 1940 obituary of a founder and long-time president of the Women's Musical Club of Toronto, Mrs. George Dickson, was "unquestionably the contribution which she made to the refinement of social behaviour." It was "with the dignity and wit of a Marquise of the *ancien régime* [that her appreciation of] every kind of artistic talent ... made her social relations 'catholic' in the fullest sense of the word." As Robin Elliott notes, private Musicales, which he suggests were performed only by women in 1897, may have been the forebears of the WMCT.[13] Mrs. Widder's Soirée Musicale suggests that the roots of the late nineteenth-century women's musical clubs sank deeper, into the older tradition of elite, private concerts at mid-century in Canada, and earlier yet in Britain and Europe. The historic periods of Mrs. Widder's operatic selections and the assignment of musical genres appropriate to people of different sex and social rank in her Soirée Musicale program were not coincidental but fundamental.

The organisational aspect of Mrs. Widder's Soirée Musicale developed, in women's musical clubs, into the administration of benevolent funding for training and debut performance opportunities for young professional musicians. It would be worth exploring whether any of the budding professionals came from the same social class as the women who ran the musical clubs that fostered professional careers. Robin Elliott cites other historians of women's clubs who endorse the opportunities the clubs provided their women members in the late nineteenth and early twentieth centuries for education, public community service, and for building the skills of "organization, public speaking, and social investigation ... [which] may have been of more importance than the aims for which the women had allegedly come together."[14] If the aim of such skills was to help women achieve full participation in the business of directing or managing the large cultural organizations of mainstream culture, then the clubs failed. Even in 2003, very few women are in positions of real power on boards of directors or as artistic directors who decide the content, casting, and implementation of large-budget performance programs. In mid-nineteenth century, Mrs. Robinson had used the domesticity of the Soirée Musicale and her amateur status to veil her run for a professional career. The Women's Musical Clubs were doing no such thing. Elliott rightly suggests that, "in all public arenas, the face of musical Toronto was dominantly male."[15] The clubs were silos of amateur status.

What of Mrs. Widder's glee-singing gentlemen? Her particular Gentleman Amateurs performed occasionally and sporadically in public concerts into the 1860s.

Mr. Barron's public record, for instance, shows his steady preference for singing glees, including "Come, silent evening" and he was often associated as director of choral concerts given by Upper Canada College boys. Mr. Wells, apart from church choir membership, is known to have sung only three times in public over the next twenty years, and Reverend McCaul composed music or organized concerts more often than he performed in them. [16] This reflects the different social status of the three men. McCaul was the administrative superior of Barron, and Wells, as a barrister, may have found singing in a church choir, as a testament to his religious faith, more appropriate than secular public performance, since he is known only to have sung on three concert occasions. The lowest man on this social scale Frederick Barron, sang in public more often than the others, but not very often at all.

Their limited public performance of glees also reflects the short life of the Gentleman Amateur as a public musical figure. Glees slid out of concert programs where women also performed and into another all male preserve. Male university students formed glee clubs, particularly after 1879, during the time when women were admitted as students.[17] As Canadian historian William Westfall suggests, access to higher education was an important new opportunity for women.[18] Nevertheless, glee singing, as an unbroken continuation of the long tradition of private, even secretive, masculine leisure pickled in drink and committed to group loyalty, staked an exclusively male sub-territory in university life. The University of Toronto Ladies' Glee Club was founded 1892, but this did not change gender segregation as a function of glee singing. All-male sports culture in universities emerged at the same time. The simplicity of these glees, unchanged from Mrs. Widder's time, was notable as a contrast to the musical complexity of other, perhaps feminine, music. As one University of Toronto glee singer pointed out in 1923, "we didn't sing these fancy songs, you may imagine."[19]

In this respect, university glee clubs shared a certain conceptual ground with Mr. Widder's attempt to isolate some aspects of traditional governance from access by a newly enfranchised group. Mrs. Widder's program was not one of political rebellion, but a celebration of the tropes of unelected political power and its relationship with the lower echelons of humanity essential to implementing that power, the working classes and the woman at home. The underlying premise of the Widder program and Frederick Widder's business scheme, that social hierarchy was natural and benevolent, seems to have been present in the segregating of university glee clubs by gender. Glee club men were doing what came naturally! Women had nothing to do with it.

The performative silence of the powerful men at the Widder concert of 1844 translated to patronage of public concerts and the founding and directing of the first major orchestral and choral organisations in Ontario.[20] Men like Widder and

Beverley Robinson (Sr.) sat on these boards of directors, and had as advisors local musicians like Humphreys. These were not profitable organisations, except for the musicians who were paid for individual engagements, so were perhaps driven by the idealism of their directors.[21] Composers and often the very music performed by formal music organisations overlapped with the Widder program selections. Further research is needed to investigate the links between conservative political ideals and the organized musical life of pre-Confederation Canada.

Mrs. Widder's Soirée Musicale program reveals that musical leisure was not leisure for all of its participants, but professional work for some, whether paid directly or as a marketing endeavour. For professional musicians throughout the nineteenth century, private concerts continued to be part of their livelihood. The 1885 Soirée Musicale at Northwold, performed only by professionals for a private party in the Toronto home of Mrs. Susan Cawthra, may be evidence that as the status and perhaps the quality of amateur musicianship declined, the purveyor of strategic domestic entertainments more commonly engaged only professionals. In the Northwold concert, while the musical genre of each selection was noted on the program, only the difference between vocal and instrumental music was made. All of the vocal selections were called "Song" but the more intellectual, instrumental material was described in terms of its musical form – a sonata, a dance, a march. There were no glees. Since all the performers were professional, the program did not need to draw attention to class distinctions among them. Men performed both songs and instrumental music, but the solitary woman sang only simple songs.[22]

In 1901, professional musician Ernest Theodore Martin advertised that he would travel to Hamilton to perform in two public recitals and "at a musicale, given at the residence of Dr. T. H. and Mrs. Husband."[23] The Soirée Musicale was still an important professional engagement in 1901. While much was changing in Canadian society, the lot of the professional musician was still to scramble after a profusion of related income streams.

Despite the social overtones of the private Soirée Musicale, where professionals performed with their amateur hosts, musician and host did not share peer status. This remained true even as society inched into the twentieth century. By the 1890s, the Canadian Augusta Beverley Robinson was working as a paid "salon singer" in England. A note from the well-known ballad composer, Jacques Blumenthal, to Miss Robinson hints at the discretion that would be required to negotiate a living wage from such performances: "Dear Miss Robertson [sic], I have just heard that you are in town from Miss Brema and as we have a few friends tomorrow Tuesday evening here (about 1/4 past ten) we shall be very glad to see you again - Miss Brema is coming too.

It would be very nice if you would bring some good songs. Yours very truly, Jacques Blumenthal."[24] Establishing payment or what was meant by "good songs" in the salon of a popular composer like Blumenthal, required refined judgement. Miss Robinson's more famous musical friend, Maud Valérie White, was equally familiar with the paid salon engagement. She wryly noted that, although she could usually stay in the room after performing, "one hardly exists for people in London unless one happens to belong to their particular set, or unless one is a well-known person of some sort."[25] The domestic Soirée Musicale as a paying concert venue for professionals was part of their fragile hold on financial health. Private concerts are still performed by professional musicians even today, and, just as in 1844 and 1890, working musicians are still not the social peers of their employers.

At the same time that Ontario audiences were paying to attend Mrs. Robinson's public charity concerts, they also paid to attend commercial Soirées Musicales with all-professional casts. The showmanship of one travelling virtuoso was enhanced by his clever reference to the domestic Soirée Musicale. In 1862, pianist Louis Moreau Gottschalk advertised a "Soirée Musicale" at which he invited audience members to ask for particular selections from his repertoire during the concert, billing this as "a source of real amusement and instruction, as well as of social intercourse."[26] Gottschalk was using the familiar conventions of the Soirée Musicale by promising the audience the experience of influencing his choice of repertoire and program sequence. In doing so, he was subtly advertising the opportunity to experience the kind of social intercourse with professional musicians familiar to the hosts of private Soirées Musicales, a combination of the spiritual uplift promised by great music well performed and pure social lust.

By combining the definitional domesticity of the "lady" with the quasi-professional level of her musical achievement, the Soirée Musicale was well suited to expand from the posh parlours of its origins to the public concert stage. It met the Victorian, middle-class need for respectability, with the Lady Amateur and her elite domesticity guaranteeing the moral propriety of the undertaking and enhancing the reputations of the paid, professional musicians who depended on direct contact with amateur students and employers for much of their living. The professionals provided the benchmark of skill against which the amateur performances would be directly measured, while helping the amateurs by teaching them skills and finding appropriate repertoire for them to perform.

The term "Soirée Musicale" was flexible in Ontario, but it always had as its core the combination of domesticity and gender-specific music. All-professional troupes presented entertainments that were like the private Soirée Musicale in name or in fact, re-enacting in public the private musical leisure of the upper classes. For example,

The Buckleys, ballad and glee singers from New York gave two "Grand Musical Soirees" in 1857. In 1886 in London, Ontario, the Saunders Family of professional musicians gave "Parlour Concerts" in their home, making a private parlour into a professional concert stage. Domesticity, with its overtones of morally valuable leisure, was projected in a variety of ways. Some concerts presented whole families of professionals performing together, with leisured amateurs tucked in. Mr. R. G. Paige's "Grand Subscription Concert" of 1853 featured his daughters Ellen, Emily, and Georgina, and a "gentleman amateur" in a program of opera, ballads (one by Glover) and a piano duet by Henri Herz.[27]

Professional performers usually had to teach to survive financially. The combination of a teacher with his amateur students, true of Mrs. Widder's program, had to change only slightly to emphasize the teachers, rather than the students' parents, as producers of the concert, in school concerts like the Rolleston House Soirées Musicales of 1891 and 1894. Sometimes the civic value of music was emphasised by such teachers as Mrs. Marshall, whose students gave a concert for charitable purpose in 1861. One of the marketing functions of combining musical genres in concert programs was to promote easy music suitable for domestic use by sheet-music-buying audiences, and the inclusion of musical genres simple enough for amateurs to perform, the glee and the ballad, was an identifying feature of the Soirée Musicale, as the travelling Buckleys with their "glee and ballad Soirées" of 1852 emphasised.[28]

The casting of nineteenth-century Soirées Musicales did not depend solely on gender but on the class of the performer, as the presence of male performers at Mrs. Widder's Musicale shows. Music in the large drawing rooms of the wealthy was accessible to a limited public, but sometimes that public paid for tickets. The public "subscription" concerts of nineteenth-century Ontario were perhaps no more than a variation on this practice, replayed in larger settings for greater profit, but equally dependent on sufficient ticket purchases made in advance of the event. Professional musicians like Humphreys and Henry Schallehn, for instance, produced a series of subscription concerts in 1849, in which they performed. In Toronto, in 1902, $1 tickets were sold to a concert in the private home of Mrs. Walter Beardmore, at which a professional string quartet provided the jewelled setting for the appearance of Mr. Alfred Beardmore. After Mr. Beardmore's name on the program, the word "Tenor" is scratched out, perhaps a restrained commentary on the aspiring singer's high notes by the professional cellist who played that evening and kept the program. The event seems to have been a pixilated variation of the old British practice of paid subscription concerts held in aristocratic homes, but this one attempting to foster the musical career of the son of the host family.[29] This may be an indication that the rigid dissociation of music with upper-class men was dissolving, but further research is needed to be sure that this was not a momentary aberration, similar to Augusta Beverley Robinson's professional career.

In Ontario after 1880, cellist Paul Hahn, whose career was markedly similar to that of James Dodsley Humphreys, played at Soirées Musicales as part of his normal activities. He was the programmer and featured performer of a private Soirée Musicale held at Benvenuto to entertain visiting royalty in 1910. Like Humphreys, Hahn performed with amateurs and with professionals, toured outside of Toronto, provided entertainment for business meetings, played in church services, worked with students by performing on graduating recitals to provide the ambience of professionalism, and turned to retail instrument sales by working for the same Nordheimer company that had bested James Humphreys' attempt to bolster his performance income by opening a retail shop in 1844.[30] Like Humphreys with his greenhouse full of roses, Hahn found recreation in nature, becoming "an authority on extinct and vanishing birds."[31] Unlike James Dodsley Humphreys, who tried retail music sales just as the Nordheimer brothers were starting their Toronto shop in 1844, Paul Hahn developed a successful retail music business from 1913, while the Nordheimer firm was in its final years of operation. The Hahn firm expanded to include the prestigious Steinway piano line only after the Nordheimer firm had closed its doors in 1927.[32]

From the beginning, the Soirée Musicale had been of use to musicians not only by bolstering their performance incomes, but also as a venue for marketing new compositions and promoting instrument sales. Samuel Nordheimer, the piano dealer and music publisher, had expanded his musical influence from publishing music requested by active Lady Amateurs like Mrs. Robinson to advising the early Toronto Philharmonic Association. Domestic amateurs bought far more pianos than single organisations like the symphony, however; so amateur students were rewarded with performance venues even more formal and public than the private drawing room Soirée Musicale. By 1876, the "First Classical Chamber Concert by Mr. Torrington's pupils" was given "at the Piano rooms of Messrs. Nordheimer."[33] The "chamber" in chamber music had developed from the private rooms of the Soirée Musicale to the public "piano rooms" of music retailers. The aura of domesticity continued to hover over the retail music business.

Musical training had become a lucrative business by 1886, when the Toronto Conservatory of Music opened as a joint-stock company aiming at maximum return on investment.[34] As the century progressed, public Soirées Musicales were increasingly relegated to schools, where their function seems to have been either to maintain the ideal of the blessed domestic angel of harp and hearth, in girls' schools like Rolleston House, or through student recitals, such as those at the commercial Toronto Conservatory of Music, to remind a supportive public of the "classy" culture of the recent past. For example the program cover for the "Soiree Musicale by the Jan Hambourg Trio," held in 1911, states "at the Conservatory music hall -- under the gracious patronage of Their Excellencies, Earl and Countess Grey The Lieutenant Governor of Ontario and Mrs. Gibson." Additional announcements include that "The assisting artist will be Miss Beatrice Delamere, Soprano. Miss Delamere will make her Toronto debut on this occasion." Tickets, $1, at "Nordheimer's."[35] The private teaching of Mrs. Widder's star tenor had been transformed into formal education leading to a professional credential in the Soirée Musicale as graduating recital, but the genteel overtones of the drawing room had not been dispersed. The term "Soirée Musicale" has persisted into the twenty-first century, where it usually makes arch reference to the historic pleasures of the cultured amateur. It is now often used to raise funds for professional performing organisations, with amateur musicians from the board of directors showing support for the ideals of classical music.[36]

The practice of the domestic Soirée Musicale came to Ontario from Britain in the baggage of wealthy émigrés and professional musicians, but local politics and history were quickly incorporated into what it meant to local participants. It is

Figure 23: Soirée Musicale, Interior, Port Dalhousie. National Archives of Canada/e002213447

impossible to know if Mr. Widder directly influenced the programming of his wife's Soirée Musicale in 1844, but the concert's thematic focus was eerily apposite to the social and political demands of his business plans of the time. Such inferences about the non-musical implications of particular repertoire are most reliably drawn from a private, amateur concert where the names of the mixed array of performers can be investigated to show the networks of their many-layered relationships. Understanding the layers of personal meaning in this private program may offer useful insights into how other audiences understood the music they heard. Where there was a direct transfer of repertoire and performers from private to public concerts, as there was with Mrs. Widder's Soirée Musicale in Ontario, the implication is that the non-musical meanings of the programming, repertoire, and performers may also have been transferred intact to the public forum. Certainly, Mrs. Widder's private concert offers a helpful interpretive model for some later public concerts in Ontario.

With these lessons from Mrs. Widder's 1844 program in mind, it was possible to make rapid headway in researching the only known photograph of a Canadian Soirée Musicale from the nineteenth century, (Figure 23), "Soiree Musicale, Port Dalhousie." The provenance of this image is not known, so the image and its title were the starting place for the research. It was assumed that the performers in this clearly domestic interior were a mix of professional and amateur, and from the women's clothing the date was estimated to be the mid-1890s. The clothing ranges from the exquisite gown of the seated woman on the right, front, to the drab bodice of the standing woman on the far left, which has narrow sleeves of an older style than the puffed and ruffled sleeves of the women in front. The cornet player's jacket sags wearily by contrast with the crisp, high-collared outfit of the seated singer, with his dapper, curled hair. The differences in apparent wealth, with the most certain candidate for professional musician, the cornettist, clad in poorer clothing, suggest that this group, like Mrs. Widder's, was composed of well-off amateurs and professional musicians.

To develop a list of professional musicians in Port Dalhousie and its neighbouring metropolis, St. Catharines, church and entertainment musicians were hunted. Comparison with photographs of the Opera House Orchestra of neighbouring St. Catharines, which performed professionally in the 1880s and 1890s, showed the cornet player in the Port Dalhousie Musicale photograph to be professional cornettist Albert Lindsley.[37] By the 1880s, more women were working in professional venues like the highly respected Opera House Orchestra, and the standing women's workaday clothing suggests that these may have been Henrietta and Elizabeth Weeks, both members of the orchestra.[38] The woman pianist is clearly coordinating the musical activities of the back row of participants, so she too may have been a professional musician. Certainly, her physical stance communicates the authority of musical skill and concentration.

The item being rehearsed or performed was a combination of recitation and music, typical of the mixed programming of the nineteenth century. Note that the seated women are reading from a book, and the musicians are poised for a cue from the pianist, suggesting a dramatic recitation punctuated by musical interludes. Combining recitations with music was a popular option for Victorian concert programs. Whether this was a purely domestic gathering of music lovers for their own enjoyment, a private concert with amateurs and professionals, or a rehearsal for an enactment of a posh musicale to be given at the St. Catharines Opera House cannot be wholly known from this photograph alone. Each of these possibilities, however, combines domesticity and public performance, amateurs and professionals, typical of an Ontario Soirée Musicale.

Applying the interpretive model of Mrs. Widder's concert to the Port Dalhousie photograph revealed new subjects and the possibility of new sources for the history of musical performance in nineteenth-century Canada. One of the theoretical purposes of this study is to integrate gender theory with business, political, and music history. Unpicking the condensed layers of gendered social identity is essential to identifying the patterns of musical genre, professionalism, and what might be called performative silence in Mrs. Widder's Soirée Musicale. This has implications for the history of the music profession in Canada, which cannot properly account for the professional careers of male musicians like James Dodsley Humphreys and Paul Hahn without understanding their relationship with amateurs like Mrs. Robinson. The dreams and expenditure of many an upper-crust Lady Amateur were critical to sustaining the professional careers of male musicians like James Dodsley Humphreys and Paul Hahn. Is the same dynamic at play in the concerts presented by amateur musical clubs today?

The role of apparently amateur musicians may be an important factor in the history of women in the Canadian music profession. When, exactly, did a significant number of women start working as professional musicians in Canada? The existing biographies of such performers as Emma Albani and Georgina Stirling tend not to take account of the significant factors of class and gender, whether within the profession itself or in the relationships between professionals and their publics. Was the relationship between client and musician different when both were women? The distinction between amateurism and professionalism, made with a sharp eye to gender and class, holds promise for future scholarship.

From my perspective as a twentieth-century professional musician, the idea of a domestic Soirée Musicale seemed rather sly. A formal concert held in a home and a program that combined amateur and professional performers in music of such varied genres seemed based on some unspoken premise. Very little documentary evidence provides direct information about how music was experienced, but the programs themselves give an enormous range of information. That the kind of information available on concert programs today is different from the ordinary run of nineteenth-century Soirée Musicale programs is telling. It is not necessary to put any information on a program, particularly in an informal situation where performers and audience know each other well. A program is a map of what the programmer intended the concert to mean. The statement of musical genres on the Widder program is the central clue to the relationship between social identity and musical genre with and it leads to the conclusion that certain musical genres refer to historically specific meanings about class and gender on concert programs has changed over time.

Concert programming can adapt quickly to changing social circumstances. The problem for the historian is to find evidence that concerts were in some way specific to time, to place, and to the individuals who participated in them. The mass of empirical information implicit in a single domestic program, however, suggests that the history of musical activity may be an unjustly overlooked source of insight into how society synthesised and negotiated the overlapping layers of politics, commerce, and personal values. Subtle nuances of social identity were played out in Mrs. Widder's drawing room. Whether, and how, this mingling through shared musical activity affected social change is a subject for further study.

The domestic Soirée Musicale was a subset of all domestic music making, for which there is otherwise little historical trace. Using the documentary evidence of this elite form of parlour music provides greater insight into all parlour music practice. The research into the broad range of sources needed to make sense of Mrs. Widder's concert led to the discovery of Mrs. Robinson's private papers, and an unusual series of insights into her conscious management of the gender constraints she and her daughter faced as musicians. Bringing attention to this outstanding amateur woman musician may encourage further research into the achievements and the influence of other middle-class women musicians of nineteenth-century Canada. Amateur status was nominal for one such woman: was anyone else in the same situation? Certainly, Mrs. Robinson's career is evidence that music provided a flexible margin for women whose options for public life were otherwise tightly limited.

It is no surprise that Victorian gender ideology thwarted some women's professional ambitions in nineteenth-century Ontario. Although Mrs. Widder's Soirée Musicale provided some wealthy women with the opportunity of real personal development, the sound of the drawing-room door locking tight in the later nineteenth-century is unmistakable. It is sorely tempting to see the juggling of so many risks and opportunities by these gifted, wealthy, women amateurs as subversive activism, but it is unwise. Music is a persuasive enchantment and the music of the Soirée Musicale perpetuated the class and gender stereotypes of its time. What can be said for women like Miss Hagerman is that although the chains of Victorian femininity were real and often painful, women's capacities for musical excellence, driving professional ambition, and magisterial subtlety in developing strategies to circumvent what could not be changed were also real. Persistent high levels of conceptual thinking and civic citizenship were as feminine as they were masculine.

Private concert giving, like music making in the home, dwindled to sporadic nostalgia in the twentieth century, but its legacy may still be woven into the meanings of musical performance today. Many of the conclusions drawn about Mrs. Widder's Soirée Musicale were also true of public concerts, even those called by other names. The domestic Soirée Musicale was a concentrated form of music making which placed a spotlight on each of its constituent features: amateur performance by ladies, amateur performance by gentlemen, professional performance by male musicians, the combination of unlike musical genres, and the domestic venue for a formal concert. Each feature existed elsewhere in the musical life of the period, but juxtaposed in the same program, they created the Soirée Musicale as a form. The surprise of this study in finding similarities between a private concert and public musical life, coupled with the strong political overtones of the private concert, raises the question of how the business of music was connected to public political and economic life. The Soirée Musicale in the nineteenth century brought the most prominent musicians and music businesses into direct, personal contact with prominent members of the political and business communities. Given the stable social values so fundamental to the very structure of the Soirée Musicale, the question of how musical life was involved in promoting those values in public policy arises. Although three other programs from the same period, two in Toronto and one in London, England, were reviewed in this study, a more comprehensive history of alternative programming themes and structures could make a useful comparison with the Widder concert.

As the interpretive kaleidoscope clicks through patterns of gender, class, and musical genre to examine Mrs. Widder's 1844 Soirée Musicale, the multiple meanings expressed in the sound of music come into focus. Music lives as sound, and as sound, it functions as but one of the tumbling, colourful components that make up each performance. The time, the place, and the participants also vary every time music is heard. The art of constructing a domestic concert program for personal use caught the clutter of a way of life and threw the ideas that underpinned it into stark relief.

On March 12, 1844, the guests, the servants, the artists, and the hosts gleamed in the candlelight of Lyndhurst at Mrs. Widder's Soirée Musicale. The light and the sound of music flowed out through the windows, through the keyholes, and through the drawing-room door propped temporarily ajar, into the night air where people hurried by, uninvited to the party. Did one man pause and smile at the sound of "Dermot Astore," as he thought fondly of his daughter singing it at home? Mr. Widder would lose his bid to lock the Clergy Reserves away from democratic governance and Mrs. Widder would sometimes stumble in her hot pursuit of social prominence, but their use of the Soirée Musicale would echo into the twentieth century.

Much changed as the kaleidoscope of time clicked through its layered patterns of historical meaning, but wherever the Soirée Musicale can be found, stable categories of class and gender, locked into an eternally "natural" hierarchy of merit, are at its core. Mrs. Widder's Soirée Musicale, like all Soirées Musicales, performed a drama of difference, in which Ideally Feminine Women, Ideally Masculine Men, and Ideally Subordinate ranks of "naturally" different types of humanity, demonstrated a harmonious vision of an ideal world.

Acknowledgements

This study was made possible by many people. My heartfelt thanks go first to Brian McKillop, who encouraged and guided this project with pragmatic erudition, enthusiasm, and good humour. His wide-ranging curiosity about the history and meaning of popular culture helped me shape the topic. The collegiality of Carleton University professors made for many an enriching conversation, and I was fortunate to study history with Deborah Gorham and Duncan McDowall, and Canadian musicology with Elaine Keillor, all committed and insightful teaching scholars. Joan White, the Graduate Secretary of the history department, was unfailingly helpful. To my fellow students, Sarah Futterer, so generous with ideas, and to Ryan Eyford, Robbyn Gulka, Ryan Shackleton, Stacey Barker, Matthew McRae, Judith Rygiel, and Janice Cavell, thank you for sharing the journey with such frankness and laughter.

I am grateful to an international community of scholars who responded to my questions, often by internet alone, with gracious advice and curiosity, including Robin Elliott, Robert Burns of Heritage Resources Consulting, Derek Scott, Richard Excell, David Kimmel, Stephen Herx, Michael Rudman, Stephen Otto, Michael Peterman, Ian Begg, Isabel Campbell, Major Paul Lansey, Sophie Fuller, and Frank Nakashima.

Finding all of Mrs. Widder's music was a mountain which inter-library loan librarians Callista Kelly and Christine Taylor conquered smiling. Many librarians and archivists gave unstinting help, and I thank each of them at Carleton University Library, especially Janet Carson, the National Library and National Archives of Canada, the Art Gallery of Ontario Library, Parks Canada, the McCord Museum, the University of Windsor Leddy Library Archives, the Public Archives of Ontario, and the Toronto Reference Library. I thank in particular Bernadine Dodge of Trent University Archives, Marion Spence at Upper Canada College, Kathleen McMorrow and her colleagues at the University of Toronto Faculty of Music Library, and Doug Fyfe for introducing me to the Spadina Historic House and Garden collection. I was privileged to be introduced to the musical ancestors of several families, including those of Paul Hahn, Barbara Larsen, Timothy Anderson, and Karey Shinn. A real joy was the late Jim McPherson, a meticulous, witty friend whose love of singers is much missed.

Sarah Bonesteel provided sensitive, thorough, and creative editorial assistance in streamlining my master's thesis into this book. It was a pleasure to work with her.

Liss-Carin Alvin gave invaluable encouragement and Eleanor Crowder reminded me of the truth of performance. Finally, thank you to my husband, Janis Kazaks, who understood that I had to learn whatever the Soirée Musicale might teach, and made it possible at home.

Appendix 1

Lyrics of Mrs. Widder's Program

PART I

1. ** "Plaudite O Popoli"[1]

CHORUS	Applaud, people, the valor of the conqueror with high songs,
	The much-celebrated hero of our country.
TANCREDI	Sweet are the tones of glory, dear the honourable victory,
	But a miserable heart knows no peace
CHORUS	We render glory to you and send to your heart.
TANCREDI	Ah! For this soul no peace arrives.
	... A cruel fate, implacable, guides me.

2. "Mira Oh Norma"[2]

ADALGISA Hear me, Norma, in pity hear me, I would fain dispel thy dark despair;
At thy feet behold thy children kneeling, / Can a mother's heart reject their prayer?
When the heart is cold that should have cherish'd / Eve'ry hope of joy it falsely gave;
Wouldst thou have me live / Ah no! Thou wouldst not,
My only haven is but the grave.

NORMA Ah in vain you thus implore me / Time cannot my joys restore me,
Yet could he feel who caus'd my anguish / How deep hath been my silent sorrow,
Then repenting, he would languish at my feet ere dawns the morrow,
Blessed hope, thy peace restore and joy shall beam once more.

CAVATINA (together)
Still in our fond hearts one bright hope is beating
Friendship shall blossom tho' love's star be fleeting,
Be thou but faithful and I will still cherish / Hope that shall fade not till life itself perish.

ADALGISA Oh what joy to hear thee thus cherish hope again

TOGETHER Thou alone hast taught me / Despair is worse than pain.
Oh Thro' clouds of sadness the sun of joy appears.
How bright the gladness that shineth thro' our tears. Yes, joy is mine.

** indicates a structural pillar in the program.

[1]Gioachino Rossini, *Tancredi, melodramma eroico in due atti*, eds., Bruno Cagli, Philip Gossett, and Alberto Zedda, *Edizione Critica delle Opere di Gioachino Rossini*. Sezione prima: opere teatrali, vol. 10 (Milan: Fondazione Rossini Pesaro,1984), pp. 29-74.

[2]Vincenzo Bellini, "Hear Me Norma," arr. S. Nelson, trans. by Ch. Jefferys (New York: James L . Hewitt & Co, 1843).

3. "My Mother Bids Me Bind My Hair"[3]

My mother bids me bind my hair with bands of rosy hue,
Tie up my sleeves with ribbands rare, and lace my bodice blue.
For why, she cries, sit still and weep, while others dance and play?
Alas! I scarce can go or creep, while Lubin is away.
'Tis sad to think the days are gone, when those we love were near,
I sit upon this mossy stone and sigh when none can hear.
And while I spin my flaxen thread and sing my simple lay,
The village seems asleep or dead: now Lubin is away.

4. "Come T'adoro"[4]

How I adore you, and how much / My heart only could say to you:
Joy is mine in my weeping/ Peace in my distress. / If on earth the throne
I could offer you / Ah! Would you not want the gift / Dearest in your beautiful heart.

5. ** Glee: "Lutzow's Wild Hunt"[5]

From yonder dark forest what horsemen advance?
What sounds from the rocks are rebounding?
The sunbeams are gleaming on sword and on lance,
And loud the shrill trumpet is sounding.
And if you ask what you there behold, / 'Tis the hunt of Lutzow, the free and the bold.

Why roars in yon valley the deadly fight?
What glittering sounds are clashing?
Our true-hearted riders maintain the right,
And the torch of freedom is flashing.
And if you ask what you there behold, / 'Tis the hunt of Lutzow, the free and the bold.

'Tis our hunt! The proud tyrant and dastardly slave
Before our hunters are flying;
And weep not for us, if our country we save,
Although we have saved it by dying.
From age to age it shall still be told / 'Twas the hunt of Lutzow, the free and the bold.

---

[3]Joseph Haydn, "My mother bids me bind my hair," *Canzonettas and Songs for Voice with Piano Accompaniment*, ed. Ludwig Landshoff (New York/London/Frankfurt: C. F. Peters Corporation, 1931), pp. 9-12.

[4]Vincenzo Bellini, *Beatrice di Tenda, tragedia lirica in two acts*, ed. Philip Gossett, synopsis Laura DeMarco (New York: Garland Pub., 1980), pp.44- 60. Translation Kristina Guiguet.

[5]Carl Maria Von Weber, "Lutzow's Wild Hunt," in *Heart Songs Dear to the American People and by them Contributed in the Search for Treasured Songs Initiated by the National Magazine*, ed., Bea Friedland (Boston: Chapple Publishing Company, Ltd., 1909), pp. 331-2.

6. ** "Vivi Tu" [6]

Ah! Live thou, I do conjure thee! / Thou who hast less cause for anguish,
Fairer hopes time may ensure thee, / But in dark despair I would languish.
Seek a refuge where though obscurely, / Truth and honor may dwell securely:
Find a region, though desert it be, / Where friendship fears not tyranny.
While so many, so many now guiltless perish, / Let one haply, aye, haply consent to live
That our mem'ry he still may cherish, /And to regret, to regret his fond tears give!
Since thy courage thou hast prov'd thee, / O'er my heart peace gains her power;
Nought save thy misfortune mov'd me, / In thy grief was all my pain!
Death can never make me cower, / Over me his triumph's vain!
Yes! the fatal moment speeding, / Let us meet no menace heeding;
For on earth, where we are reft, / To us, nor fear nor hope is left.

7. The Dream Is Past[7]

The dream is past, and with it fled / The hopes that once my passion fed;
And darkly die, mid grief and pain / The joys which gone come not again.
My soul to silence and in tears / Has cherished now for many years
A love for one who does not know / The thoughts that in my bosom glow
Oh! Cease my heart thy throbbing hide / Another soon will be his bride
And hopes last faint but cheering ray / Will then forever pass away.
They cannot see the silent tear / That falls uncheck'd when none are near
Nor do they mark the smothered sigh / That leaves my breast when they are by.
I know my cheek is paler now, / And smiles no longer deck my brow:
'Tis youth's decay, 'twill soon begin / To tell the thoughts that dwell within.
Oh! Let me rouse my sleeping pride / And from his gaze my feelings hide
He shall not smile to think that I / with love for him could pine and die.

---

[6]Gaetano Donizetti, "Ah! Live thou, I do conjure thee! (Vivi tu, te ne scongiuro)," in *Anna Boleyn* [sic] (Philadelphia: A. Fiot, 1844).

[7]Stephen Glover,"The dream is past" (New York: Firth Hall & Pond, 239 Broadway and by Firth & Hall 1 Franklin Square, [1846-1847]).

8. Crudel Perche Finora [condensed][8]

COUNT	But why, why make me suffer, longing for your reply? Why? Cruel one!
SUSANNA	In time we women grant you what we at first deny.
COUNT	Then shall we meet this evening SUSANNA If you wish, my lord
COUNT	You will not fail to be there? SUSANNA No you have my word.
COUNT	You promise? SUSANNA No - I mean yes
COUNT	The sweet promise you gave me raises my hope so high. You'll meet me in the garden?
SUSANNA	All those who know what love is, forgive me for this lie, If that's your wish, I shall.

9. I Ought to Tear Thee from My Heart[9]

I ought to tear thee from my heart / But cannot bear with thee to part,
I ought to blot thee from my mind, / And be not thus to reason blind.
Nor sense nor reason will avail, / And I my folly must bewail,
For sure 'tis madness great in me, / To ere bestow one thought on thee."

10. ** Mi Manca La Voce[10]

My voice fails me, / I feel myself dying, / Such terrible blows / Who could bear them?
My pain muffles my voice, / Such terrible blows / I know not how to bear.

---

[8]Wolfgang Amadeus Mozart, *The Marriage of Figaro*, trans. Ruth Martin and Thomas Martin (New York/London: G. Schirmer, 1951), pp. 283-288.

[9]Harriett Abrams, "I ought to tear thee from my heart," in Harriett Abrams, *A Second Sett of Italian and English Canzonetts, for One, Two, or Three Three Voices with an accompaniment for the Piano-Forte or Harp, etc.* (London: L. Lavenu, for the Author, c. 1800), pp. 10-11.

[10]G. Rossini, "Mi manca la voce," in *Mose in Egitto*, arr. C. M. Sola (London: Goulding, D'Almaine, Potter & Co., 20 Soho Squ., n.d.).

PART II

1. Herz - Piano Forte Fantasia

2. Trono E Corona[11]

Yes, Torquato, I am destined to love you:
Mocked by my ancestral blood and my throne!
It is useless to deny I am in love ... / Torquato, his madness has maddened my heart, too.
... In your fury, Destiny, take my crown and my throne.
Leave me only his heart, 'til I die. / In my unhappiness, Destiny, I defy you.
But leave me Torquato, / And I will forgive you everything.
Yes: even in his icy tomb, / His heart will beat for me.

3. Dermot Astore[12]

Oh! Dermot Astore! Between waking and sleeping
I heard thy dear voice and I wept so to say:
Ev'ry pulse of my heart, the sweet measure was keeping
'Til Killarney's wild echoes had borne it away.
Oh! Tell me, my own love, is this our last meeting?
Shall we wander no more in Killarney's green bow'r,
To watch the bright sun o'er the dim hills retreating,
And the wild stag at rest in his bed of spring flowers.
V. 2 Oh Dermot Astore! How this fond heart would falter
When I see thee by sight in the dawn
And heard thine own voice in a soft whisper utter
Those words of endearment, "Mavourneen Colleen."
I know we must part, but oh! Say not forever,
That it may be for years adds enough to my pain,
But I'll cling to the hope, that though now we must sever
In some blessed hour I shall meet thee again.

---

[11]Don White, synopsis and translation in brochure notes for Kenneth Montgomery, dir., *Torquato Tasso*, by Gaetano Donizetti, Opera Rara Production, 1974, M.R.F. Records, Inc.

[12]F. W. Nichols Crouch, "Dermot Astore" (New York: Hewitt & Jacques, 239 Broadway, n.d.).

4. Oh, Lovely Maiden, Stay[13]

AZOR   Oh! Lovely Maiden stay: Nay, turn not thus away!
               Nor let the woes that move / My breast, unpitied be
               Tis all I ask, for love I may not seek from thee!

ZEMIRA And are his words so mild! / So strangely sweet his tones!
               My heart, with terror wild, / Their stealing softness owns.

AZOR   One ray of hope would cheer me!

ZEMIRA Approach not! Approach not! Still I fear thee!

AZOR   To thee I bow, nay, fear not! To thy best service true, to thee I bow.

ZEMIRA To me! Oh yet that form I dare not view!

AZOR   Say then, shall I depart?

ZEMIRA No, stay, I'll nerve my heart! / (My Father! 'Tis for you.)
               I feel my fears subsiding, /... I do not dread him. now!

AZOR   Oh, Fairest! Still confiding, / Compassion but bestow;
               All gifts with me abiding, / To thee alone I'll vow.

ZEMIRA I ask no part of all your treasure / But for my Father sue alone.

AZOR   Thy wish my law, thy word my pleasure,
               Accept my pow'r, 'tis all thine own!

Together:
ZEMIRA Full oft the form repelling / Conceals the noble mind;
               So in the darkest dwelling / The cavern'd gem we find.

AZOR   Her gentle looks are telling / Of all that's good and kind,
               And speak her heart the dwelling / Of every grace refin'd.

5. ** Ah, per sempre io ti perdei[14]

Have I lost thee indeed forever? / Flower of beauty, must we sever?
Sad and mourning, yet I linger, / Lone and joyless, reft of thee.
Hope beguiled me with blissful dreamings / Through long years I loved and waited,
But my doom, alas, is fated, / Nought but sorrow and despair on earth now is left me.

---

[13]Louis Spohr, "Oh, lovely maiden stay, duet from *Grand Opera of Azor & Zemira*," arr. Sir George Smart (London: D'Almaine & Co., n.d. [104 New Bond Street, c. 1811]), pp. 119-126.

[14]Vincenzo Bellini, "Ah forever I now have lost thee," Toronto: A.&.S. Nordheimer Co., n.d. [1846-50]).

6. Echo Song[15]

What airy sound / Floats sweetly round, / Some spirit seems to play! /
How did that note, /
On ether float, / And steal, and steal my soul away, and steal my soul away.
Still, still I hear the changeful strain, / It mocks, it echoes, it echoes me again.
Is't Fairy ground, / Are Spirits round?

7. Come, Silent Evening[16]

Come silent evening o'er us, / In this sequestered plain
And while thou closest o'er us,
We'll chant our humble strain.
Delightful nature weareth, / Too soon the garb of night,
And beautiful appeareth, / The moon in silvr'y light. / See twilight fast descending,
Upon each dale and hill, / The sun his last rays bending, / Now glimmers on the rill.
Hark! Thro' the silence reigning, / The flute's soft murm'ring song,
While nightingales complaining, / Their melting notes prolong.

"Give me the night"[17]

[Not on Mrs. Widder's program, the following song by Joseph Knight captures the same mood as the Von Call glee.]

Give me the night! The calm beautiful night!
When the green earth reposes in heaven's own light;
When the moon and the stars keep their vigils above,
And nought is awake, save the spirit of love!
When visions of memory visit the heart,
Like dreams of the past which too soon must depart,
And the soul fond dwells on the scenes of delight,
Give me the night! The calm beautiful night!

---

[15]H. R. Bishop,"The Echo Song," arr. arr. V. de Giorgio, in *Paling's Album Series No. 7* (Sydney, Brisbane: W. H. Paling & Co. Limited, 1929), pp.8-9.

[16]Leonhard von Call, "Come, Silent Evening," in O.L. Fogle, ed. *Fogle's Male Quartet and Chorus Book: A Collection of High Grade Music for Men's Voices* (Cincinnati: Fillmore Music House, 1908), p. 211. Attributed variously to "von Call," "de Call," and, in one British edition, "von L. deCall." These lyrics and tune have been compared with German and English editions to confirm that this is the text referred to by the Widder program. It is noted in Sale appendix in 1850s as "deCall."

[17]Joseph Philip Knight, "Give me the night" (Philadelphia: John F. Nunns 70 S. Third St., n.d.).

8. Vi Ravviso[18]

As I view now, these scenes so charming, / With dear remembrance, my heart warming,
Of days long vanish'd, / Oh! My breast is fill'd with pain.
Finding objects that still remain, / While those days ne'er come again.
Maid, those bright eyes! / My heart depressing / Fill my breast with thoughts distressing
By recalling an earthly blessing / Long since dead and past away.
She was like thee e'er death oppressing / Sunk her beauties in decay.

9. ** Not a Drum Was Heard (excerpts)[19]

Not a drum was heard, nor a funeral note, / As his corse to the rampart we hurried;
Not a soldier discharged his farewell shot / O'er the grave where our hero we buried.
We buried him darkly at dead of night,
... But he lay like a warrior taking his rest / With his martial cloak around him. ...

We thought, as we hollowed his narrow bed / And smoothed down his lonely pillow,
That the foe and the stranger would tread o'er his head, / And we far away on the billow!
...And we heard the distant and random gun / That the foe was sullenly firing.
Slowly and sadly we laid him down, / From the field of his fame fresh and gory;
We carved not a line, and we raised not a stone, / But left him alone with his glory.

10. ** Vadasi via di qua[20]

Why sure! There never met / A truly jovial set / More prone than we to laugh,
Ha ha ha ha ha ... While thus our wine we quaff.
For what have we to do, Old Care! / With such as you?
No, no we'll ever laugh, ha ha ha ha ... / While thus our wine we quaff.

---

[18]Vincenzo Bellini, "As I view these scenes so charming, sung by Mr. Brough, Air in the celebrated Opera *La Sonnambula*," (New York: H. Hewitt & Co., 230 Broadway, n.d.).

[19]John Barnett, "Not a Drum was Heard: written on the Death of Gen'l Sir John Moore" (Philadelphia: G. Willig Chestnut Street, n.d.).

[20]Martini, "The Laughing Trio [Vadasi via di qua] arranged from Martini's Terzetto," J. Addison, arr. (New York: Dubois & Stodart, 167 Broadway, n.d.).

Appendix 2

Lyrics of Mr. Humphreys' 1851 Program[1]

PART I

1. *Quadrilles*– Victoria   CZERNY

2. *Chorus*– "Lutzow's Wild Hunt"   WEBER
   [see Appendix 1: "Lyrics of Mrs. Widder's Program"]

3. *Piano Solo*– Fantasies from "Lucrezia Borgia"   BEYER

4. *Glee*– "When wearied wretches"   BISHOP
   When wearied wretches sink to sleep, / How soft their slumbers lie;
   How sweet is death o those who weep, / To those who weep, and long to die!
   Saw you the soft and grassy bed, / Where flow'rets deck the green earth's breast,
   'Tis there I wish to lay my head; / 'Tis there I wish to sleep at rest.
   Lo! Now, methinks, in tones sublime, / As viewless o'er our heads they bend,
   They whisper! Thus we steal your time, / Weak mortals, 'till your days shall end.

5. *Waltz*– "Queen of the Flowers"   SIEBOTH

6. *Violin Solo*– Swiss Air and Variations   PRAEGER

7. *Chorus*– "The Pilot"   NELSON
   Oh! Pilot, 'tis a fearful night; / There's danger on the deep;
   I'll come and pace the deck with thee, / I do not dare to sleep.
   Go down! The sailor cried, go down! / This is no place for thee -
   Fear not, but trust in Providence, / Wherever thou may'st be ...

8. *Song*– Mr. Humphreys   LEE
   Hearts may warm the winter, / hearts will melt the snow,
   If, while hopes are freezing, / Friendship be not so.
   Worlds of ice may bound us, / Hearts will break their chain,
   If they rally round us / While their loves remain.
   Household gods lie scattered / Round the ruined hearth:
   Do we mourn them, shattered? / Do we weep their dearth?
   No! If love but cheer us / On our withered way,
   Friendship, too, keep near us, / What of their decay?

9. "*Rauber Galop*" [Thieves' Gallop]   KREUTZER

---

[1]Private Collection. Reproduced here to imitate original.

PART II

1. *Quadrilles–* "Fête au Couvent" [Convent Celebration]   BERGMULLER

2. *Glee–* "The Old Bell"   ALLEGHANIANS

> For full five hundred years I've swung / In my old grey turret high;
> And many a different theme I've sung / As the time went stealing by;
> I've pealed the chant of a wedding morn, / Ere night I have sadly toll'd,
> To say that the bride was coming, lone, / To sleep in the church-yard mould:
> Ding-dong, my ceaseless song, / Merry or sad but never long.
>
> For full five hundred years I've swung / In my ancient turret high;
> And many a different theme I've sung / As the time went stealing by:
> I've swell'd the joy of a country's pride, / For a victory far off won,
> Then chang'd to grief for the brave that died, / Ere my mirth had well begun …

3. *Flute Solo–* "È vezzosa si la rosa"   VACCIA

4. *Chorus–* "The brave old Oak"   NELSON

> A song for the Oak, the brave old Oak,
> Who hath ruled in the greenwood long,
> Here's health and renown to his broad green crown,
> And his fifty arms so strong!
> There's fear in his frown when the sun goes down,
> And the fire in the west fades out,
> And he showeth his might, on a wild midnight,
> When storms through his branches shout.
> Then sing to the Oak, the brave old Oak! / Who stands in his pride alone,
> And still flourish he, a hale green tree, / When a hundred years are gone …

5. *The College Polka*   MAULE

6. "Some love to roam"   RUSSELL

> Some love to roam o'er the dark sea foam, / Where the shrill winds whistle free;
> But a chosen band in a mountain land, / And a life in the woods for me.
> When morning beams o'er the mountain streams, / Oh! merrily forth we go,
> To follow the stag to his slippery crag, / And chase the bounding roe. Ho! Ho!
>
> The deer we mark thro' the forest dark, / And the prowling wolf we track;
> And for right good cheer, in the wild woods here, / Oh! Why should a hunter lack!
> For with steady aim at the bounding game, / And hearts that fear no foe,
> To the darksome glad, in the forest shade, / Oh! merrily forth we go. Ho! Ho!

7. *The Railroad Galop*   GUNGLE

8. *Chorus*– "See our Oars"   STEVENSON

   See our oars with feather'd spray, / Sparkle in the beam of day;

   In our little bark we glide, / Swiftly o'er the silent tide,

   From yonder lone and rocky shore, / The Warrior Hermit to restore;

   And sweet the morning breezes blow, / While thus in measur'd time we row.

9. Finale– "GOD SAVE THE QUEEN"   JOHN BULL

Endnotes

COVER ILLUSTRATION

[1]Achille Devéria, "Soirée Musicale – Musical Evening Party," in *Les Heures de la Pariesienne: cinquième album de la collection costumes et modes d'autrefois* (ca. 1840; reprint, with a forward by Roger-Armand Weigert, coloured by Edmond Vairel, Paris: Éditions Rombaldi, 1957), Plate XXIII. Courtesy National Library of Canada.

OVERTURE

1. Archives of Ontario (hereafter AO), Colonel Lucas Colley Foster Fonds, MU1507/ Correspondence/3, Charles Harrison to Ellen [Humphreys] Foster, Toronto, 5 Mar. 1844.

2. Architecture, Lucy Booth Martyn, *100 Years of Grandeur* (Toronto: Pagurian Press Limited, 1978), pp. 101-2. Weather, *British Colonist*, 1 Mar. 1844.

3. Richard B. Howard, *Colborne's Legacy, Upper Canada College, 1829-1979* (Toronto: Macmillan, 1979), p. 1, cited in Norma Martin, Donna S. McGillis, and Catherine Milne, *Gore's Landing and the Rice Lake Plains* (Gore's Landing, Ontario: Heritage Gore's Landing, 1986), p. 111. My thanks to Dr. Donald Smith for this reference.

4. Trent University Archives, Stewart and Gilbert Bagnani Fonds (hereafter TU), 94-016/1/1, Christopher Hagerman to John Strachan, London, England, 16 Nov. 1833. Details Hagerman's work on behalf of Upper Canada College, King's College, Bishop Strachan.

5. Gerald M. Craig, *Upper Canada: The Formative Years, 1784-1841* (Toronto: McClelland and Stewart Limited, 1963), p. 137.

6. *Dictionary of Canadian Biography* (hereafter DCB), s.v. "Hagerman, Christopher," "Wells, Joseph," "Widder, Frederick," "McCaul, John," et al. For persistent influence of many of Family Compact families, see Robert J. Burns, "The First Elite of Toronto: An Examination of the Genesis, Consolidation and Duration of Power in an Emerging Colonial Society" (Ph.D. diss., University of Western Ontario, 1974). For George Dupont Wells as musician, see David John Sale, "Toronto's pre-confederation music societies, 1845-1867" (M. Mus. thesis, University of Toronto, 1968) (hereafter Sale), p. 387.

7. Sale, pp. 312-390, a comprehensive index of all who performed in public in Toronto in the period.

8. Roderick Hamilton Burgoyne, ed., *Historical Records of the 93rd Sutherland Highlanders, now the 2nd Battalion Princess Louise's Argyle and Sutherland Highlanders* (London: Richard Bentley and Son, 1883), pp. 62, 86, 81, 386. For musical life, see Elinor Kyte Senior, *British Regulars in Montreal: an Imperial Garrison 1832-1854* (Montreal: McGill-Queen's University Press, 1981), p. 166. Thanks to the History and Heritage Unit, Department of National Defence, Government of Canada, for discussions of military social networks and scholarly references.

9. See n. 1, above. Death announcement of "Henrietta wife of Capt. G. E. Aylmer, 93rd Highlanders," in *The Patriot*, Tuesday 5 Mar. 1844. G. E. Aylmer is confirmed as a Captain in the same regiment as Haliday in Burgoyne, *Historical Records*, p. 382.

10. Major Joshua Thompson, *Militia List for Canada West* (Toronto: S. Derbishire and G. Desbarats, 1851), for militia ranks of Thomas Galt, p. 40; of McGill p. 34; of H. J. Boulton (Jr.), p. 39. For Humphreys, in Private Collection, clipping, "Military Cap from the Rebellion of 1837 headed for display at Fort York," *Antique Showcase* (September, 1987), p. 15. Frank Norman Walker, *Sketches of Old Toronto* (Toronto: Longmans Canada Limited, 1965), p. 128, quoting Henry Rowsell diary, 24 and 28 Oct. 1835.

11. For her inheritance, see David B. Read, *The Lives of the Judges of Upper Canada and Ontario from 1791 to the Present Time* (1888; reprint, Holmes Beach, Florida: Wm. W. Gaunt and Sons, Inc., 1995), p. 221. Quote from "Tory Factionalism" in *S. F. Wise: God's Peculiar Peoples: Essays on Political Culture in Nineteenth-Centu ry Canada*, eds. A. B. McKillop and Paul Romney (Ottawa: Carleton University Press, 1993), p. 93, citing John Beverley Robinson (Sr.) to John Macaulay, 25 Nov. 1810, Macaulay Papers, AO.

12. Plot summaries based on *The Concise Oxford Dictionary of Opera*, 1ˢᵗ ed. (1977 reprint) (hereafter CODO) and/or the edition of the music noted in the bibliography. See Appendix 1: "Lyrics of Mrs. Widder's Program."

CHAPTER ONE

1. Pirkko Moisala, "Musical Gender in Performance", *Women and Music*, Vol. 3 (1999), 13.

2. Christopher Small, "Musicking: A Ritual in Social Space" (lecture at University of Melbourne, 6 June 1995), <http://www.musekids.org/musicking.html,> (4 June 2003), p. 4; John Shepherd, *Music as Social Text* (Cambridge: Polity Press, 1991), pp. 176, 13.

3. Gerda Lerner, *Why History Matters: Life and Thought* (New York: Oxford University Press, 1997), p. 153.

4. Terry Cook, "John Beverley Robinson and the Conservative Blueprint for the Upper Canadian Community" in *Historical Essays on Upper Canada*, ed. J. K. Johnson (Toronto: McClelland and Stewart Limited, 1975), p. 339.

5. J. M. S. Careless, *Toronto to 1918: An Illustrated History* (Toronto: J. Lorimer and Co., 1984); *S. F. Wise: God's Peculiar Peoples: Essays on Political Culture in Nineteenth-Century Canada*, eds. A. B. McKillop and Paul Romney (Ottawa: Carleton University Press, 1993); Paul G. Cornell, " The Genesis of Ontario Politics in the Province of Canada (1838-1871)" in *Profiles of a Province: Studies in the history of Ontario*, ed. Edith Firth (Toronto: Ontario Historical Society, 1967); George Metcalf, "William Henry Draper" in *The Pre-Confederation Premiers: Ontario Government Leaders, 1841-1867*, ed. J.M.S. Careless (Toronto: University of Toronto Press, 1980); Lillian F. Gates, *Land Policies of Upper Canada* (Toronto: University of Toronto Press, 1968); Edith Firth, ed., *The Town of York 1815-34* (Toronto: Champlain Society, vol. 6, Ontario Series, 1966); J. K. Johnson, ed., *Historical Essays on Upper Canada* (Toronto: McClelland and Stewart Limited, 1975); Frederick H. Armstrong, *Handbook of Upper Canadian Chronology* (Toronto and London: Dundurn Press, 1985).

6. A. B. McKillop, *Matters of Mind: the University in Ontario 1791-1951* (Toronto: University of Toronto Press, 1994); William Westfall, *The Founding Moment: Church, Society, and the Construction of Trinity College* (Montreal & Kingston: McGill-Queen's University Press, 2002).

7. Katherine McKenna, *A Life of Propriety: Anne Murray Powell and Her Family, 1755-1849* (Montreal & Kingston: McGill-Queen's University Press, 1994); Elizabeth Jane Errington, *Wives and mothers, schoolmistresses and scullery maids: working women in Upper Canada, 1790-1840* (Montreal & Kingston, London, Buffalo: McGill-Queen's University Press,1995); Cecilia Morgan, *Public Men and Virtuous Women; the Gendered Languages of Religion and Politics in Upper Canada, 1791-1850* (Toronto: University of Toronto Press,1996).

8. Careless, *Illustrated History*, p. 75.

9. Firth, *The Town of York 1815-34*, pp. lxxxii - lxxxiii. Firth refers to "musical evenings," but does not specify glee clubs or soirées musicales.

10. William Weber, *Music and the Middle Class: The Social Structure of Concert life in London, Paris and Vienna* (New York: Holmes & Meier Publishers, Inc., 1975), pp. 37, 31.

11. Weber, *Music*, pp. 19-20; Derek Scott, *The Singing Bourgeois: Songs of the Victorian Drawing Room and Parlour* (Milton Keynes: Open University Press, 1989), p. 45.

12. Weber, *Music*, p. 19; Michael Broyles, *Music of the Highest Class* (New Haven: Yale University Press, 1992); Paul Di Maggio, "Cultural Entrepreneurship in Nineteenth-Century Boston: The Creation of an Organizational Base for High Culture in America," in *Rethinking Popular Culture: Contemporary Perspectives in Cultural Studies*, eds. Chandra Mukerji and Michael Schudson (Berkeley: University of California Press, 1991, pp. 374-397.

13. James Parakilas, ed., *Piano Roles; Three Hundred Years of Life with the Piano* (New Haven, Conn.: Yale University Press, 1999), pp. 5-6.

14. Neil McKendrick, John Brewer, and J. H. Plumb, *The Birth of a Consumer Society: The Commercialization of Eighteenth-century England* (London: Europa Publications Limited, 1982), pp. 16, 33.

15. Cyril Ehrlich, *The Music Profession in Britain Since the Eighteenth Century: A Social History* (Oxford: Clarendon Press, 1985), pp. 112, 22, 36, 41.

16. Scott, *Singing Bourgeois*, p. 127.

17. Wm. McDonnell, "See the Dawn of the Fair Bright Morning" (Toronto: Strange & Co., 1884). "Dedicated to the Hon. John Beverly Robinson, Lieutenant Governor of the Province of Ontario," on cover.

18. Scott, *Singing Bourgeois*, pp. 57, 121.

19. Weber, *Music*, p. 124.

20. Eva Öhrstrom, *Borgerliga kvinnors musicerande i 1800-talets Sverige* (Göteborg: Studies from Gothenburg University, 1987), pp. 193, 196. There is an eight-page English language abstract. For the dissenting view that Andrée's career was an important "example and influence," see Pirkko Moisala, review of *Elfrida Andrée Eett Levnadsode* [Elfrida Andrée: A Life Destiny], by Eva Öhrstrom, *Women and Music*, vol. 5 (2001), 146-8.

21. Richard Leppert, *Music and Image: Domesticity, Ideology and Socio-cultural Formation in Eighteenth-century England* (Cambridge: Cambridge University Press, 1988), p. 162, 29.

22. Leonore Davidoff, *The Best Circles - Society Etiquette and the Season* (London: Croom Helm Ltd., 1973), p. 16.

23. Moisala, *Women and Music*, vol. 3 (1999), 8.

24. George P. Upton, *Woman in Music*, 4th ed. (Chicago: A.C. McClurg and Co., 1886), p. 31, quoted in Margaret William McCarthy, *Amy Fay: America's Notable Woman of Music* (Michigan: Harmonie Park Press, 1995), p. 102.

25. Leonore Davidoff and Catherine Hall, *Family Fortunes: Men and Women of the English Middle Class, 1780-1850* (Chicago: University of Chicago Press, 1987). Deborah Gorham, *The Victorian Girl and the Feminine Ideal* (Bloomington: Indiana University Press, 1982), p. 12.

26. Jann Pasler, "The Ironies of Gender or Virility and Politics in the Music of Augusta Holmès" *Women & Music: a Journal of Gender and Culture*, vol. 2, 1998), 19; Karin Pendle, *Women and Music; a History*, 2nd edition (Bloomington, Ind.: Indiana University Press, 2001).

27. Leppert, *Music and Image*, pp. 28-9.

28. Gorham, *Victorian Girl*, p. 38.

29. Davidoff, *Best Circles*, p. 92.

30. *The Musical Times and Singing Class Circular*, 1, No. 4 (1 Sept. 1844), p. 42. This was a marketing publication by Orpheus Publications, Little Heath, England.

31. Morgan, *Public Men and Virtuous Women*, pp. 210-212.

32. McKenna, *A Life of Propriety*, pp. 13-14.

33. Nancy B. Reich, "Women as Musicians: A Question of Class" in *Musicology and Difference: Gender and Sexuality in Music Scholarship*, ed. Ruth A. Solie (Berkeley: University of California Press, 1993), pp. 125-6. Cf., Ann V. Beedell, *The Decline of the English Musician 1788-1888: A Family of English Musicians in Ireland, England, Mauritius, and Australia* (Oxford: Clarendon Press, 1992), p. 298.

34. Beedell, *Decline*, p. 127.

35. Marilynn J. Smiley, "Across Lake Ontario: Nineteenth-Century Concerts and Connections" in *Taking a Stand: Essays in Honour of John Beckwith*, ed. Timothy J. McGee (Toronto: University of Toronto Press, 1995), p. 152. Beedell's example is the London Royal Academy of Music, but women's training in music at all institutions was restricted.

36. Reich, "A Question," pp.126-134.

37. Natalie Zemon Davis, *Women on the Margins: Three 17ᵗʰ Century Lives* (Cambridge, Mass: Harvard University Press, 1995), p. 207.

38. Small, "Musicking," p. 2.

39. Helmut Kallmann, *A History of Music in Canada 1534-1914* (Toronto: University of Toronto Press, 1960; reprint 1987), p. 5.

40. Helmut Kallmann, Gilles Potvin, and Kenneth Winters, eds., *Encyclopaedia of Music in Canada* (Toronto: University of Toronto Press, 1981) (hereafter EMC).

41. Kallmann, *History*, p. 109.

42. Mary Vipond, *The Mass Media in Canada Second Edition* (Toronto: James Lorimer & Company, Publishers, 1992), p. 188.

43. Kallmann, *History*, p. 171.

44. Examples are: Arthur Loesser, *Men, Women and Pianos* (New York: Simon and Schuster, 1954); and John Shepherd, *Music as Social Text* (Cambridge: Polity Press, 1991). Gender studies also fuelled the change. See Elizabeth Wood,"Women in Music: A Review Essay," *Signs* 6, no. 2 (Winter,1980), 283-97; and Ruth Solie, "Defining Feminism: Conundrums, Contexts, Communities," *Women & Music: A Journal of Gender and Cuture* vol.1 (1997), 1-11.

45. David John Sale, "Toronto's pre-confederation music societies, 1845-1867" (M.Mus. thesis, University of Toronto, 1968) (hereafter Sale).

46. Wayne Kelly, *Downright Upright* (Toronto: Natural Heritage/Natural History Inc.,1991); Gaynor Jones,"The Fisher Years: the Toronto Conservatory of Music, 1886-1913," in *CanMus Documents, 4: Three Studies*, ed. John Beckwith (Toronto: Institute for Canadian Music, 1989), 59-146; and Dorith Cooper, "Opera in Montreal and Toronto; a study of performance traditions and repertoire, 1783-1890"(Ph.D. diss., University of Toronto, 1983).

47. Michael Rudman, "James Dodsley Humphreys: A Look at Musical Life in Mid-Nineteenth Century Toronto," *The York Pioneer*, 96 (2001), 8-25.

48. Phyllis Rose, *Parallel Lives: Five Victorian Marriages* (New York: Knopf, 1983), p. 6.

CHAPTER TWO

1. Cecilia Morgan, *Public Men and Virtuous Women; the Gendered Languages of Religion and Politics in Upper Canada, 1791-1850* (Toronto: University of Toronto Press,1996), p. 188.

2. John Shepherd, *Music as Social Text* (Cambridge: Polity Press, 1991), p. 189.

3. William Weber, "Review of Salons, Singers and Songs: A Background to Romantic French Song, 1830-1870, by David Tunley," H-France, (November 2002). <http://www3.uakron.edu/hfrance/reviews/weber2.html> (21 Nov. 2002); Jeremy Dibble, "Edward Dannreuther and the Orme Square Phenomenon," in *Music and British Culture, 1785-1914: Essays in Honour of Cyril Ehrlich*, eds. Christina Bashford and Leanne Langley (Oxford: Oxford University Press, 2000), pp. 275-298; William Weber, "Miscellany vs. Homogeneity: Concert Programmes at the Royal Academy of Music and the Royal College of Music in the 1880s" in *ibid.*, pp. 299-320; and Shepherd, *Music as Social Text*, pp. 189-197.

4. Private Collection, "Royal Academy of Music 1848: A list of pupils received into the Academy since its foundation in 1822-23," (London: Royal Academy of Music, 1848), p. 56.

5. For plot summaries, CODO. Also see Appendix 1: "Lyrics of Mrs. Widder's Program."

6. TU, 97-003/1/1, Hagerman to John Beverley Robinson (Sr.), London, 13 May 1833.

7. J. MacKay Hitsman, *Safeguarding Canada, 1763-1871* (Toronto: University of Toronto Press, 1968), p. 144; S. F. Wise, "Upper Canada and the Conservative Tradition,"in *S. F. Wise: God's Peculiar Peoples: Essays on Political Culture in Nineteenth-Century Canada*, eds. A. B. McKillop and Paul Romney (Ottawa: Carleton University Press, 1993), p. 169.

8. Aliquis [John Strachan], *Observations on the history and recent proceedings of the Canada Company; addressed in four letters to Frederick Widder, esq., one of the commissioners* (Hamilton: [no publisher], 1845), p. 43.

9. Paul G. Cornell, "The Genesis of Ontario Politics in the Province of Canada (1838-1871)," in *Profiles of a Province: Studies in the History of Ontario*, ed. Edith G. Firth (Toronto: Ontario Historical Society, 1967), p. 62.

10. Herbert Wood, *A Brief History of the King's Royal Rifle Corps, 1755 to 1948*, third edition, (Aldershot: Gale and Polden Limited, 1948), p. 9. DCB, s.v. "Rottenburg, Baron Francis de."

11. James Milne, "The Development of Canadian Military Bands after the Militia Act of 1855," unpublished manuscript for *Traditions and Customs of the Canadian Forces* (Ottawa: Department of National Defence, Directorate of History and Heritage), p. 74.

12. Major-General J.F.C. Fuller, "Sir John Moore's Light Infantry Instructions of 1798-1799," *Army Historical Research*, vol. 30 (1952), p. 68.

13. Major-General J. F. C. Fuller, "Letters of Major-General Sir John Moore, K. B.,"*Army Historical Research*, vol. 12 (1933), p. 185. DCB, s.v. "Wells, Joseph."

14. Private Collection, J. W. Beatty to Miss Humphreys, Toronto, 1 May 1912, states that Miss Humphreys' grandfather, James Dodsley Humphreys, had "arranged the concert" on 19 Dec. 1851.

15. Lillian F. Gates, *Land Policies of Upper Canada* (Toronto: University of Toronto Press, 1968), p. 196; Gerald M. Craig, *Upper Canada: The Formative Years, 1784-1841* (Toronto: McClelland and Stewart Limited, 1963), pp. 27, 34-5.

16. Gates, *Land Policies*, p. 291.

17. AO, Merritt Papers, Lands Package #30, Frederick Widder to Dr. Ripley, Secretary of the Anglican Church Society, Toronto [copies to Rev. Richard Innis, President of the Wesleyan Methodist Church, Picton; Rev. Dr. Cook, Moderator of the Scotch Church, Quebec; and the Catholic Bishop of Toronto, Toronto], Toronto, 18 Nov. 1844. Enclosed as a copy with letter to William Hamilton Merritt.

18. Cf., A. B. McKillop, *Matters of Mind: The University in Ontario, 1791-1951* (Toronto: University of Toronto Press, 1994), p. 9.

19. George Metcalf, "William Henry Draper" in *The Pre-Confederation Premiers: Ontario Government Leaders, 1841-1867*, ed. J.M.S. Careless (Toronto: University of Toronto Press, 1980), pp. 32-88.

20. *The Banner* (Toronto), 8 Mar., 1844, p. 39.

21. Metcalf, "William Henry Draper," p. 39.

22. William Westfall, *The Founding Moment: Church, Society, and the Construction of Trinity College* (Montreal & Kingston: McGill-Queen's University Press, 2002), pp. 76-7.

23. McKillop, *Matters of Mind*, p. 10. Cf., Robert J. Burns, "The First Elite of Toronto: An Examination of the Genesis, Consolidation and Duration of Power in an Emerging Colonial Society" (Ph.D. diss., University of Western Ontario, 1974), pp. 14-5.

24. TU, 94-016/1/1, Hagerman to Strachan, London, England,16 Nov. 1833.

25. Michael J. Rudman, "James Dodsley Humphreys: A Look at Musical Life in Mid-Nineteenth Century Toronto," *The York Pioneer*, 96 (2001), 24.

26. Frederick Widder to William Merritt, Toronto, 21 Nov. 1844, (emphasis is Widder's), see n. 22 above,

27. Hugh G. J. Aitken, "The Family Compact: A Force for Progress?" in *The Family Compact: Aristocracy or Oligarchy?* ed. David W. L. Earl (Toronto: The Copp Clark Publishing Company, 1967), p. 66.

28. Widder to Merritt, 21 Nov. 1844, see n. 22, above.

29. Widder to Dr. Ripley, see n. 22, above.

30. Aliquis, *passim*.

31. *Ibid.*, pp. 5, 7.

32. For the poem , see Carola May A. Omana, *Sir John Moore* (London: Hodder & Stoughton, 1953), p. v. For Harriett Abrams (ca. 1758-1822), see Susan Levin, "The Gipsy Is a Jewess: Harriet Abrams and Theatrical Romanticism," in *Romantic Women Writers: Voices and Countervoices*, eds. Paula R. Feldman and Theresa M. Kelley (Hanover, NH: University Press of New England, 1995), pp. 236-51.

33. Metcalf, "William Henry Draper," p. 38.

34. *The British Colonist*, Tuesday, 5 Mar. 1844.

35. *The Globe*, Tuesday, 9 July 1844, p. 4.

36. E.g., NLC Music, Binder's Album #22, "Prayer: from Moïse in Egitto;" #103, "Marche de Norma" arr. Bergmüller.

37. David John Sale, "Toronto's pre-confederation music societies, 1845-1867" (M. Mus. thesis, University of Toronto, 1968) (hereafter Sale), p. 79.

38. For Miss Hagerman and both Robinsons, see TU, 94-016/3/1, "Cards left on JBR and self while in England 1854," including cards from Mr. H. Schallehn, Professor of Singing, and the Countess Dowager of Glasgow. Schallehn lived in Toronto from 1847-1851, working as violinist, clarinetist, military band conductor, composer, and teacher of singing. See EMC, s.v. "Schallehn, Henry." The EMC entry suggests that the conductor of the Crystal Palace band in England in 1854 was the same Henry Schallehn of Toronto, a possibility corroborated by the card left on Mrs. Robinson in 1854.

39. F. Henry Johnson, "A Colonial Canadian in Search of a Museum," *Queen's Quarterly* 77, no. 2 (1970), p. 230, citing Egerton Ryerson, *The Story of My Life*, ed. J. G. Hodgins (Toronto: Briggs, 1883), pp. 366-7.

40. "Miss Dickens' Soiree Musicale," review of concert, at Royal Academy of Music, *Times* (London), 30 May 1835 (issue 15804), p. 5 col. C.

41. William Weber, *Music and the Middle Class: The Social Structure of Concert life in London, Paris and Vienna* (New York: Holmes & Meier Publishers, Inc., 1975),p. 31. Weber does not specify the professional or amateur status of the performers at the Soirées Musicales he describes as fashionable. For For Adolfo Ferrari (1807-1870) and Thompson, see *The New Grove Dictionary of Music and Musicians*, 2nd ed. (hereafter *New Grove*), s.v. "Ferrari, Giacomo Gotifredo. For Bennett, *ibid.*, s.v. "Bennett, Sterndale." For Regondi, who worked with the composer Blagrove, see International Guitar Research Archives, California Station University, Northridge, Department of Music, n.d., <http://www.csun.edu/~igra/bios/text/regondi.html> (10 May 2003). For Chardonnay, British Library, Add 45723, Letters and Papers Concerning the School at Penn, f. 39.

42. Schubert translation from Franz Schubert, "The Wanderer," arr., trans., F. W. Rosier (Boston: Geo. P. Reed, 17 Tremont Row, n.d.); for Costa quartet, see <http://www.door.library.uiuc.edu/sousa/band-a-f.htm>, (5 Apr. 2003); for Mercadante aria, see synopsis of opera *Il giuramento* at <http://www.opera.stanford.edu/Mercadante/Giuramento/synopsis.html>, (5 Apr. 2003).

43. For Miss Sandeman's age, see Paul Dobree, 1 Mar. 2003, <http://www.careyroots.com/PS03/PS03_371.htm>, (1 July 2003), s.v. "Helen Sandeman." Site states that Helen Jane Sandeman, 1831-1900, resided at 15, Hyde Park Gardens, married a Vicar in 1862, aged 31.

44. Cyril Ehrlich, *The Music Profession in Britain since the Eighteenth Century: A Social History* (Oxford: Clarendon Press, 1985), p. 41.

45. *New Grove*, s.v. "Spohr, Louis."

46. Rudman, *The York Pioneer* 96 (2001), p. 8.

47. John King, *McCaul, Croft, and Forineri: Personalities of Early University Days* (Toronto: The Macmillan Company of Canada, 1914), p. 100.

48. McKillop, *Matters of Mind*, p. 104.

49. Private Collection, J. W. Beatty to Miss Humphreys, Toronto, 1 May 1912, states that Miss Humphreys' grandfather, James Dodsley Humphreys, had "arranged the concert" on 19 Dec. 1851.

50. Anon., *Party Giving on Every Scale* (London: F. Warren and Co., c. 1890), p. 39. This etiquette book advised that a "really taking programme ... includes the newest things of the hour." Weber, *Music and the Middle Class*, p. 41.

CHAPTER THREE

1. Nancy B. Reich, "Women as Musicians: A Question of Class" in *Musicology and Difference: Gender and Sexuality in Music Scholarship*, ed. Ruth A. Solie (Berkeley: University of California Press, 1993), p. 125.

2. Roderick Hamilton Burgoyne, ed., *Historical Records of the 93rd Sutherland Highlanders, now the 2nd Battalion Princess Louise's Argyle and Sutherland Highlanders* (London: Richard Bentley and Son, 1883), p. 76.

3. Elinor Kyte Senior, *British Regulars in Montreal: An Imperial Garrison, 1832-1854* (Montreal: McGill-Queen's University Press, 1981), p. 173.

4. Susan Levin, "The Gipsy Is a Jewess: Harriet Abrams and Theatrical Romanticism," in *Romantic Women Writers: Voices and Countervoices*, eds. Paula R. Feldman and Theresa M. Kelley (Hanover, NH: University Press of New England, 1995), p. 242. For waiving fees, see Cyril Ehrlich, *The Music Profession in Britain since the Eighteenth Century: A Social History* (Oxford: Clarendon Press, 1985), pp. 40-1.

5. Ann V. Beedell, *The Decline of the English Musician 1788-1888: A Family of English Musicians in Ireland, England, Mauritius, and Australia* (Oxford: Clarendon Press, 1992), pp. 299-304.

6. Michael Rudman, "James Dodsley Humphreys (1810-1877), an annotated chronology (provisional form)," (photocopy, 1985), p. 2. My thanks to Mr. Rudman for his generosity in sharing his unpublished material.

7. Michael Rudman, "James Dodsley Humphreys: A Look at Musical Life in Mid-Nineteenth Century Toronto," *The York Pioneer*, 96 (2001), 9-10.

8. Henry Haycraft, "Thy bonnie Blue E'en," (Toronto: Haycraft Small & Addison, 1856). For scholarliness as a music marketing device, see Leanne Langley, "Sainsbury's Dictionary, the Royal Academy of Music, and the Rhetoric of Patriotism," in *Music and British Culture, 1785-1914: Essays in Honour of Cyril Ehrlich*, eds. Christina Bashford and Leanne Langley (Oxford: Oxford University Press, 2000).

9. David John Sale, "Toronto's pre-confederation music societies, 1845-1867" (M. Mus. thesis, University of Toronto, 1968) (hereafter Sale.), p. 353; EMC, s.v. "Humphreys, James Dodsley."

10. Private Collection, Caroline Humphreys to James Humphreys, April, 1857.

11. Beedell, *Decline*, p. 305; *The Globe*, Tuesday, 9 July 1844, p. 4. For Nordheimer credit report, see Ohio, Vol. 3, p. 29, R.G. Dun & Co. Collection, Baker Library, Harvard Business School.

12. Private Collection. This note is signed "Mary Robinson," but is written in Mary Jane Hagerman's handwriting, as found in AO, MS 787 r. 2 (Jarvis-Powell Papers). Minnie Hagerman to Samuel P. Jarvis, (Jr.), Toronto, 10 Feb. 1845. Miss Hagerman became Mrs. Robinson when she married in 1847. Since the only known Humphreys dedication to her was printed as "to Miss Hagerman" in 1843, there may be another Humphreys song so far unknown.

13. NLC Music, Binder's Album #42.

14. Henry Martin, "Sweet Madeline" (Toronto and Montreal: A. & S. Nordheimer [sic], 1867). Cover printing includes "sung by Mrs. J. Beverley Robinson."

15. Rudman, *The York Pioneer*, 96 (2001), 25; Cf., Beedell, *Decline*, p. 299.

16. Ehrlich, *Profession*, p. 48; EMC, s.v. "Holman," "Paige;" Private Collection, "Royal Academy of Music 1848: A list of pupils received into the Academy since its foundation in 1822-23," (London: Royal Academy of Music, 1848), pp. 31, 56.

17. Reich, "A Question," pp. 126-33; Richard Leppert, *Music and Image: Domesticity, Ideology and Socio-cultu ral Formation in Eighteenth-century England* (Cambridge: Cambridge University Press, 1988), p. 66; Ehrlich, *Profession*, p. 42.

18. Leonore Davidoff, *The Best Circles - Society Etiquette and the Season* (London: Croom Helm Ltd., 1973), p. 53. For letter quotes, see AO, Col. Lucas Colley Foster Fonds, MU1507/3 of Correspondence, Caroline Amelia Humphreys to Ellen Foster, Queenston , 15 Sept. 1842 (emphasis in original) and Private Collection, Caroline Amelia Ridout Humphreys to James Dodsley Humphreys, probably April, 1857.

19. Beedell, *Decline*, pp. 123, 120.

20. Helmut Kallman, *A History of Music in Canada 1534-1914* (Toronto: University of Toronto Press, 1987), p. 118, based on the 1851-2 census in Upper Canada.

21. Ehrlich, *Profession*, pp. 71-2.

22. Leppert, *Music and Image*, passim.

23. Gloria T. Delamar, *Rounds Re-sounding: Circular Music for Voices and Instruments: an Eight-century Reference* (Jefferson, North Carolina, and London: McFarland & Company, Inc., 1987), pp. 5-7.

24. Edward F. Rimbault, ed., *The Rounds, Catches and Canons of England: A Collection of Specimens of the sixteenth, seventeenth and eighteenth centuries, adapted to modern use* (c. 1875; reprint, New York: Da Capo Press, 1976), p. xxx.

25. Delamar, *Re-Sounding*, p. 7; Rimbault, *Rounds*, p. vii; William Alexander Barrett, *English glees and part-songs, an inquiry into their historical development* (London: Longmans, Green, and Co., 1886), p. 350.

26. Delamar, *Re-sounding*, p. 7.

27. William Weber, *Music and the Middle Class: The Social Structure of Concert life in London, Paris and Vienna* (New York: Holmes & Meier Publishers, Inc., 1975), p. 39.

28. Joseph Philip Knight, "Give me the night" (Philadelphia: John F. Nunns 70 S. Third St., n.d.), Private Collection, Humphreys' daughter's music album. See Appendix 1: "Lyrics of Mrs. Widder's Program."

29. Rimbault, *Rounds*, p. vii.

30. Lawrence Kramer, "*Carnaval*, Cross-Dressing, and the Woman in the Mirror," in *Musicology and Difference: Gender and Sexuality in Music Scholarship*, ed. Ruth A. Solie (Berkeley: University of California Press, 1993), p. 307.

31. AO, Colonel Lucas Colley Foster Fonds, MU1507/Correspondence/3, Charles Harrison to Ellen [Humphreys] Foster, Toronto, 5 Mar. 1844. See n. 1, "Overture," above.

32. Egerton Ryerson writing about the Widders in 1863 stated that, "they will deprecate ... any thing in which they know they cannot excel in themselves." C. B. Sissons, ed., *My Dearest Sophie: Letters from Egerton Ryerson to his daughter* (Toronto: The Ryerson Press, 1955), p. 49.

33. Katherine McKenna, *A Life of Propriety: Anne Murray Powell and Her Family, 1755-1849* (Montreal & Kingston: McGill-Queen's University Press, 1994), p. 62.

34. TU, 97-003/3/5, Minnie Forsyth Grant, "Old Time Politics and Elections" (typescript, Nov. 1917), p. 1. Mrs. Grant was the daughter of Mrs. Robinson (née Hagerman).

35. Peter J. Ward, *Courtship, love and marriage in nineteenth-century English Canada* (Montreal: McGill-Queen's University Press, 1990), p. 69; Lucy Booth Martyn, *The Face of Early Toronto: an Archival Record 1797-1930* (Sutton West & Santa Barbara: The Paget Press, 1982), p. 158 .

CHAPTER FOUR

1. Richard Leppert, *The Sight of Sound: Music, Representation, and the History of the Body* (University of California Press, 1995), p. 67, quoting anon. English pamphlet, c. 1778.

2. Natalie Luckyj, *Helen Galloway McNicoll: A Canadian Impressionist* (Toronto: Art Gallery of Ontario, 1999), p. 19.

3. Margaret William McCarthy, *Amy Fay: America's Notable Woman of Music* (Michigan: Harmonie Park Press, 1995), p. 15.

4. W. W. Bailey (text), Lamoureux [sic] (image), "The Music Lesson," *The Aldine Magazine: The Art Journal of America*, vol VII, no. 20 (1874-5), p. 391.

5. Editorial, *The Musical Times and Singing Class Circular* (London, England), 1 Dec. 1844, p. 55.

6. For all references to the Widder program, see Appendix 1: "Lyrics of Mrs. Widder's Program."

7. Derek Scott, *The Singing Bourgeois: Songs of the Victorian Drawing Room and Parlour* (Milton Keynes: Open University Press, 1989), p. 103, quoting M. W. Disher, *Victorian Song* (London: Phoenix House, 1955), p. 144.

8. Scott, *Singing Bourgeois*, p. 105. Cf., Ronald Pearsall, *Victorian Popular Music* (Detroit, MI: Gale Record Company, 1976), p. 48.

9. James Parakilas and Gretchen A. Wheelock, "1770s to 1820s: The Piano Revolution in the Age of Revolutions," in *Piano Roles; Three Hundred Years of Life with the Piano*, ed. James Parakilas (New Haven, Conn.: Yale University Press, 1999), p. 87.

10. EMC, s.v. "Nordheimer, A. & S. Co."

11. Richard Leppert, *Music and Image: Domesticity, Ideology and Socio-cultural Formation in Eighteenth-century England* (Cambridge: Cambridge University Press, 1988), p. 40.

12. Scott, *Singing Bourgeois*, p. 77.

13. Frances Roback, "Advertising Canadian Pianos and Organs, 1850-1919," *Material History Bulletin* 20 (Autumn 1984), 38.

14. *The Musical Times and Singing Class Circular* (London, England), 1 Nov. 1844, p. 30.

15. Scott, *Singing Bourgeois*, p. 53.

16. Deborah Gorham, *The Victorian Girl and the Feminine Ideal* (Bloomington: Indiana University Press, 1982), pp. 6, 37.

17. AO, Sarah Murray Collection, F 1129, MU3033/1 Northwold Soirée Musicale Program, 1885; Spadina Museum Collection, Culture Division, City of Toronto, Llawbaden Soirée Musicale program, 1907; Hahn Family Collection, Benvenuto Soirée Musicale program, 1910.

18. Booth Martyn, *100 Years*, p. 102.

19. AO, MS 787 r. 2 (Jarvis-Powell Papers). S. P. Jarvis to Mary Jarvis, Kingston, 23 Mar. 1843, and Mary Jarvis to S. P. Jarvis, Toronto, 10 Apr. 1843.

20. Robin S. Harris and Terry G. Harris, eds., *The Eldon House Diaries*, p. 170, 13 Sept. 1860. For Blanche Widder/Edward Harris/Sophia Ryerson, see 1859-60 entries (*ibid.*, pp. 133-5).

21. Gorham, *Victorian Girl*, p. 37; Richard Leppert, *Sight of Sound*, p. 67.

22. NLCMusic, Binder's Album #121, Valtoline, "The Musical Husband" (Boston: Oliver Ditson, 1842).

23. F. Simm, "An Amateur Concert," in *The Music of the Modern World, Illustrated in the lives and works of the greatest modern musicians and in reproductions of famous paintings etc.* vol. II, eds. Anton Seidl, Fanny Morris Smith, and H. E. Krehbiel (New York: D. Appleton and Company, 1895), p. 289, National Library of Canada, e002283002.

24. Charles Osborne, *The Bel Canto Operas of Rossini, Donizetti, and Bellini* (Portland, Oregon: Amadeus Press, 1994), pp. 344-6.

25. John Shepherd, "Difference and Power in Music," in *Musicology and Difference: Gender and Sexuality in Music Scholarship*, ed. Ruth A. Solie (Berkeley: University of California Press, 1993), p. 53.

26. John Shepherd, *Music as Social Text* (Cambridge: Polity Press, 1991), p. 176.

27. Carolyn Abbate, "Opera; or, the Envoicing of Women," in *Musicology and Difference: Gender and Sexuality in Music Scholarship*, ed. Ruth A. Solie (Berkeley: University of California Press, 1993), pp. 256, 235-6, 254.

28. AGO, SCA4-5-1, Marble Scrapbook, unidentified clipping.

29. AGO Bagnani SCA4-5-1 Marble Scrapbook, unidentified newspaper clipping, inscribed in ink, "January 11, 1860."

CHAPTER FIVE

1. TU, 97-003/17/1, Stewart Bagnani to Professor O'Brian, 17 July 1969.

2. Nancy B. Reich, "Women as Musicians: A Question of Class," in *Musicology and Difference: Gender and Sexuality in Music Scholarship*, ed. Ruth A. Solie (Berkeley: University of California Press, 1993), p. 132.

3. TU, 97-003/3/5, M. Forsyth Grant, "Old Time Politics and Elections," (typescript labelled 'Canadian Magazine,' Nov. 1917), p. 3.

4. Buffalo Public Library, *Buffalo Morning Express*, 6 Mar. 1852.

5. TU, 97-003/2/4, Stewart Bagnani, ed., "My Aunt Minnie," (typescript introduction to Minnie Beverley Robinson Diary, 1874 and 1876, n.d.), p. 36.

6. DCB, s. v. "Robinson, John Beverley."

7. TU, 97-003/1/1, Christopher Hagerman to Mary Jane Hagerman, Upper Canada, 10 Sept. 1832.

8. TU, 97-003/2/4, Bagnani, "My Aunt," p. 62.

9. Carolyn G. Heilbrun, *Writing a Woman's Life* (New York: W. W. Norton & Company, 1988), p. 70.

10. David B. Read, *The Lives of the Judges of Upper Canada and Ontario from 1791 to the Present Time* (1888; reprint, Holmes Beach, Fla.: Wm. W. Gaunt & Sons, Inc., 1995), p. 212.

11. J. Dodsley Humphreys, "When We Two Parted" (New York: John F. Nunns, 1843). See Mrs. W. Forsyth Grant, "Bygone Days in Toronto," *The Canadian Magazine* (January, 1914), p. 5.

12. David John Sale, "Toronto's pre-confederation music societies, 1845-1867" (M. Mus. thesis, University of Toronto, 1968) (hereafter Sale), p. 79.

13. *Ibid.*, p. 100.

14. *Ibid.*, p. 8, citing *British Colonist* 29 Dec. 1848, p. 2.

15. See n. 4, above.

16. Metropolitan Toronto Reference Library, Baldwin Room, Larratt Smith Papers S102, Larratt Smith, "Diary: November 1842 – April 1844," (typed transcript by Mary Goldie), 1 Mar. 1844, p. 360.

17. Julia Jarvis, *Three Centuries of Robinsons* (Don Mills, Ontario: T. H. Best Printing Company Limited, 1967), p. 174.

18. TU, 97-003/17/1, Stewart Bagnani to Professor O'Brian, Toronto, 17 July 1969; TU, 97-003/1/4, Mrs. Robinson to "My sweet pet," [daughter?], discusses friendship with Jarvises.

19. Reich, "A Question," p. 132.

20. Sale, pp. 117-8, 127.

21. AGO, SCA4-5-1 Marble Scrapbook, two unidentified newspaper clippings inscribed in ink "1852." Her daughter met Lind in London in the 1890s. See AGO, SCA4-5-1, Marble Scrapbook, "People We Meet" (*Home Journal*, Toronto, n.d.), p. 7, inscribed in ink "November 1895." Joan Bulman, *Jenny Lind: A Biography* (London: James Baril, 1956), pp. 176, 242, 251, 284.

22. Reich, "A Question," p. 132.

23. Frank Norman Walker, *Sketches of Old Toronto* (Toronto: Longmans Canada Limited, 1965), pp. 331, 337.

24. Sale, p. 131.

25. AGO, SCA4-5-1, Marble Scrapbook, unidentified newspaper clipping, "May 4/75" inscribed in ink, states that $803.10 was raised and $867.35 in interest earned (6% per annum), and given to the Hospital for Incurables. *Ibid.*, Clerk of City Council to Mrs. Robinson, Toronto, 7 June 1856.

26. TU, 97-003/1/4, Mrs. Robinson to Augusta Beverley Robinson, 26 Oct. [1890?].

27. AGO, SCA4-5-1, Marble Scrapbook, review of concert performance of Mrs. Robinson, Toronto, *The Globe*, 2 Apr. 1866.

28. AGO, SCA4-5-1, Marble Scrapbook, unidentified second review of same concert.

29. TU, 97-003/2/4 Bagnani, "My Aunt," p. 36.

30. My thanks to Dr. Michael Peterman for drawing my attention to this connection.

31. AGO, SCA4-5-1, Marble Scrapbook, unidentified newspaper clippings.

32. Heilbrun, *Writing*, p. 24.

33. TU, 97-003/1/4, partial list of Mrs. Robinson's repertoire by her husband includes only standard repertoire; corroborated by Sale, Appendix II, pp. 58-311.

34. Leonore Davidoff, *The Best Circles - Society Etiquette and the Season* (London: Croom Helm Ltd., 1973), p. 81.

35. Reich, "A Question," p. 127.

36. Carol Neuls-Bates, ed., *Women in Music; an Anthology of Source Readings from the Middle Ages to the Present* (Boston, Mass.: Northeastern University Press, 1996), p. 136.

37. E.g., David Read, *The Lieutenant-Governors of Upper Canada and Ontario 1792-1899* (Toronto: William Briggs, 1900), p. 224.

38. AGO, SCA4-5-1, Marble Scrapbook, General Sam Jarvis to John Beverley Robinson (Jr.), Bath, 23 July 1892.

39. AGO, SCA4-5-1, Marble Scrapbook, unidentified newspapers, inscribed in ink "1862."

40. AGO, SCA4-5-1, Marble Scrapbook, unidentified newspaper clippings, inscribed in ink "1 June 1861 Quebec."

41. AGO, SCA4-5-1, Marble Scrapbook, unidentified newspaper clipping, [1888?].

42. AGO, SCA4-5-1, Marble Scrapbook, unidentified newspaper clipping; *Ibid*.

43. TU, 97-003/1/4, Mrs. Robinson to Augusta Beverley Robinson, Toronto, 27 Oct. [1891?].

44. TU, 97-003/1/4, Mrs. Robinson to Augusta Beverley Robinson, Toronto, 17 Jan. [1891?].

45. *Ibid*.

46. Seranus [Susan Frances Harrison], "The Prisoner Dubois," in *Crowded Out! And Other Sketches* (Ottawa: The Evening Journal Office, 1886), p. 91.

47. Nina Auerbach, *Ellen Terry: A Player in Her Time* (New York, London: W. W. Norton & Company, 1987), p. 178.

48. Alden G. Meredith, *Mary's Rosedale and Gossip of 'Little York'* (Ottawa: The Graphic Publishers Ltd., 1928), p. 214.

49. AGO, SCA4-5-1, Marble Scrapbook, *The World*, 8 June 1887, p. 98.

50. AGO, SCA4-5-1, Marble Scrapbook. Because this was a family scrapbook, her husband is the probable author.

51. TU, 97-003/3/5, M. Forsyth Grant, "Old Time Politics and Elections" (typescript for *Canadian Magazine*, Nov. 1917), p. 3.

52. TU, 97-003/1/4, Mrs. Robinson to Augusta Beverley Robinson, 17 Jan. [1891].

53. TU, 97-003/1/4, Mrs. Robinson to Augusta Beverley Robinson, 26 or 27 Oct. [1890?].

54. TU, 97-0031/4, Mrs. Robinson to Augusta, Beverley Robinson, 17 Jan. [1891?]. Of the possible years for which 17 Jan. fits the sequence of events in these letters, 1891 is the most likely. Sir John A. Macdonald died in June, 1891, as Prime Minister of Canada. Other documents in the Bagnani collection confirm that Macdonald visited the Robinson home occasionally.

55. TU, 97-003/1/4, Bagnani, "My Aunt," pp. 34 50.

56. Nels Juleus, "Lady Dufferin's Theatricals," *Canadian Drama*, 2 (1985), 245-50. TU, 97-003/4/5, Minnie Forsyth-Grant, "Memories of Government House: Passing of a Famous Social Shrine" (typescript, 27 Apr. 1912).

57. AGO SCA-4-5-1, "Family," Lady Dufferin to Mrs. Robinson, n.d. Lord Dufferin was Governor-General of Canada 1872-78.

58. AGO, SCA4-5-1 Marble Scrapbook, General Sam Jarvis to John Beverley Robinson (Jr.), Bath, 23 July 1892.

59. Reich, "A Question," pp. 134-9.

60. AGO, SCA4-5-1, Marble Scrapbook, "People We Meet" (*Home Journal*, Toronto, n.d.), p. 7, inscribed in ink "November 1895."

ENCORE

1. Lawrence Levine, *Highbrow/Lowbrow: The Emergence of Cultural Hierarchy in America* (Cambridge, Mass.: Harvard University Press, 1988), p. 207.

2. Cecilia Morgan, personal communication, 17 Mar. 2003.

3. AGO, SCA4-5-1, Marble Scrapbook, two unidentified newspaper clippings, inscribed in ink "Oct 1859."

4. David John Sale, "Toronto's pre-confederation music societies, 1845-1867" (M. Mus. thesis, University of Toronto, 1968) (hereafter Sale), Appendix II, "Index of Performers," pp. 311-90.

5. Kandis Cook and Nick Till, <http://www.post-operative.org/product3.html,> n.d., (25 May 2003), p. 1.

6. AO, Sarah Murray Collection, F 1129, MU3033/1, Rolleston House program. Alan Gordon, "Jewish Businessmen in Toronto's Conservative Party, 1911-1921," *Ontario History* 88, no. 1 (1996), p. 33; and Lucy Booth Martyn, *The Face of Early Toronto: an Archival Record 1797-1930* (Sutton West & Santa Barbara: The Paget Press, 1982), p. 158.

7. Cf., Deborah Gorham, *The Victorian Girl and the Feminine Ideal* (Bloomington: Indiana University Press, 1982), p. 24.

8. Spadina Collection, Blue Box: Social-Radio, Env. 2, "Spadina Christmas 1900," and Llawbaden Soirée Musicale Programme, 1907.

9. Spadina Collection, Program for "Spadina Music in the Orchard," 14 June 1998, "Mary Austin," biographical outline, and Mary Bridgeland *et al*, choristers at Bloor Street United Church to Mary Kerr, Toronto, 27 Dec. 1879, poem on her retirement as organist to marry. EMC, s.v. "Robinson, Augusta Beverley."

10. Gorham, *Victorian Girl*, p. 58.

11. Hahn Family Collection, The Fortnightly Musical Club program, 2 Apr. 1898.

12. Robin Elliott, *Counterpoint to a City: The First One Hundred Years of the Women's Musical Club of Toronto* (Toronto: ECW Press, 1997), pp. 47, 76, 50.

13. "Late Mrs. George Dickson," *Saturday Night* 26 Oct. 1940, p. 3, cited in *ibid.*, p. 38.

14. Ramsay Cook and Wendy Mitchinson, eds., *The Proper Sphere: Women's Place in Canadian Society* (Toronto: Oxford UP, 1976), p. 199, cited in *ibid.*, p. 23.

15. *Ibid.*, p. 20.

16. Sale, pp. 317, 387, 362.

17. Rebecca Green, "Gaudeamus igitur: college singing and college songbooks in Canada," in *CanMus Documents*,4, *Three Studies*, ed. John Beckwith (Toronto: Institute for Canadian Music, 1989), p. 3.

18. William Westfall, *The Founding Moment: Church, Society, and the Construction of Trinity College* (Montreal & Kingston: McGill-Queen's University Press, 2002), p. 81.

19. Green, "Gaudeamus," pp. 26, 43, 34; A. B. McKillop, *Matters of Mind; the University in Ontario 1791-1951* (Toronto: University of Toronto Press, 1994), p. 244.

20. Sale, pp. 55-7.

21. *Ibid.*, p. 21.

22. For Cawthra, see Lucy Booth Martyn, *Face of Early Toronto*, p. 58.

23. *Canadian Music & Trades Journal*, 11, no. 2 (Jan. 1901), p. 21.

24. TU, 97-003/1/4, Jacques Blumenthal to Augusta Beverley Robinson, London, 30 Jan. 1893.

25. Maude Valérie White, *Friends and Memories* (London: Edward Arnold, 1914), p. 34. For White as a friend of Augusta Beverley Robinson, see TU, 97-003-1/4, White to Augusta Beverley Robinson, London, n.d. [c. 1890].

26. *The Globe*, 16 and 17 July 1862, p. 3, advertisement.

27. For example, "Grand Soiree Musicale with Miss Julia Hill, unequalled lady pianist, and her father," *The Globe*, 27 Dec. 1856, advertisement; David B. Payne, "Social Music in London, Upper Canada/ Canada West: Establishing a 'sort of colonial nobility'"(M. Mus. thesis, University of Western Ontario, 1998), p. 144; Sale, pp. 146, 113.

28. Sale, p. 202, "Mrs. Marshall and her pupils, Musical Soiree in Aid of the Protestant Orphans' and Boys' Homes," 25 Dec. 1861; *ibid.*, p. 146.

29. Hahn Family Collection, "Recital Given at the Home Of Mrs. Walter Beardmore, 174 Beverley Street" Program, 18 Feb. 1902; Sale, pp. 58-311; EMC, s.v. "Schallehn, Henry."

30. Hahn Family Collection, Benvenuto Soirée Musicale program, 1910. The history of Hahn's role in the Canadian music profession is yet to be written.

31. EMC, s.v. "Hahn, Paul."

32. Wayne Kelly, *Downright Upright* (Toronto: Natural Heritage/Natural History Inc., 1991), p. 83.

33. Toronto Public Library (TRL), Women's Musical Club Collection, Box 5, program.

34. Gaynor Jones, "The Fisher Years: the Toronto Conservatory of Music, 1886-1913," in *Three Studies, CanMus Documents*, 4 (Toronto: Institute for Canadian Music, 1989), p. 125.

35. Hahn Family Collection, "Soiree Musicale by the Jan Hambourg Trio," program, 23 Jan. 1911.

36. Saratoga Soiree Musicale Newsletter, 2 Mar. 1999 <http://www.metroactive.com/papers/saratoga. news/02.03.99/SaratogaSampler.num,> (7 Feb. 2001)

37. "Glimpses into our Past: Fond Memories of the Grand!" *The Standard*, 24 Dec. 1983, p. 8.

38. Elizabeth Finnie, Special Collections Librarian, St. Catharines Library, summary of article from *St. Catharines Standard*, 9 May 1921, personal communication.

Bibliography

Abbreviations

AGO	Art Gallery of Ontario, Archives, Gilbert and Stewart Bagnani Collection
AO	Archives of Ontario
CODO	*The Concise Oxford Dictionary of Opera*, 1st ed. (1977 reprint)
DCB	*Dictionary of Canadian Biography*
EMC	*Encyclopaedia of Music in Canada*, 1981 ed.
NAC	National Archives of Canada
New Grove	*The New Grove Dictionary of Music and Musicians*, 2nd ed.
NLC Music	National Library of Canada, Special Collections, Music Division
TU	Trent University, Stewart and Gilbert Bagnani Fonds

I. PRIMARY SOURCES

A. MANUSCRIPT SOURCES

1. Private Collections

Hahn Family Collection, 1880 - 1930 (Toronto)

Private Collection, 1830 - 1880 (Toronto)

2. Public Collections

Art Gallery of Ontario Archives
Gilbert and Stewart Bagnani Collection

Baker Library, Harvard Business School
Ohio, Vol. 3, R.G. Dun & Co. Collection

British Library
Mrs. Sandeman's Soirée Musicale program, 1849, shelf mark 1572/596

National Library of Canada, Music Division
133 bound music folios and nineteenth-century Ontario sheet music

Public Archives of Ontario
Colley Lyons Lucas Foster Papers, F-891
Jarvis-Powell Papers, MS 787 R2
Merritt Fonds, MS 74 R4
Sarah Murray Collection, F 1129

Queen's University Libraries, W. D. Jordan and Lorne Pierce Special Collections Music
Five bound albums of sheet music

St. Catharines Library, Special Collections, "Grand Opera House Scrapbook"
    Photograph of Opera House Orchestra of St. Catharines

Spadina Museum, City of Toronto
    Music collection of Mary Richmond Kerr Austin and Mary Paul Kerr
    Newspaper clippings

Toronto Public Library (TRL), Special Collections
    Ephemera
    Larratt Smith Papers S102
    John Ross Robertson Collection

Trent University, Archives
    Stewart and Gilbert Bagnani Fonds

University of Toronto, Faculty of Music Library
    Bound albums of sheet music

University of Windsor, Rare Books and Special Collections, University of Windsor Library
    Bound albums of sheet music

A.   MUSIC

Abrams, Harriett. *A Second Sett of Italian and English Canzonetts, for One, Two and Three Voices, with an Accompaniment for the Piano-Forte or Harp, etc.* London: L. Lavenu, for the Author, ca. 1800.

Barnett, John, "Not a Drum was Heard: Written on the Death of Gen'l Sir John Moore," Philadelphia: G. Willig Chestnut Street, n.d.

Bellini, Vincenzo, "Ah forever I now have lost thee," Toronto: A & S. Nordheimer Co., n.d. [1846-50].

_____, "As I view these scenes so charming, sung by Mr. Brough, Air in the celebrated Opera La Sonnambula," New York: H. Hewitt & Co., 230 Broadway, n.d.

_____. *Beatrice di Tenda, tragedia lirica in two acts.* Edited by Philip Gossett, synopsis Laura DeMarco. New York: Garland Pub., 1980.

_____, "Hear Me Norma," arranged by S. Nelson, translated by Ch. Jefferys, New York: James L.Hewitt & Co, 1843.

_____. *I Puritani Di Scozia, an opera in three acts with Italian and English text.* New York: Edwin F. Kalmus.

_____. *La Sonnambula, Melodramma in due atti.* Milan: Ricordi

_____. *Norma, lyric tragedy in two acts.* New York: G. Schirmer.

Bishop, H. R., "The Echo Song." Arranged by V. de Giorgio, in *Paling's Album Series No. 7.* Sydney, Brisbane: W. H. Paling & Co. Limited, 1929, pp. 8-9.

Call, v. L. de [Leonhard von Call], "Komm, stiller Abend," in *Orpheus: Sammlung auserlesener mehrstimmiger Gesaenge, ohne Begleitung.* Braunschweig: In Commision bei F. Busse, [c. 1825], pp. 71-2.

Crouch, F. W. Nichols, "Dermot Astore" New York: Hewitt & Jaques, 239 Broadway, n.d.

De Call [Leonhard von Call], "Silent Evening O'er Us," in *Fogle's Male Quartet and Chorus Book: A Collection of High Grade Music for Men's Voices.* Edited by O.L. Fogle. Cincinnati: Fillmore Music House, 1908, p. 211.

Donizetti, Gaetano, "Ah! Live thou, I do conjure thee! (Vivi tu, te ne scongiuro)," Philadelphia: A. Fiot, 1844.

Glover, Stephen, "The dream is past," New York: Firth Hall & Pond, 239 Broadway and by Firth & Hall 1 Franklin Square, n.d.

Haycraft, Henry J., "Touch once again thy breathing wire," Toronto: Haycraft Small & Addison, 1856.

___ "Thy bonnie blue e'en," Toronto: Haycraft Small & Addison, 1856.

Haydn, Joseph, "My mother bids me bind my hair," in *Canzonettas and Songs for Voice with Piano Accompaniment.* Edited by Ludwig Landshoff. New York/London/Frankfurt: C. F. Peters Corporation, 1931.

Hilliard Ensemble. *The Singing Club: Ravenscroft-Lawes-Purcell-Arne.* Harmonia Mundi s.a., HMC901153, 1985.

Humphreys, James Dodsley, "When we two parted," Philadelphia: John F. Nunns, 1843.

Knight, Joseph Philip, "Give me the night," Philadelphia: John F. Nunns 70 S. Third St., n.d.

Martin, Henry, "Sweet Madeline, " Toronto and Montreal: A. & S. Nordheimer [sic], 1867.

Martini [Martin Y Soler], "The Laughing Trio [Vadasi via di qua] arranged from Martini's Terzetto," arranged by J. Addison, New York: Dubois & Stodart, 167 Broadway, n.d.

McCaul, John, "Merrie England! A patriotic song," Toronto: A & S. Nordheimer, and Lovell & Gibson, Yonge Sreet, n.d.

McDonnell, Wm., "See the Dawn of the Fair Bright Morning," Toronto: Strange & Co., 1884.

Mozart, Wolfgang Amadeus. *Le Nozze di Figaro (The Marriage of Figaro), an Opera in Four Acts.* Translated by Ruth and Thomas Martin. New York/London: G. Schirmer, 1951.

Rossini, Gioachino. *Tancredi, melodramma eroico in due atti.* Edited by Bruno Cagli, Philip Gossett, and Alberto Zedda. *Edizione Critica delle Opere di Gioachino Rossini.* Sezione prima: opere teatrali, vol. 10. Milan: Fondazione Rossini Pesaro, 1984.

_____, "Mi manca la voce," arranged by C. M. Sola, London: Goulding, D'Almaine, Potter & Co., 20 Soho Squ., n.d.

Schubert, Franz, "The Wanderer," arranged and translated by F. W. Rosier, Boston: Geo. P. Reed, 17 Tremont Row, n.d.

Spohr, Louis, "Oh, lovely maiden stay," in *Azor & Zemira, or the Magic Rose, founded upon the fairy tale of Beauty and the Beast: Grand opera adapted for the English stage with an accompaniment for the piano forte.* Arranged by Georg Smart, translated into English by William Ball. London: Goulding & D'Almaine, [ca.1831].

Weber, Carl Maria Von, "Lutzow's Wild Hunt," in *Heart Songs Dear to the American People and by them Contributed in the Search for Treasured Songs Initiated by the National Magazine.* Edited by Bea Friedland. Boston: Chapple Publishing Company, Ltd., 1909, pp. 331-2.

White, Don. Synopsis and translation in brochure notes for Kenneth Montgomery, dir., *Torquato Tasso,* by Gaetano Donizetti. Opera Rara Production, 1974, M.R.F. Records, Inc.

B.   PRINTED PRIMARY SOURCES (NOT MUSIC)

The Aldine, The Art Journal of America, Vol. VII, no. 20 (1874-5), New York: The Aldine Company.

Aliquis [John Strachan], *Observations on the history and recent proceedings of the Canada Company; addressed in four letters to Frederick Widder, esq., one of the commissioners*, Hamilton: [no publisher], 1845.

The Banner (Toronto), March, 1844.

The British Colonist (Toronto), February-April, 1844.

The Buffalo Morning Express, 6 March, 1852.

The Canadian Courier, the National Weekly, vol. IX, No. 25, 20 May 1911.

Canadian Music & Trades Journal (Toronto), 1901.

Cooke, Maud C. *Social Etiquette, or, Manners and Customs of Polite Society*. London, Ontario: McDermid, 1896.

The Globe (Toronto), 1844-1900.

The Mirror (Toronto), February – April, 1844.

The Musical Times and Singing Class Circular (Little Heath, England, Orpheus Publications), vol. 1, 1844.

Party Giving on Every Scale by the author of 'Manners and Tone of Good Society,' 'The Management of Society,' etc. London: F. Warren and Co., c. 1890.

The Patriot (Toronto), February - April, 1844.

Read, David B. *The Lives of the Judges of Upper Canada and Ontario from 1791 to the Present Time*. 1888. Reprint, Holmes Beach, Florida: Wm. W. Gaunt and Sons, Inc., 1995.

Seranus [Susan Frances Harrison], "The Prisoner Dubois," in *Crowded Out! And Other Sketches*. Ottawa: The Evening Journal Office, 1886.

C.   ELECTRONIC (PRIMARY SOURCES)

[Costa, Michael Andrew Agnus, "Ecco quel fiero Istante,"] <http://www.door.library.uiuc.edu/sousa/band-a-f.htm>, (5 May 2003).

Dobree, Paul, <http://www.careyroots.com/PS03/PS03_371.htm>, (1 July 2003).

[Ellet, Mrs. E. F., "The Mysterious Singer," in *Godey's Lady's Book* January 1850, Philadelphia,] <http://www.history.rochester.edu/godeys/o1-50/tms.htm>, (10 October 2000).

[*Globe*, 1844-1900, Toronto], <http://www.//199.198.129.206/PageView.asp,> (2003).

[Regondi, Giulio], International Guitar Research Archives, California State University, Northridge, Department of Music, n.d., <http://www.csun.edu/~igra/bios/text/regondi.html> (10 May 2003).

[Mercadante, Saverio, *Il giuramento*,] <http://www.opera.stanford.edu/Mercadante/Giuramento/synopsis.html>, (5 April 2003).

Saratoga Soirée Musicale Newsletter, 2 Mar. 1999 <http://www.metroactive.com/papers/saratoga.news/02.03.99/SaratogaSampler.num>, (7 February 2001).

II. SELECTED SECONDARY SOURCES

A.   Books

Auerbach, Nina. *Ellen Terry: A Player in Her Time.* New York, London: W. W. Norton & Company, 1987.

Barrett, William Alexander, 1836-1891. *English glees and part-songs, an inquiry into their historical development.* London: Longmans, Green, and Co., 1886.

Bashford, Christina, and Leanne Langley, eds. *Music and British Culture, 1785-1914: Essays in Honour of Cyril Ehrlich.* Oxford: Oxford University Press, 2000.

Beckwith, John, ed. *CanMus Documents, 4: Three Studies.* Toronto: Institute for Canadian Music, 1989.

Beedell, A.V. *The Decline of the English Musician 1788-1888: A Family of English Musicians in Ireland, England, Mauritius, and Australia.* Oxford: Clarendon Press, 1992.

Booth Martyn, Lucy. *The Face of Early Toronto: an Archival Record 1797-1930.* Sutton West & Santa Barbara: The Paget Press, 1982.

_____. *100 Years of Grandeur.* Toronto: Pagurian Press Limited, 1978.

Burgoyne, Roderick Hamilton, ed. *Historical Records of the 93rd Sutherland Highlanders, now the 2nd Battalion Princess Louise's Argyle and Sutherland Highlanders.* London: Richard Bentley and Son, 1883.

Careless, J. M. S., ed. *The Pre-Confederation Premiers: Ontario Government Leaders, 1841-1867.* Toronto: University of Toronto Press, 1980.

Craig, Gerald. *Upper Canada: The Formative Years, 1784-1841.* Toronto: McClelland and Stewart, 1963.

Davidoff, Leonore. *The Best Circles - Society Etiquette and the Season.* London: Croom Helm Ltd., 1973.

Delamar, Gloria T. *Rounds Re-sounding: Circular Music for Voices and Instruments: an Eight-century Reference.* Jefferson, North Carolina, and London: McFarland & Company, Inc., 1987.

Ehrlich, Cyril. *The Music Profession in Britain since the Eighteenth Century: A Social History.* Oxford: Clarendon Press, 1985.

Elliott, Robin. *Counterpoint to a City: The First One Hundred Years of the Women's Musical Club of Toronto.* Toronto: ECW Press, 1997.

Firth, Edith. *The Town of York 1815-34.* Toronto: Champlain Society, vol. 6, Ontario Series, 1966.

Firth, Edith, ed. *Profiles of a Province: Studies in the history of Ontario.* Toronto: Ontario Historical Society, 1967.

Gates, Lillian F. *Land Policies of Upper Canada.* Toronto: University of Toronto Press, 1968.

Gorham, Deborah. *The Victorian Girl and the Feminine Ideal.* Bloomington: Indiana University Press, 1982.

Harris, Robin S. and Terry G. Harris, eds. *The Eldon House Diaries: Five Women's Views of the Nineteenth-century.* Toronto: University of Toronto Press, 1994.

Heilbrun, Carolyn G. *Writing a Woman's Life.* New York: W.W. Norton & Company, 1988.

Jarvis, Julia. *Three Centuries of Robinsons.* Don Mills, Ontario: T. H. Best Printing Company Limited, 1967.

Kallmann, Helmut. *A History of Music in Canada 1534-1914.* Toronto: University of Toronto Press, 1987.

Keillor, Elaine. *Vignettes on Music in Canada.* Ottawa: Carleton University, 2000.

Kelly, Wayne. *Downright Upright.* Toronto: Natural Heritage/Natural History Inc., 1991.

Leppert, Richard. *Music and Image: Domesticity, Ideology and Socio-cultural Formation in Eighteenth-century England.* Cambridge: Cambridge University Press, 1988.

_____. *The Sight of Sound: Music, Representation, and the History of the Body.* University of California Press, 1995.

Lerner, Gerda. *Why History Matters: Life and Thought.* New York: Oxford University Press, 1997.

Levine, Lawrence. *Highbrow/Lowbrow: The Emergence of Cultural Hierarchy in America.* Cambridge, Mass.: Harvard University Press, 1988.

Luckyj, Natalie. *Helen Galloway McNicoll: A Canadian Impressionist.* Toronto: Art Gallery of Ontario, 1999.

McCarthy, Margaret William. *Amy Fay: America's Notable Woman of Music.* Michigan: Harmonie Park Press, 1995.

McKendrick, Neil, John Brewer and J. H. Plumb. *The Birth of a Consumer Society: The Commercialization of Eighteenth-century England.* London: Europe Publications Limited, 1982.

McKenna, Katherine. *A Life of Propriety: Anne Murray Powell and Her Family, 1755-1849.* Montreal & Kingston: McGill-Queen's University Press, 1994.

McKillop, A. B. *Matters of Mind; the University in Ontario 1791-1951.* Toronto: University of Toronto Press, 1994.

McKillop, A. B., and Paul Romney, eds. *S. F. Wise: God's Peculiar Peoples: Essays on Political Culture in Nineteenth-Century Canada.* Ottawa: Carleton University Press, 1993.

Morgan, Cecilia. *Public Men and Virtuous Women; the Gendered Languages of Religion and Politics in Upper Canada, 1791-1850.* Toronto: University of Toronto Press, 1996.

Öhrstrom, Eva. *Borgerliga kvinnors musicerande i 1800-talets Sverige.* Göteborg: Studies from Gothenburg University, 1987.

Parakilas, James, ed. *Piano Roles; Three Hundred Years of Life with the Piano.* New Haven, Conn., Yale University Press, 1999.

Rimbault, Edward F., ed. *The Rounds, Catches and Canons of England: A Collection of Specimens of the sixteenth, seventeenth and eighteenth centuries, adapted to modern use.* 1875. Reprinted, New York: Da Capo Press, 1976.

Scott, Derek. *The Singing Bourgeois: Songs of the Victorian Drawing Room and Parlour.* Milton Keynes: Open University Press, 1989.

Senior, Elinor Kyte. *British Regulars in Montreal: an Imperial Garrison 1832-1854.* Montreal: McGill-Queen's University Press, 1981.

Shepherd, John. *Music as Social Text.* Cambridge: Polity Press, 1991.

Small, Christopher. *Music, Society, Education: a Radical Examination of the Prophetic Function of Music in Western, Eastern and African Cultures with its Impact on Society and its Use in Education.* London: John Calder, 1977.

Solie, Ruth A., ed. *Musicology and Difference: Gender and Sexuality in Music Scholarship*. Berkeley: University of California Press, 1993.

Thomas, Dylan. *Dylan Thomas: The Poems*. Edited by David Jones. London: J. M. Dent & Sons Ltd., 1971.

Walker, Frank Norman. *Sketches of Old Toronto*. Toronto: Longmans Canada Limited, 1965.

Ward, Peter J. *Courtship, love and marriage in nineteenth-century English Canada*. Montreal: McGill-Queen's University Press, 1990.

Weber, William. *Music and the Middle Class: The Social Structure of Concert life in London, Paris and Vienna*. New York: Holmes & Meier Publishers, Inc., 1975.

Westfall, William. *The Founding Moment: Church, Society, and the Construction of Trinity College*. Montreal & Kingston: McGill-Queen's University Press, 2002.

Wood, Herbert. *A Brief History of the King's Royal Rifle Corps, 1755 to 1948*, third edition. Aldershot: Gale and Polden Limited, 1948.

Vipond, Mary. *The Mass Media in Canada Second Edition*. Toronto: James Lorimer & Company, Publishers, 1992.

B.   ARTICLES

Cook, Terry. "John Beverley Robinson and the Conservative Blueprint for the Upper Canadian Community." In *Historical Essays on Upper Canada*, edited by J. K. Johnson, 338-360. Toronto: McClelland and Stewart Limited, 1975.

Di Maggio, Paul, "Cultural Entrepreneurship in Nineteenth-Century Boston: The Creation of an Organizational Base for High Culture in America." In *Rethinking Popular Culture: Contemporary Perspectives in Cultural Studies*, edited by Chandra Mukerji and Michael Schudson, 374-397. Berkeley: University of California Press, 1991.

Fuller, Major-General J.F.C., "Letters of Major-General Sir John Moore, K.B." *Army Historical Research*, vol.12 (1933), 179-87.

_____, "Sir John Moore's Light Infantry Instructions of 1798-1799", *Army Historical Research*, vol. 30 (1952), 68-75.

Gordon, Alan, "Jewish Businessmen in Toronto's Conservative Party, 1911-1921", *Ontario History* 88, no. 1 (1996), 31-46.

Hillier, Paul. *Liner Notes to The Singing Club*, recorded by The Hilliard Ensemble, Paul Hillier Conducting. France: Harmonia Mundi, HMC 90 1 153, 1985.

Johnson, F. Henry, "A Colonial Canadian in Search of a Museum", *Queen's Quarterly* 77, no. 2 (1970), 217-29.

Juleus, Nels, "Lady Dufferin's Theatricals", *Canadian Drama*, 2 (1985), 245-50.

Levin, Susan. "The Gipsy Is a Jewess: Harriet Abrams and Theatrical Romanticism." In *Romantic Women Writers: Voices and Countervoices*. Edited by Paula R. Feldman and Theresa M. Kelley, pp. 236-51. Hanover, NH: University Press of New England, 1995.

Milne, James, "The Development of Canadian Military Bands after the Militia Act of 1855," (unpublished manuscript for *Traditions and Customs of the Canadian Forces*), Ottawa: Department of National Defence, Directorate of History and Heritage.

Moisala, Pirkko, "Musical gender in Performance", *Women and Music: A Journal of Gender and Culture*, 3 (1999), 1-16.

Moisala, Pirkko. Review of *Elfrida Andrée Eett Levnadsode* [Elfrida Andrée: A Life Destiny], by Eva Öhrstrom, *Women and Music: A Journal of Gender and Culture*, 5 (2001), 146-8.

Pasler, Jann, "The Ironies of Gender or Virility and Politics in the Music of Augusta Holmés", *Women & Music: A Journal of Gender and Culture*, 2 (1998), 1-25.

Roback, Frances, "Advertising Canadian Pianos and Organs, 1850-1919", *Material History Bulletin* 20 (Autumn 1984), 31-44.

Rudman, Michael, "James Dodsley Humphreys: A Look at Musical Life in Mid-Nineteenth century Toronto", *The York Pioneer*, 96 (2001), 8-25.

Smiley, Marilynn J. "Across Lake Ontario: Nineteenth-Century Concerts and Connections." In *Taking a Stand: Essays in Honour of John Beckwith*, edited by Timothy J. McGee, 149-165. Toronto: University of Toronto Press, 1995.

Solie, Ruth A., "Defining Feminism: Conundrums, Contexts, Communities", *Women & Music: A Journal of Gender and Culture*, 1 (1997), 1-11.

White, Don. Libretto notes to *Torquato Tasso*, recorded by Opera Rara at the Camden Festival, Kenneth Montgomery Conducting, March 2, 1974.

C. THESES

Burns, Robert J. "The First Elite of Toronto: an examination of the genesis, consolidation, and duration of power in an emerging colonial power." Ph.D. diss., University of Western Ontario, 1975.

Payne, David B. "Social music in London, Upper Canada/Canada West: establishing a 'sort of colonial nobility.'" Master's of Music thesis, University of Western Ontario, 1998.

Sale, David John. "Toronto's pre-confederation music societies, 1845-1867." M. Mus. thesis, University of Toronto, 1968.

D. ELECTRONIC SOURCES (SECONDARY)

Anon.<http://www.fortunecity.com/victorian/riley//8//Napoleon/Prussia/Commanders/lutzow. html,> (21 Nov. 2002), p. 1.

Cook, Kandis and Nick Till. <http://www.post-operative.org/product3.html,> n.d. (25 May 2003), p. 1.

International Guitar Research Archives, California Station University, Northridge, Department of Music, n.d., <http://www.csun.edu/~igra/bios/text/regondi.html> (10 May 2003).

Small, Christopher. "Musicking: A Ritual in Social Space." 6 June 1995. <http://www.musekids.org/ musicking.html> (4 June 2003).

Weber, William. "Review of *Salons, Singers and Songs: A Background to Romantic French Song, 1830-1870*, by David Tunley," *H-France*, (November 2002). <http://www3.uakron.edu/hfrance/reviews/weber2.html> (21 Nov. 2002).